D0501975

ENCYCLOPAEDIA OF CLASSIC CARS

ROB DE LA RIVE BOX

ENCYCLOPAEDIA OF CLASSIC CARS

SPORTS CARS 1945-1975

REBO
PRODUCTIONS

© 1998 Rebo International b.v., The Netherlands
1998 Published by Rebo Productions Ltd., London

translation: Stephen Challacombe
coverdesign: Ton Wienbelt, The Hague, The Netherlands
editing and production: TextCase, Groningen, The Netherlands
Typesetting: Hof&Land Typografie, Maarssen, The Netherlands

BO364UK

ISBN 1 84053 111 8

Contents

Foreword

"What is a sports car?"
"What a dumb question! Everybody knows that!"
"You reckon?"
"Yes. A sports car is a very fast two-seater with hard suspension and good road-holding that can be raced."
"So my Porsche is not a sports car then, or what about a 2 + 2?"
"They're exceptions."
"And a rally is not a race."
"Of course it is."
"But saloon cars compete in rallies. Maus Gatsonides won one in a Ford Zephyr."
"That's another exception. His car had four doors, heating, and loads of comfort, so it could hardly be called a sports car."
"What about those cars that competed in the Mille Miglia? Were they sports cars?"
"Of course, though cars like the 300SLR with which Stirling Moss and Denis Jenkinson completed the 1,000 miles in an average speed of 100 miles per hour (160 kph) in 1955 were really racing cars. Imagine, they did that on ordinary roads used by trucks."
"In that same race there was a Mercedes diesel and also an Isetta with a two-stroke motor. The Isetta took twice as long as Moss – twenty hours – yet it still won its class."
"Yes, just like five other cars did in their classes because they were the only participant."
"So ordinary cars raced in the Mille Miglia just as they do in the Le Mans 24-hour race."
"Not really! Le Mans is home to the super-cars with turbochargers. That isn't just a recent introduction. Bentleys with blowers competed back in the Twenties and more recently there was Gijs van Lennep's turbo-booted Porsche 917K that delivered 630 bhp."
"That's true, but Gatsonides and Hoogeveen came in twenty-first place in 1950 in an Aero-Minor and five Renault 4's competed in 1951."
"They're all exceptions. They prove the rule that a sports car has just two doors, a low windscreen, and a soft-top – although a hard-top is also acceptable. At least Van Lennep didn't get wet when it started to rain."
"Yes but..."
"But nothing. Look at my car, that's a true sports car, complete with low scalloped doors and no side windows. It's a 1946 Singer Nine with four cylinder motor with an overhead camshaft, with power of a mere 36 bhp and a top speed of just under 70 mph (110 kph). Of course your Porsche can do that in first gear but then it's not really a sports car."

Both true pedigree sports cars and some more marginal cases are dealt with in this book. Although monsters such as the Mark X Jaguar and Oldsmobile have competed in and won rallies, these do not fall within the compass of this book. On the other hand, the Facel Vega and Ferrari 365 GT 2 + 2 could be regarded as family cars but they were at least two-door coupés, that were amazingly quick in spite of their comfort.

Purists may question the inclusion of cars such as the Excalibur, or replicas like the Auburn Speedster or Apal-Porsche.

Placing these in a separate section would not have made the book easier to use for reference. The cars are all arranged alphabetically under their marques.

This book is not comprehensive. Hundreds of marques and thousands of models have been excluded. Only a few are interested in the Fibersport American sports car on a Crosley chassis that was produced between 1953–54, or the French Marsonetto of 1958. Understandably, it has not been possible to include every model of Abarth produced, since there were sixteen new models in 1963 alone.

These omissions will not, I hope spoil your enjoyment of this book.

Rob de la Rive Box

Abarth

Carlo Abarth was born in Austria in 1908 but adopted his father's Italian nationality. Abarth started racing before World War I and won a bet that he could drive from Ostend to Vienna faster than the famous Orient Express. After World War II he established his business in Italy and developed the Cisitalia Grand-Prix cars jointly with Porsche. In 1949, he founded his team, or Scuderia, with drivers of the calibre of Nuvolari, Farina, and Taruffi and the following year his company started to produce special exhaust systems. Conversion kits for Fiats followed and soon production of complete cars too, such as the Fiat 600. The engine of this car was tweaked to produce 65 bhp although the true sports cars and grand-tourers that Abarth produced are far more interesting. It is impossible to mention every model that Abarth made because there are simply too many of them. In 1964, the company produced no fewer than twenty-two different types, ranging from the Fiat Abarth 595 to the two-litre Abarth Simca. This latter car was an aluminium-bodied coupé on the running gear of a Simca 1000. The motor had twin overhead

camshafts and two double Weber carburettors. It weighed 665 kg (1,466 lb), top speed: 169mph (270 kph). Another 1964 model was the Bialbero

Abarth built three specials in 1955 on a Fiat 1100 chassis. This is the 207-A with a Boano body.

The Abarth Bialbero (bialbero means twin camshaft) was shown at Turin in 1961.

The 207-A Spyder had a 1,089 cc four-cylinder overhead valve engine that developed 66 bhp at 6,000

An Abarth 750 with "double bubble" body by Zagato in the 1997 Mille Miglia.

1000, that was a Fiat 600 but with a 104 bhp motor with twin camshafts and a compression ratio of 10.8:1. Abarth built his own engines and developed a three-litre V-8 motor in 1968 with four camshafts, four double Weber carburettors, and twin-spark ignition. The engine developed 350 bhp at 8,200 rpm. Breaking records was more than a matter of good publicity for Abarth, it was his favourite pastime. On October 21, 1965, Abarth broke the "monoposto", or single-seater record for standing quarter of a mile and standing 500 metres with a 2-litre car. It was his firm's one hundredth record.

Abarth sold his company to Fiat in 1971 and the management of the 250-strong factory was taken over by Aurelio Lampredi, who had become famous through his work for Ferrari. Carlo Abarth retired to Austria, where he died on November 24, 1979, barely two months after marrying for the third time.

The Abarth name lives on though through the many classic examples that participate in races for historic cars and Fiat still produce a Fiat 500 Abarth.

Abarth sports cars

COUNTRY OF ORIGIN
Italy

Abarth Fiat 600

YEARS IN PRODUCTION
1955–1971

NUMBER MADE
Unknown

SPECIAL REMARKS
The body was recognisable as that of a Fiat 600 but the 750, 850, and even 1000 models had engines of 747 cc, 847 cc, and 982 cc.

A wolf in sheep's clothing: the 1000TC had a top speed of 119 mph (190 kph).

The 982 cc engine of the 1000TC produces 112 bhp at 8,200 rpm.

The difference between a Fiat 500 and an Abarth was minimal. The Fiat had a 594 cc engine but the Abarth's was 695 cc.

Abarth Fiat 500

YEARS IN PRODUCTION
1957–1971

NUMBER MADE
Unknown

SPECIAL REMARKS
The body was virtually unchanged by Abarth but the two-cylinder engines were of 594 cc and 695 cc, delivering 32 and 38 bhp respectively.

Abarth Fiat 850

YEARS IN PRODUCTION
1964–1970

NUMBER MADE
Unknown

SPECIAL REMARKS
Both the 850 saloon and coupé versions were marvellous creations by Abarth. The four-cylinder engines were of course tweaked and had capacities of 842 cc and 1,592 cc.

The 1966 Abarth OT 1300 was based on a Fiat 850 chassis but had a genuine Abarth 1,290 cc engine that developed 147 bhp at 8,800 rpm.

Autobianchi A 112

YEARS IN PRODUCTION
1971–1985

NUMBER MADE
Unknown

SPECIAL REMARKS
Externally, there was little difference between this car and the standard Autobianchi: the difference was to be found under the bonnet. In 1975, the Abarth version was supplied with a 52 bhp 982 cc engine instead of the standard Autobianchi 47 bhp 903 cc motor.

Abarth Simca

YEARS IN PRODUCTION
1962–1965

NUMBER MADE
Unknown

SPECIAL REMARKS
The Simca name was the only link with the cars from the French factory. The streamlined body was built of aluminium. The cars had a range of engines: 1,137 cc, 1,288 cc, 1,592 cc, and 1,946 cc.

Abarth Fiat 124 Rally

YEARS IN PRODUCTION
1972–1975

NUMBER MADE
Unknown

SPECIAL REMARKS
This 119 mph (190 km/hour) coupé was designed by Pinanfarina. The Abarth models can be recognised by their aluminium wheels, small rubber bumpers, and the matt black bonnet and boot lids.
The four-cylinder engine had a capacity of 1,756 cc.

The Abarth Simca is based on the Simca 1000. It is more suited to a race track than the road.

AC

The butcher John Portwine had made sufficient money by 1900 to be able to launch himself into the adventurous world of the motor car. Because he had more money than technical knowledge, he chose John Weller as his partner to help him build motor cars. The vehicle that resulted was however too expensive to sell readily so the company, known as Autocars & Accessories Ltd. switched over to making a tri-car which was so successful that by 1907, the company, now known as Autocarriers Ltd, moved from the tradesmen's version to develop a runabout. The company got a major impetus when the army's 25th Cycle Regiment was equipped with the vehicle. Larger cars with six-cylinder engines followed and one of these engines, with an overhead camshaft, remained in production until 1963 without any major modifications.

By the decade before World War II, the company specialised in sports cars and this trend continued after the war. In 1950, AC sold five cars per week and in 1953, the AC Ace was introduced. It was a two-seater roadster with tubular chassis and all-round independent suspension that was driven by the long-standing six-cylinder motor that by that time developed 85 bhp. The aluminium body was clearly a copy of the Ferrari 166 MM Barchetta, built by Touring in Milan, but nobody was upset at this. One of the early Aces competed in the Tulips rally and won its class. A year later, the Ace was equipped with a more powerful engine by Bristol, giving birth to the AC-Bristol. The car was unbeatable on American racing circuits with its 120 horsepower engine and one of these cars was second in its class to a Ferrari in the 1957 Le Mans. The following year an AC won the famous Le Mans twenty-four hour race.

AC was already famous but the true breakthrough happened after American Carroll Shelby suggested putting an American Ford V-8 engine in the Ace. Shelby demonstrated the car to Ford at Dearborn and Ford were so impressed that Shelby got an order for 100 of the cars to be built. Before the first AC Cobras were delivered, Ford had already ordered a further 100 cars. When the Americans brought out a new 7-litre engine in 1963 that developed 485 bhp, these were added to the Cobra. In Britain, the "small" 289 cubic inch capacity engine was still installed in the car, so that models for Britain were offered as AC 289. The car was sold in the United States as "Shelby American Cobra".

AC built other sports cars, often with a body designed by Frua, but they were not all as successful as the Cobra. The company tried once more to succeed with a middle-engined coupé,

Gurney and Bordurant won their class in the 1964 Le Mans 24 hours race with a Cobra Daytona and were fourth overall.

the subsequent AC 3000 ME. It took until 1979 though before this model was ready to go into production.

The Cobra has been copied by more than 150 companies so that if you see one the odds are ten-to-one that it is a replica. Carroll Shelby too began making once more what he more justifiably called "the only true Cobra" in 1997.

The car is available as a kit for $38,900 but can also be purchased ready-to-run, complete with an official Cobra chassis number, but these cost $500,000. This is a lot of money for a car but Shelby gives a large proportion of the sale price to a children's charity.

AC sports cars

COUNTRY OF ORIGIN
Great Britain

AC Ace/AC-Bristol

YEARS IN PRODUCTION
1953–1962 and 1954–1963

Between 1956 and 1963, almost 500 AC-Bristols were made.

The Bristol engine was an improved version of the pre-war BMW 328 six-cylinder motor.

The AC Ace was based on a design by the famous designer John Tojeiro.

NUMBER MADE
226 and 466

SPECIAL REMARKS
The AC Ace and Bristol shared the same body but had respectively 1,991 cc and 2,553 cc six-cylinder engines.

AC Aceca en Aceca Bristol

An AC Aceca coupé. These models had a 2-litre engine delivering 91 bhp.

YEARS IN PRODUCTION
1953–1962 and 1955–1963

NUMBER MADE
150 and 1,969

SPECIAL REMARKS
These were the coupé version of the AC. The body was aluminium but the chassis was partly fabricated from wood.

AC Greyhound

YEARS IN PRODUCTION
1959–1963

NUMBER MADE
80

SPECIAL REMARKS
This was the first post-war AC sports car with room for four adults. It had a 1,971 cc six-cylinder engine delivering 126 bhp at 6,000 rpm.

AC Ace en Aceca 2.6

YEARS IN PRODUCTION
1961–1963

NUMBER MADE
47

SPECIAL REMARKS
These models are AC Ace and Aceca with a 2.6-litre Ford engine and a slightly revised front end.

A Cobra dashboard (this is a 260) had more instruments than some light aircraft.

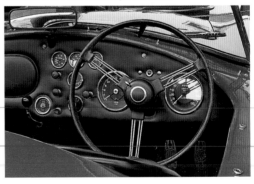

AC Cobra 260/289/Cobra 289 Mk II

YEARS IN PRODUCTION
1962 and 1963–1965

NUMBER MADE
75 and 579

The motor in an AC Cobra 260 was a Ford V-8 with a capacity of 4,261 cc delivering 264 bhp at 5,800 rpm.

Cobras can frequently be admired competing in veteran's races. A 289 is seen here at the Hockenheim-ring.

SPECIAL REMARKS
The Cobra finally made AC world-famous. The Cobra was really identical to the AC Ace with the exception of the different motors. The American Carroll Shelby had the Ace equipped with Ford V-8 engines of respectively 4,261 cc (264 bhp at 5,800 rpm) and 4,727 cc (300 bhp at 5,750 rpm).

The mixture for the Cobra 427 was provided by two quad-chambered Ford carburettors.

AC Cobra 289 427 Mk III

YEARS IN PRODUCTION
1965–1968

NUMBER MADE
27 and 348

SPECIAL REMARKS
These models had a new chassis and improved suspension. The design continued to be recognisable as an AC. The engine was a 4,727 cc V-8.

AC 428

YEARS IN PRODUCTION
1966–1973

NUMBER MADE
86

SPECIAL REMARKS
The AC 428 had a steel body, designed by Frua in Italy. This was fairly apparent since the car

When Ford introduced a 7-litre V-8 engine, the chassis of the Cobra had to be completely amended because the torque was too great for the original chassis.

By extending the wheel-base from 229 to 244 cm (90 to 96 in), the AC was made big enough to carry four people. It was introduced as the AC 428 of which eighty examples were sold.

closely resembles the Maserati Mistral from the same drawing board. The engine was a 6,997 cc V-8 that delivered 350 bhp at 4,600 rpm.

Alfa Romeo

Società Anonima Lambarda Fabbrica Automobili, better known as Alfa, was famous just before and after World War II for its sports and racing cars. With and without a turbo these cars won just about everything they entered.
Consider the Mille Miglia 1,000 mile race right across Italy: the first race in 1927 was won by an Oldsmobile but up to 1947, the race was almost invariably won by an Alfa Romeo. The exceptions were 1931 and 1940 when the race was won by, respectively a Mercedes and a BMW. Even in these races, there were eight or nine Alfa

The Disco Volante appeared in 1952–53 and was based on the Alfa 1900. Their 160 bhp motors took them to speeds in excess of 125 mph (200 kph).

An Alfa SZ (Sprint Zagato) overtakes a Spyder at the Nürburgring in 1982.

Romeos in the first ten and the competition successes were not limited to Italy. Alfa Romeo won the Le Mans 24-hour race four years in succession.
In addition to sporting cars, the Alfa factory also built even faster Grand Prix racing cars. Farina and Fangio both won World Championships in 1950 and 1951 in cars that had been developed before the war. Motor racing was a high priority with the company, even after the war, when the company was forced to make cars for a wider public, the cars retained a sporting character

The bodies of the Giulietta and Giulia Sprint were designed and built by Bertone.

Cut-away illustration of a Montreal.

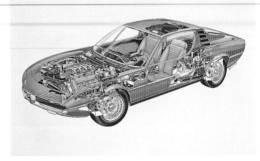

that encouraged driving. All Alfa Romeos, without exception, were suitable for rallying or club racing. The Alfa Romeo 1900s and Giulia Supers can still be seen with their 4-door bodies trouncing so-called "real" sports cars at racing circuits.

In 1947, Alfa returned with the heavy-weight 6C2500 grand-tourer but only 1,451 examples were sold in five years which was clearly too few to produce profitably.

The turn-around happened in 1950, when the factory launched the Alfa 1900 with a body of

Alfa's first model after the war was the 6C2500. It had a 2,500 cc six-cylinder engine.

unitary construction. The 1900 was initially a four-door car but the range was extended in 1954 with a two-door coupé, which established the basis for a long line of super sports cars. The 1900 was followed by the Giulietta and Giulia models that had respectively 1,300 and 1,600 cc motors. Specialist companies like Zagato and Bertone converted these models into very fast competitive cars such as the Giulietta SZ and the Giulia TZ, which were both built on a limited scale by Zagato. There were others like the Disco Volante models which bore a resemblance to a flying saucer. The 33 series successfully took on Ferrari and won between 1967 and 1977.

Alfa Romeo sports cars

COUNTRY OF ORIGIN
Italy

Alfa Romeo 6C2500

YEARS IN PRODUCTION
1939–1952

NUMBER MADE
1,591

15

Italian sports cars had their steering on the right until well into the Fifties.

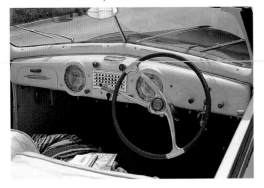

Many car body specialists created dream cars based on the 1900SS chassis. This coupé from 1956 is by Ghia-Aigle.

SPECIAL REMARKS

The Alfa Romeo 6C2500 was a status symbol for people of note and top Government officials. The sports car versions often had a very attractive body and they performed well in races such as the Mille Miglia. The 6C2500 was powered by a 2,443 cc six-cylinder motor that delivered 90–110 bhp at 4,800 rpm.

Alfa Romeo 1900

YEARS IN PRODUCTION
1954–1959

NUMBER MADE
1,932

SPECIAL REMARKS

The 1900 was Alfa's first production model. The Berlina appeared in 1950 and the sports cars a little later: the Sprint (1954–1956, 1,209 made), the Super Sprint (1955–1958, 614 made), the Super Sprint Zagato (1954–1958, 18 made), and the Touring soft-top (1952–1959, 91 made). All models had a four-cylinder 1,884 cc motor.

The dashboard of the 1900 Super Sport. Notice the column-mounted gear lever.

The Alfa SZ was nicknamed "the egg".

Bertone's Giulietta SS (Super Sprint) was an ideal normal road car.

Alfa Romeo Giulietta

YEARS IN PRODUCTION
1954–1962

NUMBER MADE
45,843

SPECIAL REMARKS
The Giulietta formed the basis for all subsequent

Alfa Romeos. In addition to the Berlina, the production models included the following models: Sprint (1954–1962, 27,141 made), Spyder (1955–1962, 17,096 made), Sprint Speziale (1959–1962, 1,366 made), and Zagatto SZ (1959–1962, 240 made). The Giulietta was produced with a 1,290 cc four-cylinder engine that delivered 100 bhp at 5,500 rpm).

The Spyder bodies (this is a Giulietta) were designed and built by Pininfarina.

The dashboard of a Giulietta with the most important instruments – the rev counter and oil-pressure gauge immediately in front of the driver.

Alfa Romeo Giulia

YEARS IN PRODUCTION
1962–1965

NUMBER MADE
22,912

SPECIAL REMARKS
The Giulia was a Giulietta with a 1,600 cc engine instead of a 1,300 cc. The Sprint coupé was made by Bertone and 11,171 of them were sold, with 10,341 Pininfarina Spyders, and 1,400 Bertone Sprint Speziale coupés. The larger four-cylinder engine had a capacity of 1,570 cc, delivering 90 bhp at 6,500 rpm.

The Giulietta Spyder was extremely successful. It remained in production for seven years, and more than 17,000 were sold.

A Giulia TZ (Tubolare Zagato) en route to a race victory

Alfa Romeo Giulia

YEARS IN PRODUCTION
1963–1977

NUMBER MADE
224,924

The Giulia GTA was in reality a much lighter and faster Sprint. Its 1.3 litre motor delivered 165 bhp, while the 1.6 litre delivered 220 bhp.

The Giulia was given an entirely new body in 1963 and several new models were added to the range: Sprint GT (1963–1977, 223,858 built), Sprint GTA (1966–1972, 942 built), and the Giulia TZ Zagato (1963–1966, 124 built). They were all equipped with the reliable four-cylinder engine from the previous Giulia, although some versions had a more powerful version. The GTA had a 133 bhp/6,000 rpm motor, and the TZ even had a 170 bhp/7,500 rpm engine beneath its bonnet.

Alfa Romeo Spider

YEARS IN PRODUCTION
1966–present day

NUMBER MADE
Not known

SPECIAL REMARKS
The Duetto Spyder could be purchased between 1966 and 1970 with 1.3, 1.6, and 1.75 litre engines. Their successors are known as the Spyder 1300 Junior, 1600 Junior, 1750, and 2000. They caught the eye because of their straight cut-off rear end. The standard engine is a four-cylinder with a capacity of 1,570 cc.

Alfa Romeo Giulia GTC

YEARS IN PRODUCTION
1966–1967

NUMBER MADE
Approx. 1,000

SPECIAL REMARKS
Carrozzeria Touring built a four-seater convertible or cabriolet on a lengthened Giulia underframe.
This car is not really a sports car and its sales were disappointing.

Alfa Romeo Zagato Junior 1300/1600

YEARS IN PRODUCTION
1969–1972 and 1972–1975

NUMBER MADE
1,108 and 402

SPECIAL REMARKS
Zagato always built very special bodies which were either adored or hated: there seems to be no midway between these two extremes. The four-cylinder engines were: 1,290 cc/87 bhp at 6,000 rpm and 1,570 cc/131 bhp at 5,500 rpm.

Alfa Romeo 2000/2600 Spider

YEARS IN PRODUCTION
1958–1961 and 1962–1965

NUMBER MADE
3,443 and 2,255

There is a six-cylinder engine with twin overhead camshafts under the bonnet of the 2600 Spyder.

SPECIAL REMARKS

The 2000 and 2600 Spyder were highly praised for their beautiful design. These two convertibles were driven by 2-litre four-cylinder and 2.6-litre six-cylinder motors. Both engines had twin overhead camshafts.

Alfa Romeo 2000 /2600 Sprint

YEARS IN PRODUCTION
1960–1961 and 1962–1965

NUMBER MADE
700 and 6,999

SPECIAL REMARKS
These Sprints were also designed and built by Bertone.

Alfa Romeo Montreal

YEARS IN PRODUCTION
1970–1977

NUMBER MADE
3,925

It was a great honour for Alfa and for Bertone to be asked by Canada to provide "the car of the future" for the 1967 World Show.

Originally, Alfa wanted to use the centrally-mounted engine of the Tipo 33, hence the air inlets behind the doors.

Bertone's design for "the dashboard of the future".

A tamer version of the Tipo 33 racing car V-8 engine was fitted to the 3,925 Montreals built.

SPECIAL REMARKS
Alfa were given the task in 1967, through Bertone, of building a prototype for the World Show in Montreal. The resulting car was a road version of the Tipo 33 (type 33) racing car. The car was put into production in 1970 but with a conventionally forward-mounted 2,593 cc V-8 that developed 200 bhp at 6,500 rpm.

Allard

Sydney Allard was born to wealthy parents in South London in 1910. When he was 18, Sydney started work in a garage as an apprentice mechanic. Simultaneously, he started his career as a racing driver, specialising at first in cross-country trials in a Morgan but a year later he was racing at circuits such as Brooklands and Donnington Park.

In 1930, he built the first Allard car: a trials special powered by a Ford V-8 engine. The car was fast and reliable and slowly but surely the interest in the successful car increased and a production line

in 1960. Allard had built a total of 1,901 cars in 15 different models.

Allard sports cars

COUNTRY OF ORIGIN
Great Britain

Allard K1

was established to cope with the increasing demand. The company switched over during World War II to making military vehicles. The company came back on the market in 1946 with the "K1", a simple two-seater convertible, powered by a Ford V-8 that had been developed by Ford at Dagenham for the armed services. In those days, there were no dealers where a car could be collected when purchased. Cars were ordered and then built to order. The Allard Motor Company sold as many cars as it could build and new two-seater and four-seater models followed, both open and enclosed, but with something in common. All of them closely resembled the pre-war trials cars built by Allard. Business was good until 1952, with the best year being 1948, when 432 cars were sold. From 1952 onwards it was easier for the British to buy a new car but Allard's fortunes dwindled. Even Allard's victory in the epic Monte-Carlo rally with a model "P" trials car with a saloon body did little to change matters. Allard tried to keep his head above water by building a smaller car, the Clipper, but it was not successful. Cars were only delivered to order after 1955, and the company closed down

YEARS IN PRODUCTION
1946–1948

NUMBER MADE
151

SPECIAL REMARKS
The first post-war Allard was available with V-8 engines from the British Ford Pilot or American Mercury. These were 3,917 cc and developed 96 bhp at 3,800 rpm.

Allard L1

YEARS IN PRODUCTION
1946–1948

NUMBER MADE
191

In 1951, the Allard J2 could be delivered with a choice of engines. Customers could choose from V-8 motors by Ford, Mercury, Chrysler, or Cadillac.

SPECIAL REMARKS
The L1 was the four-seater version of the K1. The additional space was created by lengthening the wheelbase by 6 in (15cm). The power unit was the reliable Mercury V-8.

Allard J1

YEARS IN PRODUCTION
1947–1948

NUMBER MADE
12

SPECIAL REMARKS
The Allard J1 was a sporting version of the K1 with a shorter wheelbase. It was only available with a Mercury V-8 engine.

Allard M

YEARS IN PRODUCTION
1947–1950

Many British cars immediately after the war were destined for export to America. Only a handful of these cars remained in Europe. This model M was sold to a customer in Switzerland in 1947.

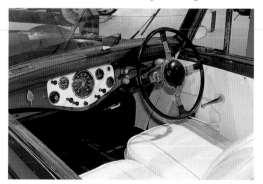

The interior of the Allard M with its abundance of leather and wood and a cranked column gear-change lever

NUMBER MADE
Approx. 500

SPECIAL REMARKS
Immediately after the war, car-makers in Britain could sell everything they could build. Allard was especially successful with the four-seater convertible that was large enough for the whole family. This car was also provided with a Mercury engine.

Allard P

YEARS IN PRODUCTION
1949–1952

NUMBER MADE
559

SPECIAL REMARKS
The Allard P was the saloon version of the M. Sydney Allard won the Monte-Carlo Rally in 1952 with a P-type Allard. The victory boosted Allard's sales. The P-type was also powered by the well-tested Mercury 3,622 cc V-8 which delivered 86 bhp at 3,600 rpm.

Allard J2

YEARS IN PRODUCTION
1950–1952

NUMBER MADE
90

SPECIAL REMARKS
The Type J2 Allard was exclusively intended for motor racing. The necessary power was provided by a 5,428 cc Cadillac V-8 engine that developed 160 bhp at 4,200 rpm.

Allard K2

YEARS IN PRODUCTION
1950–1952

A Belgian registered Allard K2 on the circuit at Zolder.

NUMBER MADE
119

SPECIAL REMARKS
The newer, improved version of the K1 with more attractive, flowing lines. The engine is a 3,622 cc V-8, delivering 96 bhp at 3,800 rpm.

Allard J2X

YEARS IN PRODUCTION
1952–1954

NUMBER MADE
83

SPECIAL REMARKS
The Type J2X was a newer version of the J2, on a lighter chassis, making it extremely fast and highly popular in America. The motor was a 160 bhp Cadillac 5,428 cc V-8.

Mr and Mrs Yamaguchi shipped this J2X from Japan so they could compete in the 1997 Mille Miglia Historica.

Allard M2X

YEARS IN PRODUCTION
1951–1952

NUMBER MADE
25

SPECIAL REMARKS
The Type M2X was a convertible version of the J2X on the new lighter 112 inch (285 cm) chassis. Unfortunately there was little demand for such a model. The M2X was delivered with V-8 engines by Ford, Chrysler, Mercury, or Cadillac.

Allard P2

YEARS IN PRODUCTION
1952–1955

NUMBER MADE
121

SPECIAL REMARKS
This car was also known as a "Monte Carlo". It was a coupé based on the M2X but with a more streamlined body. The engine was a 3,622 cc Ford V-8, delivering 86 bhp at 3,600 rpm.

Allard K3

YEARS IN PRODUCTION
1952–1955

NUMBER MADE
62

SPECIAL REMARKS
The Type K3 Allard moved away from the old, conservative lines, resembling a shorter Jaguar XK 120 but not achieving the same success. The engine was a Ford V-8.

Allard Palm Beach

YEARS IN PRODUCTION
1952–1959

NUMBER MADE
81

SPECIAL REMARKS
Allards were always famous, or notorious, for their large, powerful, and thirsty V-8 engines. The Palm Beach was the first model with smaller British Ford four or six-cylinder engines.

Allard J2R

YEARS IN PRODUCTION
1953–1955

NUMBER MADE
7

SPECIAL REMARKS
This Allard must have been regarded as "back to the roots". It had a 5,424 cc Cadillac V-8 engine that delivered 278 bhp, making this small, lightweight car extremely fast.

Allard Palm Beach MkII

YEARS IN PRODUCTION
1956–1959

NUMBER MADE
7

SPECIAL REMARKS
The final Allard model was the Palm Beach Mk II.

This attractive small car was equipped with the motor from the fast Jaguar XK120. At that time the car was too expensive as customers were able to buy much more car for their money elsewhere. Allard was unable to keep going and was forced to close down.

Alpine

Jean Rédélé was born in 1922, the son of a Renault dealer in Dieppe. He studied at the Hautes Etudes Commerciale or business school until his father handed over the business to him. At the age of 24, he was the youngest Renault dealer in France. Rédélé drove in his first rally in a Renault 4CV in 1951, was successful in the Le Mans 24-hour race, and won his class in the Mille Miglia at least three years in a row.

The first special version of a Renault 4CV appeared in 1954. This coupé was designed in Italy by Giovanni Michelotti and built in aluminium by Carrozzeria Allemano. Once a second coupé arrived from Italy, Rédélé knew what he wanted and had two prototypes built in

The in-built additional lights hint at the Alpine's rally breeding.

A scene at an Alpine club day.

steel. He introduced the first Alpine in July 1955. The Alpine Mille Miles A106 was of course based on a 4CV underframe but had a glass-reinforced polyester body. The Société des Voitures Alpine was established in Paris in October 1955 and series production began in January 1956. Renault included the car in their sales range and provided the young manufacturer with the parts that he needed. Once the Dauphine appeared, Rédélé based his Alpines on this car, calling the new version the A108. The successor to the A108, the A110, was introduced in 1963. This model was a hit and remains the most loved of the Alpines, even though it has not been built since 1976. The A110 was delivered as a coupé and a convertible and was powered by the motors from the Renaults, 8, 12, 15, or 16. The A110 was unbeatable in rallying, winning wherever they competed. Renault took-over Alpine in 1962 but this did not mean the end of the Dieppe factory, on the contrary, "real" racing cars were also built there to racing formulas such as the A 442, with which the 1978 Le Mans was won.

A new Alpine factory was built in Dieppe in 1969 and two years later a new model, the A 310 was presented at the Geneva motor show. This model was intended to support the popular A 110. The new car had the Renault R16 engine that had been tweaked from 67 up to 127 bhp. The top speed of this new racing example was 210 km per hour (131 mph). The final A 110 left the assembly line in 1977, to leave room for the A 310 V-6.

Alpine sports cars

COUNTRY OF ORIGIN
France

The great adventure began with the Alpine A 106.

There was a Renault 4 CV engine under the bonnet of the A 106

Alpine A 106

YEARS IN PRODUCTION
1955–1961

NUMBER MADE
251

SPECIAL REMARKS
Jean Rédélé established the basis of his business with the A 106. A victory in the 1955 Mille Miglia provided tremendous "free" publicity. The four-cylinder engine was 747 cc, delivering 43 bhp at 6,200 rpm.

Alpine A 108

YEARS IN PRODUCTION
1960–1962

NUMBER MADE
236

SPECIAL REMARKS
When Renault introduced the Renault Dauphine, Alpine naturally availed themselves of the new engines. The A 108 was powered by an 845 cc four-cylinder engine that delivered from 31 to 68 bhp.

Alpine A 110

YEARS IN PRODUCTION
1963–1976

NUMBER MADE
8,139

SPECIAL REMARKS
The A 110 made the company world famous. The car was ideally suited for everyday use but was also an excellent rally car. The four cylinder engines ranged from 956 to 1,647 cc.

The A 110 was World Rally Champion in 1971 and 1973.

The A 110 was also available until 1969 as a convertible.

An A 110 en route to victory at the Zolder circuit.

The Alpine A 310 was a futuristic looking coupé in 1971.

Alta sports and racing cars were both single seat and two-seaters

Alpine A 310

YEARS IN PRODUCTION
1971–1976

NUMBER MADE
2,340

SPECIAL REMARKS
The A 310 was the successor to the A 110. The four-cylinder engine originated from the Renault R16. Whether the car was better looking than its predecessor is a question of personal taste. The four cylinder engine was 1,605 cc and delivered 127 bhp at 6,250 rpm.

Alta

Geoffrey Taylor's firm Alta had its best years before World War II. Taylor began to build trials cars in 1928 in one of his father's stables. In itself this is not remarkable but was truly impressive was that Geoffrey Taylor built his own engines, and very good engines they were too, with aluminium blocks and a cylinder head with twin overhead camshafts. These engines had capacities ranging from 1,074 to 1961 cc. The largest of these, when equipped with a Rootes turbocharger could deliver at least 180 bhp.
During the war, the Alta factory produced parts for the aircraft industry but returned in 1947 to cars. Alta built sports cars and racing cars, and some which were suitable for both purposes. There was even an Alta Formula 1 racing car with its own Alta engine but the car never competed, although the engine helped secure

the first British Grand Prix victory in 1955 since 1920 when it powered a Connaught. By that time, however, the Alta factory doors had been closed for some years.

Alta sports cars

COUNTRY OF ORIGIN
Great Britain

Alta 2 Litre

YEARS IN PRODUCTION
1945–1947

NUMBER MADE
14

SPECIAL REMARKS
Alta was not very successful with its post-war cars. Even though there was a huge demand for cars, the company had difficulty in selling its cars.

Alta made its own engines, with twin overhead camshafts, and on request with turbocharger.

Alvis

Pre-war Alvis cars can be compared with a Bentley or Aston Martin. These were thorough-bred sports cars or very sporty family cars. The extremely long bonnet was a characteristic of an Alvis. Alvis picked up after the war where it left off, with the TA14 limousine, which somewhat resembled the Jaguars of that time.

In 1950, the company built 32 type TB-21 sporty convertibles but made little profit from them. Business picked-up slightly after the Swiss coachbuilder Graber put an elegant body on an Alvis rolling chassis. Graber was the official importer for Switzerland and in 1954, he was able to offer his customers four different models. When one of these was displayed at the Paris Motor Show the following year, only the new Citroën DS 19 got more attention. From 1955, the bodies were built in Britain to drawings by Graber but the production in Britain was less efficient than in Switzerland, making them more expensive than when built in Switzerland. An Alvis TC 108 G, with the G standing for Graber, cost £3,500 in 1955, more or less what a well-maintained cottage would fetch at that time. The cars were good looking though and the renowned magazine The Autocar began its

description with: "one of the most attractive and best proportioned cars to be shown at the Earls Court Motor Show is the 3.0 litre Alvis, the favourite of the true car enthusiast." From 1958, Alvis bodies were built by Park Ward, who also built bodies for Bentley and Rolls-Royce. The new type was known as the Alvis TD21 but Graber continued to build in Switzerland and produced a further 126 cars. The Series II TD21 Alvis appeared in 1962, alongside a Graber "Special" convertible that had space for five people and a top speed of 106 mph (170 km/hour). This car cost 36,500 Swiss francs at that time. If this seems a great deal of money, a Bentley cost 87,000 Swiss francs then.

Graber's final version was the TE21 with vertically-mounted twin headlights. Alvis was taken over by Rover in July 1965 and the Alvis TF21 could be purchased until 1966. When Rover was in turn taken over by Leyland Motors, it meant the end of the line for Alvis cars. From then on the name was solely used for military vehicles.

Alvis sports cars

COUNTRY OF ORIGIN
Great Britain

Alvis TB14

YEARS IN PRODUCTION
1949–1950

NUMBER MADE
Approx. 100

SPECIAL REMARKS
The Alvis TB14 was the sporting version of the TA14, built to a pre-war design with a four-cylinder engine of 1,892 cc that delivered 56 bhp at 4,400 rpm.

A 1956 Graber Special built in Switzerland.

Alvis TA21

YEARS IN PRODUCTION
1950–1953

NUMBER MADE
1,314

SPECIAL REMARKS
The TA21 was the successor to the TA14 but it still had a rather old-fashioned appearance. The engine, however, was now a 2,993 cc six-cylinder that delivered 84 bhp at 4,000 rpm.

Alvis TB21

YEARS IN PRODUCTION
1951–1952

NUMBER MADE
31

SPECIAL REMARKS
The TB21 was a convertible sports car that was supposed to compete with the Jaguar XK120. It had a six-cylinder 2,993 cc engine that delivered 95 bhp at 4,000 rpm. The BB21 was succeeded by the TC21.

A 1954 Alvis TC21 soft-top sports car.

Alvis, as exemplified by this 1954 TC21, remained typically English with right-hand drive and ample leather and wood trimmings, despite being built in Switzerland.

The TD21 Series II can be recognised by its modern twin headlights.

The TD21 Series II was a spacious five-seater.

Alvis TD21

YEARS IN PRODUCTION
1956–1963

NUMBER MADE
1,086

SPECIAL REMARKS
After the Swiss coachbuilder Hermann Graber had constructed a body on an amended rolling chassis, Alvis put this new car into production. It had a six-cylinder, 2,993 cc engine that delivered 104–115 bhp at 4,500 rpm.

Alvis TE21

YEARS IN PRODUCTION
1963–1967

NUMBER MADE
353

SPECIAL REMARKS
These two-door convertible and coupé also originated on the drawing board of Graber. The engine was a six-cylinder 2,993 cc that delivered 150 bhp at 4,750 rpm.

The TF was the final model to bear the Alvis marque on its radiator grill.

Alvis TF21

YEARS IN PRODUCTION
1963–1967

NUMBER MADE
106

SPECIAL REMARKS
The final model Alvis to be sold was the TF21, which had a slighter more powerful engine (153 bhp) than the TE21 and an entirely new dashboard.

American Motors

After the troubled companies of Hudson and Nash merged in 1954 to become the American Motors Corporation, AMC became number four behind the "big three" of Detroit. The distance between AMC and number three, Chrysler, widened further though and the company reported a loss of $12,500,000 in 1966. The forecast for 1967 was even worse so the president of the company, Roy Abernathy, was fired and his successor, Toy Chapin managed to

achieve a profit of $4,500,000. Chapin was responsible for several fine cars, such as the Javelin.

The Javelin was a response to the Ford Mustang and Chevrolet Camaro. Various engines could be installed, from a "small" 3.8 litre six-cylinder (147 bhp) to a 5.6 litre V-8 that delivered 284 SAE bhp, which made the car dangerously fast. The cars were raced successfully and in 1967 there was precious little between the Javelins and the Ford Mustang team that actually carried off the Trans-Am series. American sports car enthusiasts constantly demanded true American sports cars, yet when they bought one, it was usually of European origin. This forced the Detroit motor manufacturers after a few years to cease production. This also happened with the Kaiser-Darrin and the Nash-Healey. Only a giant and wealthy company like General Motors could manage to keep a sports car such as the

Corvette in production, even though the response was minimal. American Motor's AMX-2 (AMX-1 was a prototype) was also unable to pull it off. AMC did manage to sell 6,725 in the first year (1968) and even 8,293 the following year but this dropped to 4,000 in 1970. When the forecasts for 1971 looked worse, the car disappeared from the production line.

The AMX-2 had hardly begun production when designer Dick Teague started work on the successor, the AMX-3. With a length of 171 in (435 cm), the successor was 6 in (15 cm) shorter than its predecessor. The engine was now mounted in front of the rear axle, admidships in the car.

Teague insisted that a true sports car should be configured this way. When it was clear that the AMX was not going to succeed, the AMX-3 project was scrapped after only two prototypes had been built.

AMC sports cars

COUNTRY OF ORIGIN
USA

The long bonnet (or hood) and short rear end were typical for the time.

A M launched the Javelin on the market in 1971.

AMC Javelin

YEARS IN PRODUCTION
1968–1974

NUMBER MADE
238,098

SPECIAL REMARKS
The Javelin was a response to the Ford Mustang and Chevrolet Camaro. It had V-6, 3,799 cc/147 bhp or V-8, 6,383 cc/330 bhp engines.

The last AMX cars were built in 1970, when 4,000 were sold.

The standard engine of the AMX was a 5,622 cc motor that delivered 284 SAE bhp.

A prototype of the AMX-3 which never went into production.

The 340 bhp engine of the AMX-3 was mounted in front of the rear axle.

Is it a Porsche-Abarth? No, an Apal replica.

AMC AMX

YEARS IN PRODUCTION
1968–1970

NUMBER MADE
19,134

SPECIAL REMARKS
The AMX appeared to be smaller than the Javelin but it was only supplied with a 6,383 cc V-8 engine that delivered 330 bhp at 5,000 rpm.

Apal

The Apal company (Application Polyester Armé Liège) was set-up in 1963 by Edmond Pery to build replicas of famous sports cars. The cars were built on a VW Beetle chassis and looked exactly like the Porsche-Abarth. This was followed by coupés and soft-tops with Renault engines but Porsche and Triumph engines were also fitted.
No fewer than 375 cars of Formula V were built between 1965 and 1967. Ten coupés were built in 1968 with a centrally-mounted engine followed by a series of dune buggies. The best known Apal model is the replica Porsche 356 Speedster.

Apal sports cars

COUNTRY OF ORIGIN
Belgium

Apal 1200

YEARS IN PRODUCTION
1963–1966

NUMBER MADE
Unknown

SPECIAL REMARKS
The majority of its sports coupés and soft-tops were built on a VW Beetle chassis.

Arnolt MG/ Bristol/Aston Martin

The young engineer Stanley Harold "Wacky" Arnolt's very first job during the Great Depression must have seemed such bad luck. The Waukesha Engineering Company for whom he worked became bankrupt and as payment in lieu "Wacky" was given the patent for an outboard motor. That was in 1939, but two years later he had two factories running night and day to produce "Arnolt SeaMite" motors for the US Navy. These outboard motors made his fortune and when the peace treaty was signed, Arnolt's factories – there were now six of them – switched over to making consumer products.
Arnolt was one of the first American to import an MG TC from Britain in 1946. A year later he had several garages in Chicago and by 1952, he was the BMC (British Motors Corporation) importer for the American mid-west after selling 1,000 Morris Minors in one deal. He was already at that time the dealer for Bristol cars and Solex mopeds.
When he visited a motor show in Turin, Wacky ordered 200 MG chassis with bodies by Bertone, which he sold in the United States as Arnolt-MG. When, after they had delivered 100 chassis,

Franco Scaglione still worked for Bertone when he designed the Arnolt-Aston-Martin.

The Arnolt-MG was available with either spokes or pressed steel wheels.

MG could supply no more, the Arnolt-Bristol was created, also with a Bertone body. These later cars could be raced and this was proved in 1955, when these Bristols were placed first, second, fourth, and fifth in their class in the 12-hour Sebring race.

After a meeting with David Brown, who owned Aston Martin, four Arnolt Aston Martins were built on DB2/4 chassis. These cars were exhibited at the New York Motor Show in 1954. These cars were similarly designed by Franco Scaglione and built by his employers, Bertone.

Arnolt sports cars

COUNTRY OF ORIGIN
USA

Arnolt-MG

YEARS IN PRODUCTION
1952-1956

Arnolt-MG: 35 were built as convertible with the remainder being coupés.

NUMBER MADE
Approx. 100

SPECIAL REMARKS
To provide Bertone with the capital required for the 200 MG chassis, "Wacky" Arnolt bought half the Bertone company. The engines were 1,250 cc with four-cylinders, delivering 55 bhp at 5,200 rpm.

Arnolt-Bristol

YEARS IN PRODUCTION
1956-1960

NUMBER MADE
142

SPECIAL REMARKS
When MG could no longer deliver the TC chassis, Arnolt switched over to the Bristol. This had a six-cylinder, 1,971 cc engine, delivering 132 bhp at 5,500 rpm.

A 1953 Arnolt-Bristol that cost $3,995 in USA.
A Bristol 404 cost $9,946.

The instruments of an Arnolt-Bristol were mainly hidden behind the wide spokes of the steering wheel.

A rare bird: the ASA 1000 convertible.

Arnolt-Aston Martin

YEARS IN PRODUCTION
1954

NUMBER MADE
4

SPECIAL REMARKS
The Arnolt-Bristol was a subsequent design by Franco Scaglione. The engine was a 2,580 cc six-cylinder that delivered 127 bhp at 5,000 rpm.

There were only four Arnolt-Aston Martin's made. The rolling chassis was shipped from Britain to Turin and then exported from there to America.

ASA

A small car that had been designed by Bizzarini for Enzo Ferrari was displayed at the 1961 Turin motor show.

The "Ferrarina", as the car became known, had an aluminium four-cylinder engine with an overhead camshaft and a capacity of 1,032 cc, delivering 97 bhp at 7,000 rpm. The coupé body

was built on a tubular chassis and had space for two people.

Several months later, the convertible version was shown at the Geneva Salon. Both cars had been built by Bertone. The car never went into series production in the Ferrari works because Enzo Ferrari sold the production rights to Oronzio de Nora, owner of a chemical works. Ferrari was paid about $150,000. Nora gave his son, Niccolo, the family's old factory. Cemsa-Caproni had once built aircraft in the factory but production of the new car was very slow to get going.

The car was called the ASA Mille, with ASA being an abbreviation of Autocostruzioni Societa per Azioni. The car, with its top speed of 125 mph (200 km/hour) was very fast but virtually none were sold. This was doubtless due to the high price. In the autumn of 1965, the ASA 411 came into being with a larger 1,092 cc engine and a coupé body by Marazzi. The ASA 1000 coupé body had been built by Touring of Milan but the making of the polyester body for the convertible was entrusted to Corbetta.

That same year, a 150 bhp 1.8 litre engine was introduced, with an overhead camshaft of

A dashboard just like a real Ferrari.

course, and two twin Weber carburettors. The ASA Tipo 613 Roll-Bar, with a "targa" roof, was introduced in Geneva in 1966.
This car was powered by a 1.3 litre six-cylinder engine.

ASA sports cars

COUNTRY OF ORIGIN
Italy

ASA 1000

YEARS IN PRODUCTION
1962–1968

NUMBER MADE
100

SPECIAL REMARKS
Only 100 examples were sold of the ASA 1000, of which 70 were coupés. The four-cylinder engine had a capacity of 1,032 cc, delivering 97 bhp at 7,000 rpm.

Bizzarrini was responsible for the design of this four-cylinder engine.

Aston Martin

Aston Martin started out in a small way and never became a big company. In 1913, Bamford & Martin built a first special by putting a Coventry-Simplex motor in an Isotta-Fraschini chassis. The car appeared to be readily saleable but World War I put an end to its production. A second car followed in 1919, now with an Aston Martin chassis. The car's name was derived from the Aston-Clinton hill climb that was won by the first prototype. More cars followed, with satisfied customers.
The biggest financier, famous driver Count Lozuis Zborowski, was killed at Monza in 1924, putting the company into financial difficulties. The factory was sold for £3,600 and became Aston Martin Ltd. The cars built by Aston

The first ASA 1000 coupés were built by Carrozzeria Bertone.

Rudge nave plates on the wheels as with true Ferrari cars.

The Aston Martin works team won fifteen out of thirty-five races in a DB3S. The car shown is from 1954.

The rear window of the early Astons was also the boot lid.

Martin were very successful on racing circuits but did not sell well. The company took until 1932 to sell 15 cars.

Aston Martin did not really flourish until 1947 when it was in the hands of David Brown. He showed a completely new DB1 model in September 1948 (the initials were short for David Brown) and this was followed in 1950 by

The DB2/4 had a six-cylinder, 2,922 cc engine which had power of 162–214 bhp, depending on the tuning and choice of carburettors.

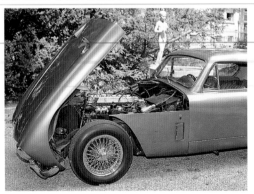

the DB2 with a 2.6 litre engine designed by W.O. Bentley for Lagonda, which was also owned by Brown. When the DB2 was succeeded in April 1953 by the DB2/4, 410 were sold.

Aston Martins had competed regularly at Le Mans since 1928. When three DB2 cars took part in 1950, Aston achieved its first class victory. Five Astons took part in 1951 and everyone of them finished. This achievement can be judged against the fact that of 60 starters, 30 failed to finish. Aston Martin did better still in 1959: of the 31 prototype cars that started, only three survived the 24 hour race, and two of these were Aston Martin racing cars. The DB3 and DB3S were other successful Aston Martins that were built solely for circuit racing in the early 1950s.

Aston Martin made and sold the very fast sporting coupés and convertibles in order to finance its expensive racing cars. The company even tried its hand at Grand Prix racing in 1959 and 1960.

The successful DB4 first left the factory in 1959, complete with an aluminium body, designed by the Italian firm of Touring. This car had twin overhead camshafts, in common with all Aston Martins since the DB1. More than 1,200 had been sold when the DB5 arrived on the scene in 1964. The following model was the DB6, the last Aston Martin with a six-cylinder engine. The DBS of 1969 had a superb V-8 under the bonnet. David Brown sold the company to William Willson in 1972 for the symbolic sum of £1. In return Willson had to take on the company's debts but these proved to be too great for the company to restart. By 1975, the loans could no longer be paid and production had to cease. The business was saved in June 1976 by American investors.

The DB4 GT had a 90 in (230 cm) wheelbase instead of 98 in (249 cm)

Aston Martin sports cars

COUNTRY OF ORIGIN
Great Britain

Aston Martin DB1

YEARS IN PRODUCTION
1948–1950

NUMBER MADE
15

SPECIAL REMARKS
The first designs for the DB1 were made before World War II. The four-cylinder, 1,970 cc engine delivered 90 bhp at 4,750 rpm.

The Aston Martin 2-litre. When the DB2 appeared in 1953, the first models were retrospectively called DB1.

Aston Martin DB2

YEARS IN PRODUCTION
1949–1953

NUMBER MADE
407

The DB2 six-cylinder engine produced 105–123 bhp at 5,000 rpm.

SPECIAL REMARKS
The six-cylinder, 2,580 cc engine of the DB2 was designed by W.O. Bentley and delivered 116 bhp at 5,000 rpm.

Aston Martin DB2/4 Mk 1

YEARS IN PRODUCTION
1953–1955

NUMBER MADE
565

SPECIAL REMARKS
The addition of the "4" indicated that this DB2 had space for four persons. The engine had six-cylinders, with a choice of 2,580 or 2,922 cc capacity, and delivered 127 or 142 bhp.

Aston Martin DB2/4 Mk 2

YEARS IN PRODUCTION
1955–1957

NUMBER MADE
199

SPECIAL REMARKS
The Mark 2 DB2/4 was shown in October 1955 at the London Motor Show. It had a six-cylinder, 2,922 cc engine that delivered 142 bhp at 5,000 rpm.

Aston Martin DB2/4 Mk 3

YEARS IN PRODUCTION
1957–1959

NUMBER MADE
551

SPECIAL REMARKS
The DB2/4 Mk 3 was the final version of this successful design. The 2,922 cc six-cylinder engine was significantly more powerful than its predecessors, delivering 164 bhp at 5,000 rpm.

Aston Martin built 1,700 plus DB2 cars: the DB2/4 Mk 3.

Aston Martin have always given great thought to the dashboard. It was (and still is) both sporty and clearly set out.

The DB2/4 Mk 3 was made between March 1957 and July 1959.

Aston Martin DB4

YEARS IN PRODUCTION
1958–1963

NUMBER MADE
1,110

SPECIAL REMARKS
The body of the DB4 was designed by Carrozzeria Touring but the car was built in England. The engine was a 3,670 cc six-cylinder one that delivered 243 bhp at 5,500 rpm.

Aston Martin DB4 GT

YEARS IN PRODUCTION
1960–1963

NUMBER MADE
100

SPECIAL REMARKS
The DB4 GT was built on a shorter chassis and was more intended for the race track than the open road. Its 3,670 cc six-cylinder engine delivered 302 bhp at 6,000 rpm.

The DB4 GT engine had twin spark plugs per

There was no room in the boot of the DB4 GT for any luggage.

Aston Martin DB4 GT Zagato

YEARS IN PRODUCTION
1960–1963

NUMBER MADE
19

SPECIAL REMARKS
The rarest member of the Aston Martin family was the DB4 GT Zagato. This car was technically identical to the standard GT but the body shape was far more interesting. Its 3,670 cc

The Aston Martin DB4 GT with body by Zagato.

Nineteen Astons were built with Zagato bodies between 1961 and 1963.

six-cylinder engine delivered 302 bhp at 6,000 rpm.

Aston Martin DB5

YEARS IN PRODUCTION
1963–1965

NUMBER MADE
1,018

SPECIAL REMARKS
James Bond made the DB5 world famous. The convertible model is designated "Volante". The "Vantage" had a more powerful engine. Engines: 3,995 cc six-cylinders, 282 bhp at 5,500 rpm or 314 bhp at 5,750 rpm.

Aston Martin DB6

YEARS IN PRODUCTION
1965–1970

NUMBER MADE
1,575

SPECIAL REMARKS
The DB6 was given a new roof line which provided more space for rear seat passengers. The 3,995 cc, six-cylinder engines delivered 282 bhp at 5,500 rpm or 325 bhp at 5,750 rpm.

Aston Martin DBS

YEARS IN PRODUCTION
1967–1973

NUMBER MADE
800

SPECIAL REMARKS
The DBS was technically identical to the six-cylinder DB6 but had a different body. The 3,995 cc, six-cylinder engines delivered 282 bhp at 5,500 rpm or 325 bhp at 5,750 rpm.

Aston Martin DBS V8

YEARS IN PRODUCTION
1969–1989

NUMBER MADE
1,755

SPECIAL REMARKS
The DBS was also available from September 1969 with a V-8 engine with four camshafts, and fuel injection that delivered 375 bhp at 5,000 rpm.

The DB6 was made between 1965 and 1970 and almost 2,000 examples were sold.

ATS

A number of top technical specialists at Ferrari left the firm in the autumn of 1961 following a row with the director, Enzo Ferrari. The multimillionaire Count Volpi took several of them under his wing to work in his Scuderia Serenissima and provided the finance for a new company, ATS (Automobili Turismo Sport SpA) in Bologna. The first cars that Carlo Chiti built in his new role as chief engineer were single-seaters for Grand Prix racing. Unfortunately for all concerned, these cars were not successful. This was followed by building a GT coupé which was shown to the press at the 1963 Geneva show. It was a wonderful looking car with a body by Allemano.

The engine was a 2,467 cc V-8 that had power of at least 210 bhp. The ATS 2500 GT was never raced and did not sell well. The ATS name had been damaged by the Formula One debacle and there was reluctance to spend a great deal of money on an entirely unknown make. When 12 of the cars had been made, the factory had to

The aluminium V-8 engine of the 2500 GT had twin overhead camshafts and four twin Weber carburettors. The engine was positioned in front of the rear axle.

The ATS 2500 GT had an aluminium body that was made by Allemano.

close down. Count Volpi took the drawings with him to his Palazzo in Venice and used them later for his Serenissima sports cars.

ATS sports cars

COUNTRY OF ORIGIN
Italy

ATS 2500 GT

YEARS IN PRODUCTION
1963–1964

NUMBER MADE
12

SPECIAL REMARKS
A number of former Ferrari employees wanted to show with the ATS 2500 GT that they could build top-class cars without the inspirational leadership of Enzo Ferrari. The 2,468 cc V-8 engine delivered 210–245 bhp at 7,700 rpm.

This cut-away drawing by Cavara appeared in the ATS brochure.

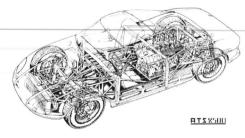

Audi

The Audi name is one of the oldest German car marques. Audi was founded in 1909 by August Horch a month after he left his own Horch works after a row with the management. Audi cars were usually characterised by their sturdiness, and more up-market appeal, often with a straight-eight engine with overhead camshaft.

Competition in Germany in the late Twenties was fierce and the demand for expensive cars was fairly low, bringing the factory, which employed more than 1,000 people, to financial crisis in 1928. The owner of DKW, J.S. Rasmussen, bought the company and formed Auto Union in 1932 from Audi, DKW, Horch, and Wanderer. The last car to come out of the factory until after World War II was made in 1940. Production did not restart until 1965. The first new generation Audi cars were really a DKW with a face-lift. It was some years before the family cars got a look of their own. A sportive Audi 100S was shown at the IAA in Frankfurt in the autumn of 1969. This was a two-door coupé on a shortened Audi 100 underframe. The body provided space for four occupants but was only 523/8 in (133 cm) high. The four-cylinder engine was bored out to 1,871 cc and fitted with twin carburettors, so that the overhead valves could deliver 115 bhp at 5,500 rpm to the front wheels. The synchro-mesh four-speed gear box was operated by a floor-mounted gear lever and the front wheels had disc brakes. This was not an unnecessary luxury, since the car had a top speed of 116 mph (185 km/hour). The 100S remained in production until 1976 and 30,687 of them were sold.

With a length of 173 in (4.40 m), the Audi 100S was certainly not a small car.

Audi sports cars

COUNTRY OF ORIGIN
Germany

Audi 100S

YEARS IN PRODUCTION
1969–1976

NUMBER MADE
30,687

SPECIAL REMARKS
The Audi 100S was more of a sporty coupé than a true sports car but this did not trouble the public with whom it was quite popular. The 1,871 cc, four-cylinder engine delivered 115 bhp at 5,000 rpm.

Austin

The Austin name was once very famous but is now almost forgotten. Herbert Austin began to make cars in 1905 and soon became once of the largest British car manufacturers. The Austin range was always all encompassing – the company made both small cars and big limousines.

Pre-war Austins were not really sporting, although the tiny Austin Seven, which was the forerunner of all mini cars, did compete in races and rallies.

After World War II the policy changed and a few sports models were added to the range, such as the A40 Sport which came out in 1951 and was developed for the American market. The car still had a separate chassis but also had independent front suspension and an overhead valve engine. The bodywork was produced by Jensen which explains why the car resembled the Jensen Interceptor of the period.

The initial A40 was succeeded in 1952 by the A40 Somerset.

The bodywork of the Austin A40 Sport, like this 1952 example, was built by Jensen.

The Austin A90 Atlantic was built from 1949–1952 but it was not a success.

A further example was the A90 Atlantic which was developed following a business trip by Leonard Lord, the then head of Austin, to the United States. Lord studied the American market and thought the A90 Atlantic would be successful. Masses of chrome, rounded lines, and a powerful engine were intended to bring the dollars streaming to Britain. The Atlantic also had electrically-operated side windows and a motorised hood which were unheard of in a European car. The Atlantic was a failure despite these features. The Americans bought just 350 of them and the rest of the world didn't show much interest either. The total production was a mere 7,981 cars.

The new generation Austin Seven became better known as the "Mini", The Mini-Cooper was very successful in both rallying and production car racing.

Austin sports cars

COUNTRY OF ORIGIN
Great Britain

Austin A40 Sport

YEARS IN PRODUCTION
1950–1953

NUMBER MADE
4,011

SPECIAL REMARKS
The A40 Sport was specially developed for the American market. It had a 1,200 cc engine that developed 46 bhp at 5,000 rpm.

Austin A90 Atlantic

YEARS IN PRODUCTION
1949–1952

NUMBER MADE
7,981

SPECIAL REMARKS
The A90 Atlantic had everything the Americans could want but they did not take to it and it flopped. The 2,660 cc four-cylinder engine developed 88 bhp at 4,000 rpm.

Austin Healey

Donald Healey was totally immersed in motor cars: he raced them, won rallies such as the Monte Carlo rally, and was technical director of Triumph before building cars in his own name after the war (see Healey). In 1952, he built a special from Austin parts. When he showed this Austin Healey (still then without a hyphen) at the Earls Court Motor Show, the head of Austin, Leonard Lord, was so impressed that he bought the production rights before the show had even opened.
The first Austin-Healey had a simple chassis with the 2,660 cc four-cylinder engine from the Austin A90. The overhead valve engine delivered at first 90 and subsequently 110 bhp, which gave a top speed of 106 mph (170 km/hour). The Americans

One of the first series of Austin-Healey 100/4 BN1 with a 2.6 litre four-cylinder engine and three-speed gear box.

The headlights of the Austin-Healey Sprite were mounted on the bonnet to meet the US minimum-height requirements.

were crazy about this attractive two-seater. Very soon, even faster models appeared, such as the 100/M with a four-speed gearbox and 110 bhp instead of 90 bhp engine. There was also the 100/S with an aluminium cylinder head that developed 132 bhp. With this engine, the car accelerated from 0–60 mph in 7 seconds (0–100 km/hour in 7.8 seconds). This car was the first production car with four disc brakes and an aluminium body. It became famous at American racing circuits where it retained the upper hand for some time.

When the British Motor Corporation developed a new six-cylinder engine, this was also used in the Austin-Healey. The 100/6 had a 2 in (5 cm) longer wheelbase, giving more comfort for the passengers than in the earlier four-cylinder models. The windscreen could no longer be pushed flat on the bonnet but on the other hand, this was the first model with external door handles and a Laycock de Normanville electric overdrive. The 100/6 had a 21 cc smaller capacity motor in spite of the two extra cylinders, and since it was also a heavier car, this affected the performance. To overcome this, the Austin-Healey 3000 appeared to become the best-selling Austin-Healey, which had no more teething problems.

This "Big Healey" as enthusiasts call it, eventually had disc brakes on the front wheels. The Mk 2 had a new gear box and three SU carburettors which helped to achieve a further 8 bhp from the engine. Because American environmental and safety legislation was becoming increasingly tougher, the Mk 3 had twin carburettors and the car had improved power-assisted brakes. The car continued to sell well in the United States but it eventually became to expensive for the British makers continually to adapt the car, so production ceased in 1968.

For those with less money, Austin built the Austin-Healey Sprite, quickly better-known by its nickname "frog-eye" because of the headlights that were mounted on the bonnet to comply with American legislation.

The car was a design by Gerry Coker and was a real two-seater without any creature comforts. The car was powered by a 948 cc engine from the Austin A35. No-one seemed to mind that this limited its top speed to 81 mph (130 km/hour).

After Syd Enever and Les Ireland had studied the car in every aspect, the Mk 2 was born, with the headlights in the wings. The boot lid was also equipped with a luggage rack. The car was continuously improved: the Mk 3 had windows that could be raised and lowered by a winder, door handles on the outside, and a slightly more powerful motor. The final version with a 1,275 cc engine was the Mk 4 and it had a hood that was fixed to the body so that it no longer had to be packed away in the boot.

The Mk 5 can be recognised by its Rostyle wheels. This model was more elaborately equipped inside. When the contract with Donald Healey was ended, the final 1,022 Sprites were sold as "Austin Sprite".

Austin-Healey sports cars

COUNTRY OF ORIGIN
Great Britain

Austin-Healey 100/4

YEARS IN PRODUCTION
1953–1956

NUMBER MADE
13,398

SPECIAL REMARKS
Donald Healey sold his prototype "Austin Healey" to Austin before the London Motor Show had opened. It had a 2,660 cc four-cylinder engine that developed 90 bhp at 4,500 rpm.

The spartan dashboard of the 100/4

The 100/6 of 1956, known as BN4 by the factory, had a 2 in (5 cm) longer wheelbase than the 100/4.

Austin-Healey 100/4M

YEARS IN PRODUCTION
1955–1956

NUMBER MADE
1,159

SPECIAL REMARKS
The 100/4M had a four-speed instead of three-speed gear box and a more powerful engine with 112 bhp at 4,500 rpm.

Austin-Healey 100/4S

YEARS IN PRODUCTION
1954–1956

NUMBER MADE
55

SPECIAL REMARKS
The 100/4S was specially made with a lightweight aluminium body for racing. The 2,660 cc four-cylinder engine delivered 134 bhp at 4,700 bhp.

Austin-Healey 100/6

The dashboard of the 100/6 was a sober affair.

The more spacious cockpit meant that two small children could be carried in the back.

The motor of the 1956 100/6 delivered 102 bhp. Three years later this had been increased to 117 bhp.

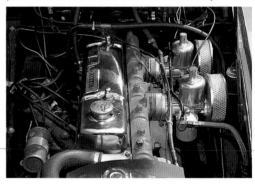

YEARS IN PRODUCTION
1956–1959

NUMBER MADE
14,436

SPECIAL REMARKS
The 100/6 was entirely renewed: the engine was now six cylinders and the longer wheelbase of the chassis improved passengers' comfort.
The 2,639 cc engine developed 102 bhp at 4,600 rpm.

The 3000 Mk 3 was made from 1959 to 1968.

The 3-litre Mk 3 engine gave 124 then 148 bhp, for a top speed of 119 mph (190 km/hour).

A sight for sore eyes! This 3-litre engine from a Mk 2 is made a thing of beauty.

Austin-Healey 3000

YEARS IN PRODUCTION
1959–1968

NUMBER MADE
42,926

SPECIAL REMARKS
The "Big Healey" was the best seller of the Austin-Healeys. Its 2,912 cc six-cylinder engine provided 150 bhp at 5,250 rpm.

Austin-Healey Sprite

YEARS IN PRODUCTION
1958–1971

The frog-eyed look

The headlights were incorporated into the wings in the later Sprites like this 1963 Mk 2.

The interior of a Mk 2 Sprite.

AANTAL
129.350

SPECIAL REMARKS
The "Sprite" was the common man's Healey.
The following versions were produced:

Sprite Mk1	1958-1961	48,987
Sprite Mk2	1961-1964	31,665
Sprite Mk3	1964-1966	25,905
Sprite Mk4 and 5	1966-1969	14,350
Austin Sprite	1969-1971	8,443

Autobianchi

The Bianchi company was founded in Milan back in 1897 by Edoardo Bianchi. The company specialised in large, luxury cars but also built a number of sports cars. Bianchi Tipo Corsas were second and third in the Brescia Grand Prix in 1923. The final pre-war cars were made by the company in 1939 and it was not until 1957 that the company brought out a new car, now under the Autobianchi name. In the earlier years after restarting, the company turned-out Fiats with special bodies but when this was no longer profitable, the business was taken over by Fiat in 1963. The factory built special Fiats in small quantities, prototypes, but also cars for which there was no space on the main factory production lines. Autobianchi built the Stellina in 1964, a sports car based on the Fiat 600 but with a body designed by Tom Tjaarda. This was followed in 1965 by the Bianchina, based on the underframe of a Fiat 500. The A112 was developed jointly with Lancia and built in large numbers, followed by a luxury version of the

Bertone built this "Runabout" for the 1969 Turin show. The car was based on the underframe of an A112.

This is how Pininfarina would like to have built the A112.

Lancia Y. The A112 was a great success and could be bought as a Lancia, Autobianchi, or Abarth. The Abarth version had a 70 bhp engine that gave it a top speed of 100 mph (160 km/hour).

A number of "carrozzeria" such as Pininfarina and Bertone built specials based on an Autobianchi, and these always attracted a great deal of attention at motor shows.

Autobianchi sports cars

COUNTRY OF ORIGIN
Italy

Autobianchi Bianchina

YEARS IN PRODUCTION
1960–1968

NUMBER MADE
9,300

The Autobianchi Bianchina was based on the underframe of a Fiat Nuova 500.

The Bianchina was made between 1957 and 1968 with 44,800 being sold.

BIJZONDERHEDEN
The Bianchina convertible was based on the underframe of a Fiat 500. The twin-cylinder engine was 499 cc, giving 21 bhp at 4,500 rpm.

Autobianchi-Stellina

YEARS IN PRODUCTION
1963–1965

NUMBER MADE
Unknown

SPECIAL REMARKS
Although the Stellina was a relatively large car, it was driven by the 767 cc four-cylinder engine from the Fiat 600 that developed 32 bhp at 4,800 rpm.

Autobianchi-A 112

YEARS IN PRODUCTION
1969–1986

NUMBER MADE
1,254,178

SPECIAL REMARKS
The A112 was a particularly lively car, especially when fitted with the Abarth engine (see Abarth). It was fitted with four-cylinder engines ranging from 903–1,050 cc that developed 44 bhp at 5,600 rpm up to 70 bhp at 6,600 rpm.

A total of 1,254,178 A112 cars were sold.

Avanti II

When Studebaker stopped making its cars, former Studebaker dealers Nate Altman and Leo Newman purchased the right in 1964 to continue building the Avanti but also the majority of the parts and tools. They also employed Eugene Hardig, the already retired former chief engineer of Studebaker. The Avanti

The Avanti II, retaining the classic lines but with wheels that are not suited.

Avanti II sports cars

COUNTRY OF ORIGIN
USA

Avanti II

YEARS IN PRODUCTION
1966–present day

NUMBER MADE
Unknown

SPECIAL REMARKS
Only 909 Avanti II cars were sold in the ten years from 1966 to 1975. The engine is a 5,354 cc V-8 that provides 304 bhp at 5,000 rpm.

II, as the car was now named, was fitted with a Chevrolet Corvette engine because the Studebaker engines were no longer available. The body was identical to the original Avanti. The first cars were delivered in 1976.

Nate Altman died in 1976 and was replaced for a while by his brother Arnold. It is not certain whether Avanti cars are still being made. The last cars were made in 1991 but the factory continued to sell spare parts until 1997, when it finally closed.

An Avanti II in front of the South Bend factory

A new Avanti was always superbly trimmed.

Bandini

Ilario Bandini (1911–1992) was born the son of a farmer in Forli, Italy. He was apprenticed as a mechanic and set-up his own business in 1938.

He never styled himself as a garage owner, rather as motor manufacturer and inventor, with several patents to his name. He was also awarded an honorary engineering degree by an American university.

Bandini certainly produced beautiful cars: probably 73 in all since 1947. Most of these were small racing cars, which were extremely popular immediately after the war but he also later made some wonderful sporting coupés and grand tourers. His cars were often equipped with tuned Fiat engines but he also made good use of the American Crosley engine. In the period from 1947–1952, this four-cylinder engine was quite advanced, with a push-rod driven overhead camshaft. The Crosley engine was often equipped by Bandini with his own cylinder head, with twin camshafts and a replacement crankshaft, also of his own making. The cylinder capacity was determined by the length of piston stroke. In the best years for the Bandini works (during the early Fifties), fifteen mechanics were employed and one car per month was turned out.

In 1960, Bandini even built no fewer than seven different versions of his own engine with capacities ranging from 750–1,300 cc. When mid-car mounted engines became the vogue, Bandini was one of the first to incorporate this into his cars, for his soft-tops and coupés, for racing cars, or even the sporting Sunday driver.

One of Bandini's last creations was the Bandini Bialbero of 1968.

Bandini sports cars

COUNTRY OF ORIGIN
Italy

NUMBER MADE
Unknown

SPECIAL REMARKS
The 750 cc class of Bandini cars were especially highly regarded. With their highly-tuned engines, they were capable of speeds of 100 mph (160 km/hour). Bandini not only worked his

A Bandini 750 tries to overtake a Lagonda M45 in the 1991 Mille Miglia.

There was not really any luggage space.

The engine can be seen through the rear plastic window. This 987 cc powered car could reach 144 mph (230 km/hour)with its power of 89 bhp at 7,200

Not a smaller Ferrari Testarossa but a 1957 Bandini 750.

magic on the engines in his cars but also on the suspension, which was incomparable with that fitted to most small cars.

a sports car with a top speed of almost 125 mph (200 km/hour).

Bentley

It is a long time since the Bentley won Le Mans 24-hours five times in a row. The pre-war sports cars with their 8-litre engines, equipped with superchargers (or turbo in today's language) for extra power, were all conquering. No more real Bentley sports cars were produced after World War II but the Bentley Continental R drove like

Bentley sports cars

COUNTRY OF ORIGIN
Great Britain

Bentley R Continental

YEARS IN PRODUCTION
1952–1955

NUMBER MADE
207

SPECIAL REMARKS
The Bentley Continental R was a very fast 2 + 2 that was ideal for long journeys along boring motorways. The 4,566 cc six-cylinder engine provided 150 bhp.

A fine car from whichever point of view you look at the Bentley.

The body of the Bentley Continental R was built by H. J. Mulliner. About 200 of this model were sold.

Berkeley

Charles Panter had a factory in which shot-up aircraft were repaired during the World War II which he switched over to making caravans after the war. He soon became one of the leading British caravan makers and made so much money that he wanted to start to make small cars. He found a partner in Laurie Bond who had been involved with producing small cars for some time and together they launched the Berkeley marque. Three prototypes were built in Biggleswade in 1956 which were shown at that year's Motor Show.

The reinforced polyester bodies consisted of three parts: a floor-pan, front, and rear body sections that were glued together. The engines were supplied by a motorcycle manufacturer. The front wheels were chain driven. Until 1959, Berkeley fitted their cars with two- and three-cylinder engines but these were the cars' weakest

The Berkeley B60 was introduced in 1956 with a 322 cc Anzani twin-cylindered engine that delivered 15 bhp and had a top speed of 69 mph (110 km/hour).

link. The company had some success in 1959 with a three-wheeler that had a single rear wheel, in the manner of early Morgans. By the time Panter changed over to using the Ford Anglia engine in 1960, it was already too late. Only two of these latter cars were built before the business was wound up.

Berkeley sports cars

COUNTRY OF ORIGIN
Great Britain

Berkeley B60

YEARS IN PRODUCTION
1956–1957

NUMBER MADE
146

SPECIAL REMARKS
The Berkeley B60 was powered by an Anzani twin-cylinder engine of 322 cc capacity that delivered 15 bhp at 5,000 rpm.

Berkeley B65

YEARS IN PRODUCTION
1957

NUMBER MADE
1,272

SPECIAL REMARKS
The Anzani motorcycle engine was replaced by a twin-cylinder 328 cc Excelsior motor delivering 18 bhp at 5,000 rpm.

The interior of the Berkeley SE 328 was very basic. Note the gear lever which operated a motorcycle gearbox and the very simple dashboard.

49

Berkeley B90

YEARS IN PRODUCTION
1957–1959

NUMBER MADE
682

BIJZONDERHEDEN
Met een driecilinder Excelsior-motor kon de B90 als twee- en als vierzitter worden geleverd. Motor: 492 cc en 30 pk/5000 tpm.

Berkeley B95/105

YEARS IN PRODUCTION
1959

NUMBER MADE
194

SPECIAL REMARKS
The figures 95 and 105 indicate the top speed of this car in miles per hour (144/152 km/hour). The engines were Royal Enfield 692 cc twins of 41 bhp at 5,500 rpm in the 95 and a more highly tuned version that gave 51 bhp at 6,250 in the 105.

Berkeley T60

YEARS IN PRODUCTION
1959

NUMBER MADE
1,830

SPECIAL REMARKS
The T60 was a step back in time. The two front wheel of this tri-car were driven by a twin-cylinder Excelsior engine. There was very little demand for this new model. The engine had a capacity of 328 cc and gave 18 bhp at 5,000 rpm.

British cars in the Fifties still had miniscule taillights that were tiny red glows.

Berkeley Bandit

YEARS IN PRODUCTION
1960

NUMBER MADE
2

SPECIAL REMARKS
The Bandit was a modern sports car with an engine from the Ford Anglia. Unfortunately only two prototypes were ever built. The engine was 997 cc, giving 41 bhp at 5,000 rpm.

Beutler

The best known Swiss coachbuilding firm of Beutler in Thun became bankrupt on September 8, 1987. Brothers Fritz and Ernst Beutler – Fritz was the builder and technical expert while Ernst was the designer and draughtsman – set-up the company immediately after the war, mainly producing special bodies for existing chassis.

A 1951 Beutler Special based on a Jowett Jupiter.

Beutler's speciality was Porsche specials. This is a four-seater 356 from 1957.

Beutler convertible of 1947 on an MG Y chassis.

The company began with a Healey, that was then an entirely new English marque. After they had supplied several Healey specials, they built a number of specials on Bristol running gear. In 1949, Beutler's built a number of convertibles based on brand new Porsches from Austria. Porsche became a trusted supplier of chassis and the brothers made a number of different versions, including even a four door saloon.

COUNTRY OF ORIGIN
Switzerland

NUMBER MADE
Unknown

SPECIAL REMARKS
The Beutler brothers were always looking for niches in the market left by the mainstream makers.
Hence they built a Porsche with enough room for four grown-ups and a four door VW Beetle, plus a number of superb sports cars.

A Simca with Beutler coachwork.

Beutler managed to turn a VW Beetle into a sports

Bitter

Peter Monteverdi and Erich Bitter had a great deal in common with each other. Both were racing drivers who imported Italian cars before they started to build cars with Italian bodies and both had to give up their work prematurely because they could not compete with the big car makers.

Erich Bitter was born the son of a cycle maker in Schwelm in Germany in 1933. His career began as a professional racing cyclist but he quickly became a driver with NSU, Volvo, Jaguar, Ferrari, Porsche, but most of all with Abarth. Alongside this he was also an importer of rally parts and equipment and later of Abarth and Intermeccanica sports cars. He began making cars based on the running gear of the more expensive Opels in 1969. When Bob A. Lutz, later to become the boss of Chrysler, ruled the roost at Opel, a "dream car" known as the Astra was developed jointly with the Italian coachbuilder Frua.

General Motors were concerned that this car would spoil sales of the Corvette, so the Astra project was cancelled. Bitter grabbed the opportunity to take over the design and built his first Bitter CD in 1972.

The energy crisis stood in the way of large scale production of the V-8 powered car and up to 1979, only 400 were sold. When Opel stopped making the Diplomat, Bitter was forced to switch to parts from the Senator. The new car was known as the SC. The business failed in 1986 and Erich Bitter emigrated to the United States.

Bitter sports cars

COUNTRY OF ORIGIN
Germany

Bitter CD

YEARS IN PRODUCTION
1973–1979

This Bitter CD could be mistaken for a Lamborghini or Ferrari.

The Bitter CD combined fine Italian lines with sound German engineering.

The bodies of the Bitter CD were made by Baur in Stuttgart. The engine was a 5,354 cc V-8 from the Opel Diplomat.

NUMBER MADE
395

SPECIAL REMARKS
Erich Bitter's cars combined Italian design with the indestructible engineering of American cars or Opel. The engine was a 5,354 cc V-8 that delivered 230 bhp at 4,700 rpm.

Bizzarrini

Giotto Bizzarrini was an important man at Alfa Romeo and Ferrari, who designed the 250 GTO, among other projects.
He left Ferrari following a row with Enzo Ferrari in 1962 and set-up his own business. He

designed the first cars for Lamborghini and Iso Rivolta and then produced the Bizzarrini Grifo Stradale in 1965. This car was actually identical to the Iso Grifo that he had designed for Renzo Rivolta. The mechanical parts originated from Chevrolet Corvette. The body, initially of aluminium and subsequently of glass-reinforced polyester, was made by Piero Drogo in Modena. Within a year, the name of this car was changed to Bizzarrini 5300 Strada.
Bizzarrini brought out a smaller version of the Stradale car in 1966, powered initially by a 1.5 litre Fiat engine and later by a 1.9 litre Opel GT engine. The final model of this series was called the Bizzarrini Europa. There were also a further four sports cars – three soft-tops and one coupé with "winged" doors, that was sold as the Bizzarrini P538. All these four cars were driven by transverse-mounted engines placed in front of the rear axle. The motors were a V-8 Corvette engine or V-12 Lamborghini power unit. One of these sports cars was sold to Giugiaro, from which he created his famous "Manta" special exhibition car.
Bizzarrini had to cease production of his superb cars in 1969 for financial reasons. He worked as a consultant for his former competitors for some years but is now engaged in the restoration or building of cars for extremely wealthy customers.

The Strada looks identical to the Iso Grifo, except the headlights are behind glass and the roof is lower.

A Bizzarrini still attracts a great deal of attention.

The Europa was a smaller Bizzarini with an Opel GT engine.

The 5.4-litre engine in a Bizzarini was a Corvette unit that delivered 365 bhp.

Bizzarrini sports cars

COUNTRY OF ORIGIN
Italy

Bizzarrini Grifo

YEARS IN PRODUCTION
1964–1969

NUMBER MADE
227

SPECIAL REMARKS
The Iso Grifo provided the basis for the Bizzarrini A3C racing car, which was subsequently called the Grifo Strada. The engine was a 5,354 cc V-8 that delivered 360 bhp at 5,400 rpm.

Bizzarrini 1500

YEARS IN PRODUCTION
1966

NUMBER MADE
5

The interior of a Bizzarini was practical and sportive.

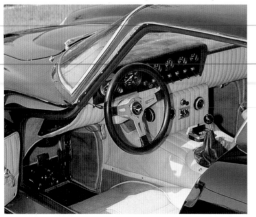

SPECIAL REMARKS
The smaller version of the Strada was sold as the 1500. It had a 1,481 cc four-cylinder Fiat engine that provided 90 bhp at 5,400 rpm.

Bizzarrini Europa

YEARS IN PRODUCTION
1966–1969

NUMBER MADE
15

SPECIAL REMARKS
When the 1500 did not sell, it was replaced by the GT Europa 1900 with a 1,897 cc four-cylinder Opel GT engine that delivered 135 bhp at 5,600 rpm.

Bizzarrini P 538

YEARS IN PRODUCTION
1968–1969

NUMBER MADE
4

The Bizzarrini Strada had a body designed by Bertone for the Iso Rivolta, that was built by Drogo in Modena.

Bizzarini built four cars of the P538 type in the 1960s. It is now a popular replica car.

SPECIAL REMARKS

The Bizzarrini P538 was not really built for the public market but for racing. The P538 was powered by either a Chevrolet Corvette or Lamborghini engine.

BMW

The Bayrischen Flugzeugwerke (Bavarian Aircraft Factory) was founded in 1916 and from this company the Bayrischen Motoren Werke (BMW) or Bavarian Motors Factory was created in 1921. The marque emblem of a rotating propeller stems from these origins. The company began in the Twenties by making motorcycles, then in 1928, the Dixi works were purchased and the company began building English Austin Sevens for the German market. This BMW-Dixi was the first mass-produced German car with more than 32,000 being sold. This was quickly followed by own designs, including very sporty coupés and soft-tops.

During World War II, more than sixty per cent of the BMW factory was destroyed and the remainder was taken as spoils of war by the Russians. BMW was not able to restart making cars until 1952. The first car to come of the new production lines was the 501, which was a luxury model with a six-cylinder engine, but it sold poorly.

BMW decided to replace the six-cylinder engine with a V-8, creating the 502 and 503, with which to compete with Mercedes. The success of these models was limited and the factory switched over to making the Isetta "bubble car" from which the 600, 700, and finally the 1500 developed. The 1500 was the forerunner of today's BMW. The 700 could also be ordered as a sports car or even in a racing version, with mid-mounted engine. Mercedes brought out its 300SL sports car in 1954 and BMW followed suit with its 507 – a two-seater with bodywork designed by

The 507 still looked good with a hard top.

After BMW took over the firm of Hans Glas,
the BMW engine was used for some time in the
1600 GT.

Count Albrecht Goertz, in common with the
503. The larger models with V-8 engines were
continuously improved and achieved their
zenith with the 3200 CS. BMW bought the firm
of Glas in 1966, adding the Glas 1300 and 1700
coupés to its range. BMW made a coupé version
of almost every model and often there was also
a convertible or soft-top as well. The BMW 507
was the high point of sports car design for the
renowned Germany marque.

BMW sports cars

COUNTRY OF ORIGIN
Germany

BMW 700

YEARS IN PRODUCTION
1959–1965

NUMBER MADE
13,758

SPECIAL REMARKS
The BMW 700 was a sports car for those with a
modest pocket. The car was sold as a coupé and
soft-top. The engine was a twin-cylinder 697 cc
unit that delivered 40 bhp at 5,700 rpm.

BMW 502

YEARS IN PRODUCTION
1954–1955

NUMBER MADE
Not known

SPECIAL REMARKS
The first post-war car made by BMW was the
501. A V-8 model, known as the 502 was added
in 1954. Both were fine touring cars that were
powered by a 2,580 cc engine that produced 95
bhp at 4,800 rpm.

BMW 503

YEARS IN PRODUCTION
1955–1959

A 1956 BMW 502 with bodywork by the Germany
firm of Autenrieth of Darmstadt.

The BMW 501 did not sell well. Its engine was
replaced by a V-8 to create the 502 and 503.

The BMW 507 lost the battle for the market between
itself and the Mercedes 300SL. Only 257 of this BMW
were sold.

SPECIAL REMARKS
Many special body companies have create cars based on the BMW 503 but the standard factory body was a marvellous sports car. The engine was a 3,168 cc V-8 that yielded 140 bhp at 4,800 rpm.

BMW 507

YEARS IN PRODUCTION
1955–1959

NUMBER MADE
412

SPECIAL REMARKS
This two-seater was supposed to compete with the Mercedes 300Sl but this was not entirely successful. The engine was a 3,168 cc V-8 that delivered 150 bhp at 5,000 rpm.

The V-8 engine in the BMW 507 provided 150 bhp which was more than ample for speeds in excess of 125 mph (200 km/hour).

The interior of a BMW 507. The wooden Nardi steering-wheel is an accessory.

The final model with the V-8 engine was the 3200 CS, designed by Giugiaro, when he was still working for Bertone.

BMW 3200 CS

YEARS IN PRODUCTION
1961–1965

NUMBER MADE
538

SPECIAL REMARKS
The final tourer with the V-8, which had by then become legendary, was the BMW 3200 CS. The car was almost perfect in engineering terms. The 3,168 cc power unit delivered 160 bhp at 5,600 rpm.

BMW 3.0 CSL

YEARS IN PRODUCTION
1973–1975

NUMBER MADE
39

A 3.0 CSL from the Swiss team of drivers Walter Brun and Cox Kocher competes at Zandvoort circuit in 1973.

Although BMW dealers could order the 3.0 CSL (Coupé Super Light) for anybody, the car was not really suitable for every day road use.

The Bond Equipe was powered by a Triumph Herald engine.

SPECIAL REMARKS
The CSL appeared to be a perfectly normal coupé but with its power of more than 200 bhp, it was really a racing car. The 3,003 cc six-cylinder engine delivered 210 bhp at 5,600 rpm.

Bond

Three-wheeled cars have always been more popular in Britain than elsewhere in Europe, due perhaps to the lower road tax for three-wheeled cars. Various manufacturers produced cars to meet this interest, one of whom was Laurie Bond, who was also associated with the failed Berkeley three-wheelers. Bond produced his first small car in 1949. Power was fed through a single front wheel. Bond added a "real car" to his range in 1963 when he introduced the Bond Equipe GT sports car which was a 2 + 2 with a glass-fibre reinforced polyester body. The chassis, doors and front windscreen were those of a Triumph Herald and the engine was that of a Triumph Spitfire, while the dashboard was from a Triumph Vitesse. This meant that the car could easily be maintained by a Triumph dealer. A true four-seater was added in 1965, the GT4S with its characteristic twin headlights. The Bond 2-litre GT was launched at the 1967 Motor Show. The car was equipped with mechanical components and the six-cylinder engine of a Triumph Vitesse.

Bond still continued with his three-wheelers and so there was also a sporting tri-car with a 700 cc four-cylinder engine that drove the two rear wheels. Getting in and out of this Bond Bug always drew the attention because the upper part of the body had to be lifted. The final Bond four-wheeled car was made in 1970 but the Bug was sold until 1975.

Bond sports cars

COUNTRY OF ORIGIN
Great Britain

Bond Equipe GT

YEARS IN PRODUCTION
1963–1971

NUMBER MADE
451

SPECIAL REMARKS
The Bond Equipe was sold as both a convertible and coupé. The body was made of glass-reinforced polyester, with the mechanical components originating from Triumph. The four-cylinder engine was 1,147 cc, delivering 63 bhp at 5,750 rpm.

Bond Equipe GT4S

YEARS IN PRODUCTION
1965–1971

NUMBER MADE
2,505

SPECIAL REMARKS
The Bond GT4S had room for the entire family. It 1,147 cc four-cylinder engine delivered 67 bhp at 6,000 rpm.

The Vitesse engine of the 2-litre version provided 95 bhp, making speeds of 103 mph (165 km/hour) possible.

Bond Equipe 2 litre

YEARS IN PRODUCTION
1967–1970

NUMBER MADE
1,432

SPECIAL REMARKS
When Triumph introduced a six-cylinder 2-litre engine that provided 95 bhp, Bond was able to use it in his 2-litre Bond Equipe.

Bond Bug

YEARS IN PRODUCTION
1970–1974

NUMBER MADE
2,270

SPECIAL REMARKS
Tri-cars or three-wheelers have been more popular in Britain than other countries. Bond was a specialist in this field. The 701 cc four-cylinder engine provided 32 bhp at 5,000 rpm.

The Bond Bug sold well in spite of its unusual shape.

Bonnet

The initials DB (separate entry) represent Charles Deutsch and René Bonnet who built sports cars, usually with parts by Panhard. The two men went their separate ways in 1961 and started new businesses. René Bonnet sold cars bearing his own name that incorporated Renault parts. His first car was the Djet 4 GT coupé with an 1100 cc engine mounted in front of the rear axle. This four-cylinder unit delivered 70 bhp but if customers wanted more power, the Gordini 95 bhp engine was fitted. The car was not particularly attractive looking but was fast and reliable. The car won its class in 1962 and 1963 at Le Mans in the 24 hour race. Bonnet also built Le Mans and Missile models but these did not sell so well.

Besides these "road" cars, Bonnet also built Formula 2 racing cars with help from Renault but when the cars were not successful, Renault stopped its financial help. Bonnet ran into financial difficulties in 1964 and sold his company to Matra, who continued building the Djet.

Five Bonnets competed in the 1963 24 Hours Le Mans. One achieved class victory but car number 41 was thirteenth over the line so missed out on classification.

A Djet III en route to a veteran's race.

Bonnet sports cars

COUNTRY OF ORIGIN
France

Bonnet Djet

YEARS IN PRODUCTION
1962–1963

NUMBER MADE
Not known

SPECIAL REMARKS
The Djet was available with a 996 cc/65 bhp or 1,108 cc/80 bhp engine.

Bonnet Djet 4 GT

YEARS IN PRODUCTION
1961–1964

NUMBER MADE
Not known

SPECIAL REMARKS
Although not pretty, the Djet 4 GT was very fast.

Borgward

When times were hard in the Twenties, Borgward built his first car. This was an inexpensive three-wheeler that was enthusiastically received. Things were so good for Carl Friedrich Wilhelm Borgward that he was able to take-over the famous Hansa-Lloyd company and built Hansa 1100 and 1700 models among others. The Hansa 2300 was launched in 1939 and sold as a Borgward but during the war, the factory and its 8,000 workers switched to building army lorries and tanks. Allied bombing flattened the factory to the ground in 1944. It did not take Borgward long to reintroduce Hansas after the war but with an entirely new post-war design. The Borgward Isabella appeared in 1954 to become one of the finest and most successful German cars of that period, selling over 200,000. Carl Borgward was technically excellent but his business logic was often difficult to understand. Each of his three business, Borgward, Lloyd, and Hansa, had its own dealer network and own research and development department. Only Borgward as the head of the company brought the strands together. Rather than spend money on motor racing which he regarded as expensive and at risk of causing bad publicity if the cars did not win, Borgward used record breaking to gain publicity. Borgward Hansa 1500 cars broke at least twelve records at the Monthléry circuit. One of these was to average 107½ mph (172 km/hour) for 1,000 miles (1,600 kilometres). A Goliath tri-car rather than one of their delivery vans broke 38 world records on the same circuit. The vehicle drove for two hours at an average speed of 97 mph (155 km/hour), which is quite a feat for a 700 cc twin-stroke engine. Borgward took

This Borgward 1500 GT coupé was launched at the Frankfurt motor show in March 1953.

The Isabella looked particularly good in duo-tone.

on Porsche with the Borgward 1500 in 1953. The cars were very successful in their class in races such as the 1,000-kilometre race at the Nürburgring, where Brudes finished third behind the much more powerful Ferrari and Jaguar. Two of these cars competed in November 1953 in the Carrera Pan-Americana race over 3,100 kilometres in Mexico. Brudes crashed in the first stage and Hartmann was disqualified after a fuel injector broke, making him seven seconds too late across the line. When this happened, he had

been 200 kilometres from the finish and one and a half hours ahead of the eventual winner.

The 350 cc Lloyd showed its metal in May 1954 when it achieved fourteen international records, which included covering 5,000 miles (8,000 kilometres) at an average speed of 70.06 mph (112.1 km/hour). This expensive hobby, plus bad management, brought Borgward into financial difficulties. It was so severe that the company went into voluntary liquidation in September 1961, although this proved subsequently not to have been necessary. Borgward died of a heart attack, aged 74, on 28 July, 1963.

The 1500RS engine delivered 115 bhp which is excellent for a 1.5 litre overhead valve motor.

The 1500RS was designed for both circuit racing and long distance races such as the Carrera Pan-Americana in 1953.

Only five were built of the 1500: three in aluminium and two in steel.

Borgward sports cars

COUNTRY OF ORIGIN
Germany

Borgward 1500 RS

YEARS IN PRODUCTION
1953

NUMBER MADE
Not known

SPECIAL REMARKS
The Borgward 1500 could hold its own against Porsche as the works driver Brudes often proved. The engine was a 1,498 cc four cylinder that delivered 80 bhp.

Borgward Hansa 1800

YEARS IN PRODUCTION
1953–1954

NUMBER MADE
Not known

SPECIAL REMARKS
The Borgward Hansa 1800 Sport had a top

The dashboard of the Borgward 1500 Sport

The 1,498 cc engine delivered 95 bhp at 6,000 rpm and had a compression ration of 9:1.

The Borgward Isabella, named after Borgward's wife.

speed of more than 94 mph (150 km/hour). The engine was a 1,758 cc four-cylinder that delivered 60 bhp at 4,200 rpm.

Borgward Isabella

YEARS IN PRODUCTION
1957–1961

NUMBER MADE
Not known

SPECIAL REMARKS
It seems quite impossible to uncover how many Isabellas were made but it is fairly certain that only 29 convertible models of this car were sold. The engine was a 1,493 cc four cylinder that delivered 75 bhp at 5,200 rpm.

Brabham

Jack Brabham's name is world-famous. Jack was three times World Champion Grand Prix racing driver, including the 1966 season, in a car he built himself. Brabham has built racing cars for numerous classes and formulas but also sports or super cars.

These sports cars too were really intended for circuit racing although a few, such as the Repco-Brabham-Ford two-seater, could be driven on the public highway.

COUNTRY OF ORIGIN
Great Britain

NUMBER MADE
Not known

This Repco-Brabham had a 1,150 cc Ford Cosworth engine but could also be supplied with a four-cylinder Lotus engine.

The "work-place" of a Brabham cockpit provides no unnecessary luxury.

The Bricklin SV–1 was made in 1974–1975.

SPECIAL REMARKS
Jack Brabham has made many different sports cars that were primarily intended for racing. Only a few were provided with detuned engines that could be used in normal traffic.

Bricklin

The Bricklin sports car was developed and sold by American Malcolm Bricklin. The car had the letters SV added to the name to denote "safety vehicle".
Bricklin attempted to use safety as a sales draw to the car but this was only moderately successful. The majority of Bricklins were painted orange to make them stand out and none of the cars had an ashtray because smoking in a car can be dangerous.
The doors were wings that hinged up towards the roof but were never completely water-tight. There were many other faults with the car which were never rectified and after 2,880 cars had been sold, the company went bust with a loss of $23 million.

Bricklin sports cars

COUNTRY OF ORIGIN
USA

Bricklin SV

YEARS IN PRODUCTION
1974

NUMBER MADE
2,880

SPECIAL REMARKS
780 of the SV1 were sold and 2,117 of the slightly improved SV2. The 5,896 cc V-8 engine developed 223 bhp at 4,400 rpm.

Bristol

Towards the end of World War II, it was clear that the Bristol aircraft factory making bombers would need to switch over to a different line. It was decided to make sporting cars aimed at the top end of the market. The intention was for Bristol to co-operate with Frazer-Nash who had built sports cars using BMW 328 engines before the war. The cars were to be known as Frazer-Nash-Bristol but when the first car was shown at the international motor show in Geneva in1947, it was simply known as a Bristol. The model was clearly a successor to the Frazer-Nash 326 of 1939. The engine of the Bristol was an improved version of the BMW 328 motor, delivering 90 bhp. The chassis also had similarities with a BMW. The head of Bristol, H.J. Aldington, who had headed Frazer-Nash before the war, had taken the drawings of the BMW 327/328 back to Britain with him in 1945 as war reparations. The Bristol 400 was a strong and fast car in which drivers could travel long distances without becoming tired. The cars that followed had these same qualities. The rolling chassis was popular

The Bristol 400 chassis was very popular with special car body builders. The car shown has a body by Pininfarina from 1947.

with several special car body builders. Specialists like Pininfarina, Beutler, and Zagato used it for some of their finest creations. The 400 was followed by the 401. 402, and 403, for which the body was developed by Carrozzeria Touring of Milan. Bristol cars were also raced and some special versions were developed for the track. The 450 was an coupé with unusual wings that raced two years in a row at Le Mans. In 1954, these cars finished 7th, 8th, and 9th to win their 2-litre class convincingly. This achievement was repeated in 1955. BMW engines were installed up to an including the 406, but after this V-8 motors were fitted that mainly originated from Chrysler.

Bristol sports cars

COUNTRY OF ORIGIN
Great Britain

Bristol 400

YEARS IN PRODUCTION
1947–1950

NUMBER MADE
700

SPECIAL REMARKS
The Bristol 400 still had various characteristics of the pre-war BMW 328. The engine was a 1,971 cc six-cylinder that developed 86 bhp at 4,500 rpm.

Bristol 401/402

YEARS IN PRODUCTION
1948–1952

NUMBER MADE
650 and 20

Between 1948–1952, 650 examples were sold of the Bristol 401.

The 405 was the last Bristol with a 1,971 cc engine.

The special spare-wheel compartment behind the front wheel arch.

Back in 1953, the Bristol 403 had a top speed of 103 mph (165 km/hour)

The BMW style grill was no longer used from the 405 onwards.

SPECIAL REMARKS
The body of the 401 coupé and 402 convertible was designed by Carrozzeria Touring. The 1,971 cc six-cylinder engine developed 86 bhp at 4,500 rpm.

Bristol 403

YEARS IN PRODUCTION
1953–1955

NUMBER MADE
300

SPECIAL REMARKS
The Bristol 403 was an improved 401, with higher performance engine and better brakes. The 1,971 cc six-cylinder engine delivered 107 bhp at 5,000 rpm.

Bristol 404/405

YEARS IN PRODUCTION
1953–1955 and 1954–1958

NUMBER MADE
40 and 297

SPECIAL REMARKS
The 404 could be recognised by the rear-mounted grill, the 405 by its four doors. The engine was a 1,971 cc six-cylinder that delivered 107 bhp at 5,000 rpm.

Bristol 406

YEARS IN PRODUCTION
1958–1961

Seven type 406 Bristols were given special bodies by Zagato in Italy.

NUMBER MADE
174

SPECIAL REMARKS
The 406 had a new body and therefore a new number. This was the final Bristol with a "BMW" engine. It was a 1,971 cc six-cylinder that developed 107 bhp at 5,000 rpm.

Bristol 406 Zagato

YEARS IN PRODUCTION
1960–1961

NUMBER MADE
7

SPECIAL REMARKS
The rolling chassis of the 406 was extremely popular with special car body builders, including Zagato, who managed to sell seven of them. The engine was a 1,971 cc six-cylinder that developed 107 bhp at 5,000 rpm.

Bristol 408/409

YEARS IN PRODUCTION
1964–1965 and 1966–1967

NUMBER MADE
83 and 74

SPECIAL REMARKS
The Bristol 408 was a 407 with twin headlights and a new grille. The 409 had a more powerful engine and better brakes. The engine was a 5,130 cc V-8 that developed 253 bhp at 4,400 rpm.

Bristol 410/411

YEARS IN PRODUCTION
1967–1969 and 1969–1976

NUMBER MADE
79 and 287

SPECIAL REMARKS
Safety was featured strongly in the brochure for the 410. The emphasis was on the stronger chassis and separate braking circuits. The 411 was powered by a Chrysler V-8 motor that initially had a capacity of 6.3 litres and then 6.5 litres after 1973. These engines developed 254 bhp at 4,400 rpm and 340 bhp at 5,200 rpm respectively.

Bugatti

The fame of the Bugatti name is largely based on the success of the cars built by Ettore Bugatti before World War II when few others were building racing cars and when motor racing was at a low ebb. The fact that the Bugattis were so pretty helped make them famous but it was largely Ettore Bugatti's charisma that made the company successful. His natural successor would have been

his son Jean but he was killed in 1939. The company were already largely engaged in general engineering before the war although a number of prototype cars were built but with Ettore's death in 1947, any ideas of building these were scotched. The company survived on sub-contract defence work but, with the money made from the war in Indo-China, the marque was briefly revived by son Roland, who had taken the reins in 1951. There was a wholly unsuccessful Formula One car (Type 251) and in 1956, the company introduced the Type 252 two-seater sports car with a V-12 engine. This car too went no further than the prototype and when the defence orders too dried up, Bugatti were forced to sell out to Hispano-Suiza.

The Type 52 Bugatti can be admired at the museum in Mulhouse, France, run by the Schlumpf brothers.

Bugatti sports cars

COUNTRY OF ORIGIN
France

Bugatti Type 101

YEARS IN PRODUCTION
1951–1956

NUMBER MADE
6

SPECIAL REMARKS
The Type 101 was the first car with which the company intended to continue its pre-war success. The engine was from the earlier Type 57 but with a supercharger (or turbo) its 3,257 cc motor could deliver 190 bhp at 5,400 rpm.

Bugatti Type 252

YEARS IN PRODUCTION
1956

NUMBER MADE
1

SPECIAL REMARKS
The Bugatti Type 252 never went beyond a prototype. This now stands in a museum in Mulhouse run by the Schlumpf brothers.

After the war, Bugatti no longer made their own bodies. This is a Type 101 with a body made in 1965 by Ghia in Turin to a design by Virgil Exner.

The dashboard of a Type 101 Bugatti. Note the small gear lever to the right of the steering wheel.

One of the six Type 101 Bugattis that was built.

Buick

A 1975 Buick Regal. The car had a choice of 3.8 litre V-6 or 5.7 litre V-8 in either a 145 or 165 bhp version.

Detroit never became widely renowned for making sports cars. Although powerful engines were made, the American car manufacturers gave them enormous bodies, perhaps with a little sporting gesture. These cars absorbed the roads like sponges and had little road-holding and often very poor brakes. It might be a slight exaggeration to say that they were only capable of driving straight on an American expressway at the speed limit of 50 mph (80 km/hour) for there were a few exceptions that were sound sporting cars, albeit not in the same vein as an MG, Austin-Healey, or Porsche. Buick too, who were mainly makers of family saloons (or sedans as they call them), made some attractive sporting cars such as the Riviera, the "small" Skylark, and its successors, the GS400.

Compare this 1969 Buick Wildcat with an MG or Porsche. In its class, it was a very sporty car that was sold as a sports coupé with two bucket seats and a 7 litre 360 bhp engine.

Less than 1,000 Buick Skylarks were sold in 1954. It had real spoke wheels and a V-8 engine that delivered 202 SAE.

The 1970 Buick GSX was a faster version of the Skylark with a 7.5 litre V-8 engine delivering 355 SAE, with a top speed of 144 mph (230 km/hour).

The spoiler on the boot was intended to make the car more stable but it had no effect so the car could only be driven fast on straight roads.

The 1975 Skyhawk was the smallest car Buick had ever built in its sixty-year history. The 2 + 2 was "only" 180 in (456 cm) long.

Buick sold the Skylark GS in 1968 with a straight six or V-8 engine. The first was 4,093 cc and there was a choice of 5,724 or 6,554 cc with the V-8

Buick sports cars

COUNTRY OF ORIGIN
USA

Buick Rivièra

NUMBER MADE
Unknown

The 1963 Buick Riviera was equipped with a 6,572 cc V-8 engine rated at 330 SAE at 4,400 rpm that had a top speed of 119 mph (190 km/hour).

SPECIAL REMARKS
The Riviera was only available with a V-8 engine. The engine size grew in line with the trends of those times and so by the 1966 model the capacity was 6,5722 cc with power of 330 SAE at 4,400 rpm.

The 1963 Riviera was only available with an automatic gearbox.

Caterham

Caterham Cars purchased the rights of the Lotus Seven in 1973. The Lotus Seven had made Lotus famous. It was available as either a kit car or ready to run model between 1957 and 1973 and Lotus sold about 3,000 of them. Initially Caterham continued producing the Series 4 with which Lotus had ceased production with but after only 38 of these were made, they went back in time in 1974 to the Series 3 that proved more popular. Although the body shape of the Caterham Super Seven is virtually unchanged, the car has been continuously improved. The cars are usually fitted with Ford or Lotus twin-cam engines which can accelerate the car from 0–60 mph (0–100 km/hour) in about five seconds.

The Caterham Seven is also available as a kit car.

Caterham sports cars

COUNTRY OF ORIGIN
Great Britain

Caterham Seven Series 3

YEARS IN PRODUCTION
1974–present day

NUMBER MADE
Unknown

SPECIAL REMARKS
In common with its forerunners, the Caterham Seven is a spartan means of transport.
The chassis has virtually no springing, two seats, and an engine powerful enough to drive a truck.

The Caterham Super Seven was born old.

The customer has a wide choice of engines.

Cheetah

When General Motors decided to withdraw from motor racing in 1963, this spurred Californian Bill Thomas into making his own cars. Bill was well-known in the United States for developing and tuning Corvette engines. With a little back-hand money from Chevrolet, he took on the dominance of the Mustangs and Cobras. He set-up a factory in Anaheim, California for which the rent was paid by Detroit. The first Cheetah soon saw the light of day. The Corvette V-8 engine was bored out to 6.2 litres and delivered 520 bhp. The car was only 140 in (356 cm) long, making it 20 in (51cm) shorter than a VW Beetle.

The first two Cheetahs had aluminium bodies but the following cars had polyester ones. This was not an improvement because when the car was driven fast the bonnet inflated like a balloon and the doors were blown open. The car was capable of reaching 212 mph (340 km/hour). The chassis and frame of the Cheetah were formed from about 150 ft (45 m) of chrome molybdenum tube of the highest quality which was cut to size and welded together.

The first two Cheetah's had aluminium bodies but the subsequent models were of polyester.

A highly tuned engine was fitted and the car was finished with a polyester body shell.

Thomas was not able to build the 100 cars required for homologation that was required to compete in races for "normal" touring cars. The Cheetah was therefore only able to compete in class prototype races against the more powerful Chaparrals, McLarens, and Lolas but still managed to win eleven races in 1964 despite this handicap. Thomas had built between 13 and 27 cars (depending on your source of information) when the factory was destroyed by fire. He could not find the will to start again from scratch and restricted himself to developing and tuning engines.
The rights to the Cheetah body were bought by Dean Morrison who sold them as kits.

With its length of 140 in (356 cm) the Cheetah was a mini-car. Its 520 bhp engine made it dangerously fast.

Cheetah sports cars

COUNTRY OF ORIGIN
USA

Cheetah

YEARS IN PRODUCTION
1963–1965

NUMBER MADE
Unknown

SPECIAL REMARKS
The Cheetah was intended to compete against the Corvette, Mustang, and Cobra but was forced to compete in a different class. It was powered by a 6.2 litre V-8 engine that delivered 520 bhp.

The production numbers for the Cheetah are unknown but this photo shows that at least one was built as a roadster.

Chevrolet

There has only been one true American sports car and that is the Chevrolet Corvette. Despite the efforts of its competitors, none of the others were able to match it. Yet for all its later success, the Corvette's birth was almost still born.
The chief designer of General Motors, Harley Earl, instructed one of his colleagues, Bob McLean, to design a two-seater sports car in 1951. The car was to be shown as a "dream" or concept car at the annual "Autorama" shows that were held in all the major cities. When the doors opened to the ballroom of the Waldorf Astoria, all eyes were on one car: a dazzling white sports car with fiery red interior. It was the new Corvette. These concept cars were usually scrapped at the end of the season but Earl had other plans for the Corvette. If the public liked the car, it could go into production with minor alterations. In that first year, 315 examples of the car were delivered.

The Corvette was based on an entirely new chassis and had a polyester body, with parts from different models of Chevrolet. In spite of this, building of the first cars was problematical with much of it being manual work. This restricted the numbers that could be built. The first series of 315 cars was not even sufficient to provide every American dealer with one Corvette. All the first cars were painted white

When Chevrolet were unable to build enough Corvettes for every dealer, they decided to give the cars to film stars and other famous people. The cars were probably sold very cheaply but provided considerable free publicity.

Chevrolet sold 19,776 Camaro sedans in its first year (1967) and 25,141 convertibles.

with red interior trim. Because of shortages of parts, the cars were fitted with different engines and some were fitted with Chevrolet Bel Air wheel trims.

Since the future lies with the young and the interest in the Corvette was substantial, particularly from the younger generation, Chevrolet decided to build a new factory in St. Louis where 10,000 Corvettes could be built each year. A smaller factory would have sufficed, because the car was difficult to sell. It cost, largely due to the hand work involved, more than twice a normal Chevrolet convertible. In reality the Corvette was not a sports car. The engine was an elderly six cylinder and the design was dated in other respects too.
The side windows had to be attached using screws, which had been common practice in the 1920s. It was not surprising that the factory had 1,100 unsold cars at the end of 1954. Critics said that Chevrolet had made a huge blunder with the Corvette but this was subsequently to be proven mistaken. From 1956 sales took off spectacularly.

Another sporting car from the Chevrolet stable was the Camaro which emerged in late 1966 as a 1977 model to compete with Ford's "pony car"

The finest of the first series of Corvettes were the 1956 225 bhp V-8 with three-speed manual gearbox or the 1957 injected 4.6 litre V-8 with its 283 bhp.

the Mustang. The Camaro was not built with winning races in mind, although this happened, rather as a sporting car for those who wanted something other than a Corvette. The Camaro was right from the outset available as a five-seater sedan or convertible with engines ranging from a six-cylinder 3.8 litre to a 5.7 litre V-8.

The initial Camaro models were available with a choice of three gearboxes: a three-speed column change, four-speed floor-change, or automatic gear box.

When Corvette fans refer to a "Ducktail", they mean the 1961 and 1962 models.

The soft-nosed Stingray was built from 1973–1982. Both the front and rear of the car has flexible plastic parts that were less easily damaged.

The Corvette Sting Ray was an entirely new model built from 1963–1967. The car shown is a 1965 model. The Stingray was the later 1968–1977 car.

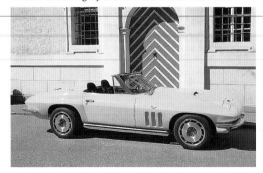

Chevrolet sports cars

COUNTRY OF ORIGIN
USA

Chevrolet Corvette

YEARS IN PRODUCTION
1953–present day

NUMBER MADE

Year	Quantity
1953	314
1954	3.640
1955	700
1956	3.467
1957	6.339
1958	9.168
1959	9.670
1960	10.261

SPECIAL REMARKS
The original Corvette was almost impossible to sell. The plastic construction was too complicated and therefore too expensive. The 3,858

cc six-cylinder engine only developed 152 bhp. It was not until 1960 that Chevrolet managed to sell more than 10,000 Corvettes.

By this time the customer had a choice of different V-8 engines of 4,637 cc capacity but with power ranging from 230–315 SAE.

A 1959 Corvette for the American market with speedometer in mph and Fahrenheit on the temperature gauge

The dashboard of the 1953/1955 Corvette looks rather primitive. Note the tachometer beneath the radio.

The second series of Stingrays as opposed to the earlier Sting Rays were made from 1968–1972.

The second generation Corvette (1956–1957) caught the eye with its duo-tone paintwork.

Three Corvettes took part in the Le Mans 24 hour race in 1973. Two managed to finish twelfth and eighteenth but the third had to retire after three hours.

The third generation of Corvettes from 1958–1960 had four headlights.

A 1969 Camaro also looks great under the bonnet.

Chevrolet Camaro

YEARS IN PRODUCTION
1967–present day

NUMBER MADE
Unknown

The Camaro could also be raced as can be seen from this 1974 photo taken at the Zandvoort circuit.

The Z-28 version of the Camaro of 1969 had stiffened front suspension, a twin exhaust, 15 x 7 wheels, and a 350 bhp engine among other modifications.

"Go-faster" body stripes.

SPECIAL REMARKS
The Chevrolet Camaro shared its body with the Pontiac Firebird. Both cars were reasonably successful in competition with the popular Ford Mustang.

Cisitalia

Immediately after World War II the demand for cars was so great that car factories sprouted from the ground like mushrooms, in Italy as elsewhere. Wealthy Piero Dusio built cars in Italy more for his own pleasure than to earn a crust. The first Cisitalia cars left the workshop in 1945. The mechanical parts were derived from Fiat. The engines were so highly tuned that they were able to hold their own in the small Cisitalia sports and racing cars against larger cars. The small single-seater for Formula Junior became renowned and many racing drivers who later became famous won their first races in one. Italian car body builders built some fine cars on Cisitalia chassis. A Cisitalia 202 Berlinetta of 1947 with a body by Pininfarina is displayed as a work of art in the New York Museum of

Cisitalia and Pininfarina became famous through the 202 Berlinetta.

Modern Art. The money that Dusio earned from his smaller racing cars and sports cars was lost on his notorious Grand-Prix car.

The car was designed by Porsche and far ahead of its time in 1948, with four-wheel drive and a centrally-mounted flat 12-cylinder engine with four camshafts and a turbocharger. The car ran well but never raced, having virtually bankrupted Piero Dusio, who emigrated to Argentina. He left the business in the hand of his son Carlo who founded a new Cisitalia company in 1950 and concentrated on building sports cars.

The parts of a Fiat 1100 with a Rocco Motto body.

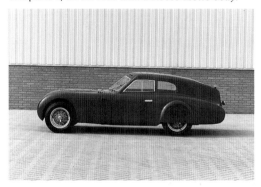

The inside of a Cisitalia 202 Motto coupé.

Things became much worse for Cisitalia from 1953 with much less demand for its well-made sports cars. The works switched, like others to building special bodies for Fiat saloons but closed down in 1964.

Cisitalia sports cars

COUNTRY OF ORIGIN
Italy

Cisitalia 202

YEARS IN PRODUCTION
1947–1952

NUMBER MADE
About 190

SPECIAL REMARKS
More power was achieved with Fiat engines by fitting twin Weber carburettors, increasing the compression ratio, and use of different crankshafts. The 1,089 cc engine delivered 65 bhp at 5,500 rpm.

This coupé was made to the order of Ir. Giovanni Savonizzi in 1947 on a 202 chassis.

The Savonizzi coupé taking part in the 1991 Mille Miglia. It was driven by Taruffi.

The dashboard of a Cisitalia 202.

Carrozzeria Stabilmenti Farina designed the body of
this 1949 example of a 202

Cisitalia sold a total of about 190 coupés and
convertibles of the type 202

The Citeria with its hard-top in place.

Beaufort, and Hans Hugenholz senior. The two-
seater roadster also had a detachable hard-top
and tubular chassis with glass-reinforced
polyester body. It was powered by a two-cylinder
BMW engine. The drivers managed speeds of 84
mph (135 km/hour) on the straight and everybody was very enthusiastic but the car never
went into production because the price of 7,450
Dutch guilders (about £2,500) was not attractive
in 1958 when a Volkswagen convertible could
be bought for 4,525 Dutch guilders (a little over
£1,500). The man behind the project, Puck van
Beekum, was unable to pay his debts and tried
to settle matters with forged cheques. By the
time he had served two and a half years in prison
the project was dead.

Citeria sports cars

COUNTRY OF ORIGIN
The Netherlands

NUMBER MADE
Not known

SPECIAL REMARKS
The Citeria was powered by an air-cooled twin-
cylinder engine from a BMW 600.

The Citeria from 1958 with a BMW 600 engine and
polyester body.

Citeria

Citeria was a failed attempt by a Dutch entre-
preneur to create a new sports car. The prototype was launched with much hype at the Dutch
motor racing circuit of Zandvoort on November
17, 1958 with television coverage and person-
alities including Stirling Moss, Carel Godin de

Citroën

Although Citroën did not make sports cars as such, some of their models were sufficiently sportive to embarrass the competition in rallies and races. The famous DS was introduced as a convertible (the DS Cabriolet) in 1961 with a body by Henri Chapron of Paris who was responsible for many special Citroën bodies. When the Italian firm of Maserati was in financial difficulties once more in 1968, Citroën bought the majority of the shares in Maserati. The resulting co-operation led to Citroën SM or Citroën Maserati being built in Modena. The Italian contribution was the production of the V-6 Maserati engine with double twin camshafts. The remainder of the engineering rested on parts from France. The SM remained in production until 1975.

The Citroën DS was also available as a convertible from 1961–1971.

Citroën sports cars

COUNTRY OF ORIGIN
France

Citroën DS Cabriolet

YEARS IN PRODUCTION
1961–1971

NUMBER MADE
1,253

SPECIAL REMARKS
Although the Citroën DS was never offered as a sports car, it won many rallies. The four-cylinder was offered as a 1,911, 1,985, or 2,175 cc versions.

Everything was a bit different in the Citroën DS: the single-spoke wheel, the unusual gear-change lever, and the knob instead of a brake pedal.

Citroën SM (Citroën Maserati)

YEARS IN PRODUCTION
1970–1975

NUMBER MADE
12,920

The Maserati engine had a capacity at first of 2.7 then later 2.9 litres, with double twin overhead camshafts and power respectively of 180 and 188 bhp.

The Citroën SM or Citroën Maserati resulted from co-operation between Citroën and Maserati. The car was introduced at the 1970 motor show in Geneva.

SPECIAL REMARKS
The SM had many technically advanced features: hydraulics from France and mechanical engineering from Italy.

Clan

Paul Haussauer and John Frayling designed the Lotus Europa for Colin Chapman. When Chapman turned down the plans for a successor, they decided to build it themselves. The British government were sufficiently impressed with their plans to provide guarantees that enabled them to build a small factory at Washington near Durham, where the Clan Crusader was built. The two-seater had a glass-reinforced polyester body and an engine from a Hillman Imp. This four-cylinder engine was rear mounted at an angle of 45°. The car weighed a mere 1,348 lb (613 kg) so that the engine was powerful enough to achieve a top speed of 100 mph (160 km/hour). The company unfortunately had little success with the car, which was expensive at £1,400. The company tried to sell the car as a kit but when the oil crisis hit there was little demand for sports cars and the company was forced to close down in 1974.

Clan closed down in 1974. In the three years of the company's existence, 315 Clan Crusaders were built.

Clan sports cars

COUNTRY OF ORIGIN
Great Britain

Clan Crusader

YEARS IN PRODUCTION
1971–1974

NUMBER MADE
315

SPECIAL REMARKS
The mechanical parts of the Crusader were from the Hillman Imp. The 875 cc engine delivered 51 bhp at 6,100 rpm.

The Government support was rewarded with at least one export!

Conrero

Virgilio Conrero had already established his name as an engine tuner when he started to make his own cars in 1951. Most of his models were based on an Alfa Romeo but he was quite

This 1953 car has an Alfa Romeo 1900 engine. Conrero's modifications included desmodromic valve operation built into the cylinder head.

It looks like an ordinary Alfa Romeo Sprint Veloce but this car is modified by Conrero to go 13 mph (20 km/hour) faster than others of its type.

happy to use an Alfa engine with a gearbox from a Lancia Aurelia. Later on he mainly used Osca engines. The Alfa Romeo shown with chassis number 009 was powered by an Osca engine. The chassis is from a 1951 Alfa Romeo 1900.

Conrero sports cars

COUNTRY OF ORIGIN
Italy

Conrero-Alfa Romeo

YEARS IN PRODUCTION
1951–1960

NUMBER MADE
Not known

Costin-Nathan

Frank Costin was an aerodynamics expert who had designed aircraft for de Havilland and also designed some 40 sports and racing cars. He designed the Lotus 8 and Elite for Chapman but also the Vandervell Formula One and the first Marcos (the "cos" is derived from Costin). In 1965 he designed a car with a three-ply timber body for Roger Nathan that became the Costin-Nathan.

These cars were extremely fast and impossible to beat in the 1 litre class in 1966. A Costin-Nathan not only won its class in the 500 kilometre race at the Nürburgring but also broke the lap record. Roger Nathan drove one of the cars in the 1967 Le Mans race but was forced to retire after four hours with electrical problems. Frank Costin died of cancer on February 5, 1995, aged 75.

A Costin-Nathan at Le Mans. The bonnet is held back by a piece of string.

A wonderfully restored Costin-Nathan participating in a veteran's race

Costin-Nathan sports cars

COUNTRY OF ORIGIN
Great Britain

Costin-Nathan

YEARS IN PRODUCTION
1961–1971

NUMBER MADE
Unknown

SPECIAL REMARKS
Costin became an expert during the war in the design of wooden gliders, such as those used in the Battle of Arnhem. Wood continued to be his favoured material after the war.

Cunningham

Briggs Cunningham was a millionaire owner of a car museum at Costa Mesa and also a car builder. Besides this, he was also an all-round sportsman who competed in all manner of races. He won the Americas Cup in his yacht Columbia in 1958, and had competed each year from 1951 to 1955 at Le Mans.

In order for a car to be homologated for Le Mans, a specific number have to be made but this was no problem for Cunningham. He built the necessary 27 cars and sold them as sports cars for every day use.
The cars never achieved victory at Le Mans but came close several times. A C-5R was third behind two Jaguar C-types in 1953. The other two Cunninghams running that year finished seventh and tenth.

The Cunningham C-2R was for true tough guys. There was no soft-top hood or side windows.

Results of Cunning hams at Le Mans

model	year	number entered	result
C-2R	1951	3	18th, 2 retired
C-4R	1952	3	4th, 2 retired
C-5R	1953	3	3rd, 7th, 10th.
C-4R	1954	3	3rd, 5th, retired
C-6R	1955	1	retired

Cunningham sports cars

COUNTRY OF ORIGIN
USA

Cunningham C3

YEARS IN PRODUCTION
1951–1955

NUMBER MADE
27

SPECIAL REMARKS
The C3 was the best selling Cunningham and in reality it was a less highly tuned C2 racing car with parts from Chrysler, including a 5,425 cc V-8 engine that developed 223 SAE at 4,400 rpm.

A Cunningham C-4R. In common with most cars of this make it has a V-8 Chrysler engine

The dashboard of the C-2R with an instrument panel like an aircraft.

Daimler

The Daimler name tends to conjure up the stately limousines use by H.M. The Queen yet this oldest of British car makers – making cars since 1896 – has also built sports cars. These include some fine cars such as the "Double Six" from the Thirties that was powered by a straight twelve-cylinder engine.

After World War II, the company mainly specialised in making cars for the very wealthy with the odd sporting model but too few cars were sold and it was a relief when Jaguar took them over in 1960. The Daimler marque still exists but is now merely a Jaguar with a different name plate. The first true sports car built by Daimler after the war was the Conquest Century Roadster that was introduced at the London Motor Show in 1954. Unfortunately this car was somewhat ponderous due to its solid and chassis that made the car so heavy. The car was advertised as a "100 miles-per-hour car" but it struggled to exceed 94 mph (150 km/hour). Daimler was more successful with the SP250 or Dart, as it became known in Britain, which was the surprise of the 1959 New York Motor Show. Everything about the car was new: a reinforced polyester body, disc brakes all round, and a fine V-8 engine. Unfortunately the Dart was too late on the scene to prevent the demise of the Daimler company. Indeed the initial problems with the car probably hastened matters. Too little money was spent on thoroughly testing and developing the car so that it was launched with all manner of teething problems. The chassis was too flimsy so that it twisted, causing the body shell to crack. The necessary improvements were only carried out after Jaguar had taken over. The 1961–1964 cars had far fewer problems.

The Daimler D18 had a 2.5 litre engine with twin carburettors that delivered 85 bhp, yet it was more of a tourer than a sports car.

The Conquest Century Roadster was a two-seater with space behind the seats for a child, dog, or luggage.

Daimler sports cars

COUNTRY OF ORIGIN
Great Britain

Daimler D18

YEARS IN PRODUCTION
1949–1953

NUMBER MADE
608

SPECIAL REMARKS
The first post-war Daimlers were made in July 1946 and they even included a sporting convertible such as the D18 which had a 2,522 cc six-cylinder engine that provided 86 bhp.

Daimler Conquest Century

YEARS IN PRODUCTION
1954–1957

NUMBER MADE
173

SPECIAL REMARKS
The Conquest Century was only available as a roadster until 1956 when a coupé also became available. The six-cylinder 2,433 cc engine delivered 101 bhp at 4,400 rpm.

Daimler SP250

YEARS IN PRODUCTION
1959–1964

NUMBER MADE
2,650

SPECIAL REMARKS
The SP250 was known as the Dart in Britain but this name belonged to Dodge who prevented its wider use. The superb V-8 engine was 2,548 cc, delivering 140 bhp at 5,800 rpm.

The SP250 or Daimler "Dart" was sold in what were large quantities for Daimler. The car was only really good after Jaguar ironed out its teething problems.

The dashboard of the SP250 or Daimler "Dart". The red mark on the tachometer is at 6,000 rpm.

Davrian

The spiritual father of the Davrian sports cars was Adrian Evans who built the first prototype

in 1968. These coupés with glass-reinforced bodies and engines and parts from Hillman Imps went into production soon afterwards. The motor was rear-mounted as standard but the cars could also be supplied with centrally-mounted engines. In common with many British specialist cars, these cars were also available as a kit and

almost 200 kits were sold in 1972). In addition to the four-cylinder Hillman engine, Volkswagen and Mini engines could also be fitted but most cars found their way to the road or circuit with a Hillman Imp engine. A new model, known as the Dragon, appeared in 1981, with a Ford Fiesta engine.

This car was built at a new factory in Wales but sales dropped back sharply in 1983 and the factory was forced to close.

Davrian sports cars

COUNTRY OF ORIGIN
Great Britain (Wales)

Davrian Imp

YEARS IN PRODUCTION
1972–1973

NUMBER MADE
Approx. 200

SPECIAL REMARKS
The Davrian Imp was mainly sold as a kit car. Volkswagen engines could be installed but the majority of customers chose the 875 cc Hillman Imp engine that could be tuned to the customer's requirements.

A Davrian Imp on a racing circuit.

The Davrian was lightweight, only 460 kg (1,102 lb).

D-B

Before World War II, Charles Deutsch and René Bonnet (see separate entry) had already started to make specials based on Citroën running gear. Once the war was over, the friends continued their activities and the first D-B cars with up-rated Citroën engines were built. The pair switched over to using Panhard engines in 1949, initially for a small single-seat Formula 3 racing car but sports cars followed. The D-B cars were fast with reliable engines, even though they were in an advanced state of tuning. D-B cars won major races such as Le Mans and the Mille Miglia and on more conventional short courses. Bonnet wanted to switch to using Renault engines in 1961 while Deutsch preferred to remain with Panhard and the resulting row led

to the two going their own way. The first time they met after the schism was at Le Mans in 1962. One of Deutsch Panhard-powered cars won the 701–850 cc class and was sixteenth overall, while Bonnet's Renault-engined car won the 851–1,000 cc class and was seventeenth overall.

D-B sports cars

COUNTRY OF ORIGIN
France

D-B HBR 5

YEARS IN PRODUCTION
1955–1961

NUMBER MADE
Approx. 660

SPECIAL REMARKS
The best known car by Deutsch and Bonnet was the HBR 5 which was shown for the first time at Paris in 1954. The twin-cylinder air-cooled Panhard engine initially was 851 cc/58 bhp, but later 954 cc/70 bhp.

A 1958 D-B convertible.

D-B named this 1960 model the "Super Rallye".

D-B cars – this is an HBR 5 – had air-cooled Panhard engines.

A 1957 D-B Le Mans with reinforced polyester body and Panhard mechanical parts.

Delahaye

The firm of Emile Delahaye was one of the oldest car makers in France, having started in 1894.

Before 1940, his cars had been regarded in the same class as Talbot, Delage, Bugatti, and Hispano-Suiza. After World War II, Delahaye co-operated with Talbot.

The company built some magnificent cars from 1946 onward that were powered by six-cylinder engines of 3,557 or 4,455 cc. Most of the cars were sold as rolling chassis on which a specialist coachbuilder provided a body to the customer's specific requirements. The cars included Grand Prix racing cars, both before and after the war, and these performed well.

The best days for the exclusive luxury car were over. In 1950, the company still built almost five hundred cars but by 1953 only three were made and the production lines were switched to building military vehicles and trucks.

A 1947 Delahaye with a Franay body.

The French singer, Charles Trenet, had this 1949 car built.

Delahaye sports cars

COUNTRY OF ORIGIN
France

Delahaye 135

YEARS IN PRODUCTION
1939–1955

NUMBER MADE
Approx. 2,000

SPECIAL REMARKS
The 135 was the principal model from Delahaye for a substantial period of time. The cars were mainly supplied as rolling chassis to be equipped with magnificent bodies.

The 3,557 cc six-cylinder engine delivered 95 bhp at 3,200 rpm. The 135 MS had triple carburettors and delivered 135 bhp at 4,200 rpm.

Delahaye 175

YEARS IN PRODUCTION
1948–1951

NUMBER MADE
Approx. 150

Whether you find it beautiful or ugly, this 1948 Delahaye with coachwork by Saoutchik is certainly impressive.

This 1949 Delahaye 135M was shown at the Paris
Motor Show.

The 135MS had triple carburettors.

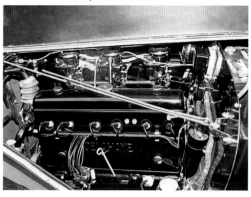

SPECIAL REMARKS
The Delahaye 175 had modern mechanical parts
and was finally provided with hydraulic brakes.
The 4,455 cc engine delivered 140 bhp at 4,000
rpm and had a top speed of 100 mph (160
km/hour).

Delahaye 235

YEARS IN PRODUCTION
1951–1955

The dashboard of the 135M was not designed for
good function. Note the small gear-change lever on
the left of the steering wheel.

The body of this 135MS was built by Figoni and
Falaschi.

NUMBER MADE
Approx. 85

SPECIAL REMARKS
The 235 was intended to replace the successful
135MS but it came too late to prevent the
company from ceasing to make cars. The 3,557
cc six-cylinder engine delivered 152 bhp at 4,200
rpm.

Carrozzeria Ghia built the body of this 1951
Type 235.

This Delahaye 235 with a Chapron body won first
prize in the 1982 Pebble Beach Concours d'Elegance.

Denzel

Austrian garage owner and amateur racing driver Wolfgang Denzel started making sports cars in 1949. His cars were made using Volkswagen parts. The first cars were shown at the Geneva Salon with the maker's name "WD" and this only changed to Denzel in 1957. Customers found the VW engines lacking in power so he switched to Porsche engines and with a Porsche-powered car, Denzel won the Rally of the Alps in 1954, which provided him with valuable publicity. The original open roadster was followed by a less successful coupé. When Denzel realised that he could never successfully compete against Porsche, he closed his works and returned to life as a garage owner. In 1980, Denzel was the importer for Volvo, Ferrari, BMW, Mitsubishi and several other makes and he had showrooms and workshops in virtually every major town in Austria.

Denzel sports cars

COUNTRY OF ORIGIN
Austria

More than 300 Denzels were made between 1949-1957.

A Denzel 1300 photographed during the 1991 Mille Miglia.

Denzel WD

YEARS IN PRODUCTION
1953–1960

NUMBER MADE
Unknown

SPECIAL REMARKS
The Denzel WD could be supplied with various engines provided they were of VW Beetle or Porsche origin. The tuned 1.3 litre four-cylinder Beetle engine delivered 65 bhp but this could be increased by using a turbocharger.

De Tomaso

Alejandro de Tomaso came to Europe in 1955 from Argentina to try his luck as a racing driver. His success on the circuit was only moderate but he met the wealthy Elizabeth Haskell in Italy and married her. The couple raced in Europe and North and South America with Maserati and Osca but did not achieve any fame. This changed when De Tomaso started to build cars. Most of his earlier cars did not proceed beyond the prototype stage and the first production model did not leave the factory until 1964.
The Vallelunga was a small coupé with Ford Corsair engine mounted in front of the rear axle, that had a reinforced polyester body. The next model, the Mangusta, was an enlarged version of

The Mangusta seen here is an enlarged version of the Vallelunga.

The interior of a Pantera GTS.

the Vallelunga and it was powered by a large Ford V-8 engine. The body was designed by the not-then-famous Giorgetta Giugiaro. These De Tomaso cars had to compete directly in the market with Mercedes and Jaguar. De Tomas became famous for his Pantera, which continues in production to current times.

This model was financed by Ford of America and sold through Mercury dealers but the high number of faults in the cars led to any profits being eroded by guarantee claims. De Tomaso, who was born in 1928, became seriously ill in

The Vallelunga was De Tomaso's first production car.

the 1990s and the business is now in the hands of his youngest son, Santiago.

De Tomaso sports cars

COUNTRY OF ORIGIN
Italy

De Tomaso Vallelunga

YEARS IN PRODUCTION
1964–1966

NUMBER MADE
50–60

SPECIAL REMARKS
It is unclear who designed the body of the Vallelunga. Alejandro certainly knows and insists that he did but the car world seriously doubts this. The engine of the Vallelunga was from a Ford Corsair that was converted in Italy to develop 102 bhp at 6,000 rpm.

De Tomaso Mangusta

The Corsair engine of Vallelunga chassis no. 001.

YEARS IN PRODUCTION
1967–1970

NUMBER MADE
401

SPECIAL REMARKS
Mangusta means mongoose. This is the only animal that has no fear of a Cobra and this explains De Tomaso's choice of name.

In reality, De Tomaso was less successful with the Mangusta than Shelby was with the Cobra. The 4,778 cc V-8 engine delivered 305 bhp at 6,000 rpm.

The engine was very accessible in the Mangusta.

De Tomaso Pantera

YEARS IN PRODUCTION
1970–present day

NUMBER MADE
Approx. 10,000

SPECIAL REMARKS
The Pantera was designed by Tom Tjaarda when he worked for Carrozzeria Ghia. The 5,796 cc Ford V-8 engine was centrally-mounted and could be delivered at various levels of tuning.

The Pantera GTS with an engine tuned to 350 bhp was introduced in 1973.

De Tomaso Deauville

YEARS IN PRODUCTION
1972–1985

NUMBER MADE
244

SPECIAL REMARKS
Tom Tjaarda also designed the Deauville. This car had a 5,796 cc Ford V-8 engine that delivered 270 bhp at 5,600 rpm.

The Deauville was De Tomaso's only four-door car.

De Tomaso tried to attract potential Mercedes. BMW, and Jaguar customers with the Longchamps. That was partially successful.

De Tomaso Longchamp

YEARS IN PRODUCTION
1973–1986

NUMBER MADE
412

SPECIAL REMARKS
The Longchamps was the next best selling De Tomaso after the Pantera. The car was an unusual combination of Italian good looks and American technology. The car was powered by a 5,796 cc Ford V-8 engine that developed 270 bhp at 5,600 rpm.

Devin

American Bill Devon got the idea to build cars when he saw a friend's Italian Ermini sports car with a Scaglietti body. He must have thought that such cars would make money. He took a mould of the body so that he could make them

Devin cars could be fitted with small European or large American V-8 engines.

Devin sports cars

COUNTRY OF ORIGIN
USA

Devin SS

YEARS IN PRODUCTION
1958–1962

NUMBER MADE
Unknown

SPECIAL REMARKS
The majority of Devins were sold as kits. The customer found his or her own engine, which could vary from a four-cylinder VW Beetle motor to a large V-8.

in reinforced polyester. The Ermini was a small car so that the body could only be fitted to a small chassis such as those of Fiat or the American Crosley. Meanwhile, Scaglietti had designed an Ermini body that was suitable for a Ferrari chassis, Because this car was known as a "Monza", Devon sold his cars under the name "Devin Monza". The bodies were mainly sold as kit cars but after 1958, the business also made complete sports cars. These were virtually the same shape as the Monza but were fitted to an improved tubular chassis that was better suited to its purpose. This model was designated the Devin SS, with the initials being short for Super Sport. The SS lived up to its name and won many club races.

The Devin D was a kit car that was designed to use with the VW Beetle floor pan. Because this kit only cost $1,495, it was a very popular model but the sales soon dropped off steadily and Devin was forced to shut down in the autumn of 1962.

Diva

Tunex Conversions, which was already renowned for engine conversions, decided in 1965 to build complete cars. These were to be built by an entirely new company, Diva Cars Ltd. The cars were intended for both the racing circuit and use on public roads. The cars were characterised by their luxury finish, including leather upholstery and trim.

The first coupés were offered as kits for the do-it-yourself builder with a choice of three different Ford engines. One of these cars was exhibited at the London Racing Car show of 1966 with a Hillman Imp engine but this car was less successful than the first GT models. The Valkyr was added in

This Devin from America competed in European races for veteran sports cars.

The Diva 1500 was a road car that could be raced.

Note the two fuel tank caps.

1966 with a centrally-mounted engine but it was less successful than the GT. Three years later, production of sports cars ceased.

Diva sports cars

COUNTRY OF ORIGIN
Great Britain

Diva GT cars are popular at races for historic racing cars. This one is on the Monthléry circuit.

Diva sold 65 GT models. This is a 1965 model.

Diva GT

YEARS IN PRODUCTION
1962–1968

NUMBER MADE
Approx. 65

SPECIAL REMARKS
The first Diva GT was built by Tunex Conversions but this formed Diva Cars Ltd to build the remainder. The car was also available as a kit car, powered by 997–1,598 cc Ford engines.

DKW

DKW became famous for several reasons. The works built front-wheel drive cars back in 1931 when this was pioneering technology, although now commonplace. The company used almost exclusively two-stroke engines and for its time the quality of the cars was excellent, making DKW very popular.

After the war, it was not until 1949 until a new car was brought out. The Auto Union GmbH in Düsseldorf had to start again from scratch, because its former factories were in Eastern

The DKW Monza was not a true production car. When DKW brought out a similar model, the expensive Monza became unsaleable.

DKW built 1,640 of the 1000 Sp convertible. Note the fashionable fins on the rear wings.

DKW sports cars

COUNTRY OF ORIGIN
Germany

DKW Monza

YEARS IN PRODUCTION
1955–1958

NUMBER MADE
155

SPECIAL REMARKS
The DKW Monza was not a true DKW and it disappeared when DKW brought out their own sports car. The Monza's engine was a three-cylinder two-stroke of 896 cc/38 bhp or 981 cc/44 bhp at 4,500 rpm.

American service personnel would be able to buy the DKW very cheaply with their dollars but few did. The main reason why not, was the two-stroke engine.

Is it a 1957 Ford Thunderbird?

Germany. In 1958, the company was sold to Mercedes-Benz, who sold it to Volkswagen in 1965. Volkswagen subsequently changed the name of Auto-Union to Audi.

The majority of DKW cars were family saloons but sporting enthusiasts soon discovered that these cars were ideal for competing in rallies. The two and later three-cylinder engines could be highly tuned and formed a reliable power source for many specials. In 1955 an unusual sports coupé by Dannenhauer and Stauss with a reinforced polyester body was seen at the IAA in Frankfurt. The spiritual father of the DKW special was the racing driver Günther Ahrens. Ahrens broke five records with the car at Monza and the car then became known as the DKW Monza.

The Stuttgart coachbuilders built another fifteen bodies before production was taken over by Karosserie Massholder. This company built about another ninety Monzas. When the Wenk company had built another fifty bodies, the Monza was finished. This was because DKW had introduced a cheaper model themselves to the market, known as the 1000 Sp. This 2 + 2 was available in 1958 as a coupé or convertible. These were no racing cars but they looked very sporting and resembled the 1955 Ford Thunderbird.

DKW 1000 Sp

YEARS IN PRODUCTION
1958–1965

NUMBER MADE
6,640

SPECIAL REMARKS
The success of the expensive Monza encouraged people in the head office in Düsseldorf to introduce their own sports car. Their 1000 Sp (Sp for sport) had a 981 cc three-cylinder, two-stroke engine that developed 55 bhp at 4,500 rpm.

Between 1958–1965 5,000 DKW 1000 Sp were sold.

The three-cylinder engine of the 1000 Sp. Note the position of the radiator, behind the engine.

The DKW still had a column gear-change lever.

Dodge

Brothers John and Horace Dodge opened their factory in Detroit in 1901. In 1902, the company received an order from Oldsmobile to make 3,000 gearboxes and they also built complete engines for Ford.

The company started to make its own complete cars in 1914, sold as a Dodge Brothers. In the company's best year of 1920, both brothers died of pneumonia. The company had become the second largest car maker in the US. Dodge was taken over by the Chrysler empire in 1928.

Dodge surprised everyone with the Charger sports coupé in 1966. The car was directly descended from the Charger II concept car that was exhibited at many shows. The Charger was pitched against the Plymouth Barracuda. Until 1969, the Charger was only available with a V-8 engine. The customer had a choice of eight different engines which grew in capacity and power each year.
A prototype racing Charger was raced in 1969. This car went into production as the Charger Daytona and Plymouth Road Runner in 1970. The cars were characterised by the huge fins above the boot (see Plymouth).

The Dodge Challenger was introduced to support the Charger in August 1969. This car was available as coupé and convertible and was supplied as standard with a six-cylinder 3.7 litre engine.
There was also a special version, the Challenger R/T (for road and track). Dodge celebrated its sixtieth birthday in 1974 when all the models except the Challenger were given a facelift. The Challenger was withdrawn.

The sporting Dodge Charger appeared in 1966. The headlights were behind the grill and could be turned outwards.

A 1963 Polara with a body of unitary construction and 6,286 cc V-8 engine. At 4,600 rpm this engine delivered 305 SAE with a twin carburettor, or 335 bhp with a quadruple carburettor.

Dodge sports cars

COUNTRY OF ORIGIN
USA

The Dodge Monaco in 1972 was the most expensive Dodge model. It was supplied with V-8 engines of 5.2–7.2 litres. All cars had automatic gearboxes and power steering.

Dodge Charger

YEARS IN PRODUCTION
1966–1987

NUMBER MADE
Unknown

SPECIAL REMARKS
The first 1966 Dodge Charger had a 5,210 cc

The Polara was available in America with bucket seats.

In 1971, the Charger cost $2,707 with a six-cylinder engine and a few hundred more with a V-8

V-8 engine that developed 233 SAE at 4,400 rpm. The car was optionally available with a 6,286 cc 330 SAE at 4,800 rpm or 6,974 cc 421 SAE engine.

Dodge Challenger

YEARS IN PRODUCTION
1970–1974

NUMBER MADE
Unknown

SPECIAL REMARKS
The Challenger was supplied from the beginning with a six- or eight-cylinder engine and as coupé or convertible.

The Challenger was Dodge's response in 1970 to the Ford Mustang and Chevrolet Camaro.

The R/T (road & track) was the quickest version of the Challenger. It was only equipped with a V-8 engine.

Buyers of the Challenger could choose between a six- or eight-cylinder engine.

The Dual Ghia was an improved version of Virgil Exner's Dodge Firearrow.

Dual Ghia

Dodge had a concept car, known as the Firearrow, built by Ghia in 1953. Gene Casaroll, whose company transported Chrysler products, was so impressed by the car that he asked the head of Dodge, William Newberg, if he could make the car. Newberg agreed and hence the first Dodge chassis were sent to Italy. The Dual-Ghia, as the car was dubbed, was an instant success and Casaroll decided who was permitted to buy one.

Frank Sinatra drove one, together with Eddie Fisher, Hoagy Carmichael, and Lucille Ball, but Sammy Davis Junior and Dean Martin were refused. Casaroll did not make money from the car because he sold them for under $8,000 but since each car required more than 1,500 man hours of labour, he lost $4,000 on every car made.

When Dodge changed over to a body of unitary construction in 1958, this meant the end for the Dual-Ghia. Between 1956–1958, 117 of them were made of which 102 were convertibles, two hardtop coupés and thirteen prototypes.

The fashion of the time: small fins above each wing.

Dual-Ghia sports cars

COUNTRY OF ORIGIN
Italy/USA

Dual-Ghia

YEARS IN PRODUCTION
1956–1958

NUMBER MADE
117

SPECIAL REMARKS
The Dual-Ghia was an old concept: Italian lines and American engineering. The Chrysler V-8 engine was powerful enough to accelerate the heavy car from 0-60 mph in about 7 seconds. (0–100 km/hour in 7.9 seconds).

Duesenberg

The cars built by Fred and August Duesenberg in the 1920s and 1930s were some of the finest looking cars ever built. It is not surprising therefore that demand exists for replicas of these classics. Fred Junior, son of August, got Virgil Exner to design a new car, known as the Duesenberg II, which was built by Ghia in Italy. The car had a highly-tuned Chrysler V-8 engine and every bit of luxury anyone could imagine but unfortunately it remained a prototype.

Four years later in 1970, Duesenberg again made the headlines with the news that the Duesenberg Corporation of Gadena, California were making

The hood of the Duesenberg was rather basic but then such a car should be driven in with the hood down.

replicas. The success was due to the fact that these new cars had more in common with the originals.

The body of the replica was very similar to the SSJ Roadster and it was powered by a turbo-charged Chrysler engine in common with many cars of the original Duesenberg era. The fact that the car was built on a Dodge truck commercial vehicle chassis did not seem to matter.

It is uncertain if the Duesenberg III is still made but there are certainly workshops in America that are still making Duesenberg replicas.

COUNTRY OF ORIGIN
USA
YEARS IN PRODUCTION
From 1966

NUMBER MADE
Unknown

SPECIAL REMARKS
Different replica Duesenbergs are constantly appearing in the market. Companies come and go and re-appear. Duesenberg replicas are still built today.

The dashboard is recreated as it appeared in pre-war Duesenbergs.

Fred Duesenberg Junior had this Duesenberg II built in Italy in 1966. It remained a prototype.

Elva

Frank Nichols was a garage owner who had won his spurs as a racing driver when he founded Elva in 1955. The name is derived from the French elle va meaning "she goes". The first cars were single seater Formula Junior racing cars but in 1958 Elva brought out a sports car that could be used to do the shopping in and to race on the track. The car was named the "Courier".

The prototype had an aluminium body but the production models had reinforced polyester body shells, which were cheaper and simpler to make. The engine was from an MGA which weighed 66 lb (30 kg) more than the 1,265 lb (575 kg) of the Courier. The car was available as a coupé or convertible and ready-to-run, or as a kit car which enable British owners to save 30 per cent of the tax. Elva also built cars that were solely intended for racing but these are not dealt with in this book. When the American importer was sent to prison leaving debts for a number of cars, Elva was plunged into serious financial problems and sold some of the production rights of the Courier to Trojan Ltd who brought it out as the Mk III. This car was constructed with rectangular section rather than round tube but Trojan did not build the car very long. In 1965, the project was sold on

again to a Tony Ellis who attempted to blow new life into it with a turbocharged engine. The project came to nothing and the car disappeared from the market in 1968.

Elva sports cars

COUNTRY OF ORIGIN
Great Britain

Elva Courier

YEARS IN PRODUCTION
1958–1968

NUMBER MADE
Approx. 600

SPECIAL REMARKS
The Courier was a typical British "mixture" with a tubular chassis, MG or Ford engine or whatever was available, and transmission from Triumph. The four cylinder engines were 1,489, 1,498, 1,588, or 1,622 cc.

A total of 670 Elva Couriers were built. This is a Mk III.

The final Elva was the Mk IV which were built in 1963.

EMW

Thoughts in Germany quickly turned to building cars after peace was signed following World War II. This was difficult for BMW because its factories at Eisenach were now in the Russian zone, forcing them to start again in Munich. The Russians and East Germans annexed the BMW factories and started to make the pre-war types 321, 340, and 327. They were not permitted to use the white BMW emblem so in its place they used a new red and white emblem. When the

The East Germans were not allowed to use the BMW name and emblem: this was their solution.

rights were granted to the BMW works in West Germany, the East Germans re-named their cars Eisenach EMW. The pre-war designs remained in production until 1955 when the factory started to make its own models such as the Wartburg.

EMW sports cars

COUNTRY OF ORIGIN
Former East Germany (DDR)

EMW-327/2

YEARS IN PRODUCTION
1952–1955

NUMBER MADE
Not known

SPECIAL REMARKS
Until 1953, the East Germans sold a sports car under the name EMW/2. Subsequently they named it "Eisenacher Sport-Kabriolett und Coupé". The engineering was based on pre-war BMW 327 and 328 models. Even the Bristol factory had long since stopped using parts from these times.

The EMW 327 of 1953 was really a 1939 BMW.

The speedometer and instrumentation of an EMW 327/2 originated from 1939.

Enzmann

Few cars were built in Switzerland after World War II so that there was astonishment when an Enzmann was exhibited at the IAA in Frankfurt in 1957. The car had been built by garage owner Emil Enzmann of Lucerne who developed the Enzmann 506 with his six sons. One son who was closely involved in the project was Emil Enzmann Junior, despite being a busy general practitioner. The car was designated "506" late into the project because that was the stand number at the Frankfurt show. In common with many specials of those days, the car was based on the running gear of a Volkswagen Beetle with a polyester body. The design was by Emil Junior. The 506 had no doors, making the body stronger and construction much simpler. The driver and passenger had to climb in over the side. The Enzmann could be supplied as a kit on request but the majority of the one hundred plus cars made in Schüpfheim between 1957–1968 were delivered ready-to-run. In addition to a VW Beetle engine, Porsche engines were also available.

Up to 1961, Enzmann purchased VW rolling chassis from the Wolfsburg factory. When this service was withdrawn, Enzmann were forced to strip down new cars, which forced up the price. Consequently in recent years the cars have only been built to order or sold as body kits. The moulds for the twenty-five plastic sections from which the body is constructed were kept. When new interest was shown in the Enzmann after

The body of an Enzmann is constructed from 25 sections glued together.

The dashboard of an Enzmann is just as primitive as that of a VW Beetle.

A few of the coupé version were made but lack that special quality of an Enzmann.

twenty-five years, Dr. Emil Enzmann put them back in production so that complete cars or kits can now be purchased.

COUNTRY OF ORIGIN
Switzerland

YEARS IN PRODUCTION
1957–present day

NUMBER MADE
Not known

How to get in to an Enzmann.

The Volkswagen or Porsche engine was mounted in its customary place – in the rear.

SPECIAL REMARKS
The Enzmann was available with either a tuned VW Beetle or Porsche 356 engine. Only a small number of cars were sold as kits.

Ermini

Countless tuners and car body builders occupied themselves during the 1950s with the Fiat 1100. They converted the engine or built different bodies on the existing chassis. One of these was Pasquale Ermini, who used the Fiat 1100 engine block but cast his own cylinder heads, often with twin overhead camshafts. He put these engines with a five-speed gearbox in a tubular chassis of his own design. The early 1950s were Ermini's most successful. His cars won their class of the classic Targa Florio and Giro Sicilia (Round of Sicily) races in 1950, with Piero Scotti coming fourth overall in the Sicilian race. The cars also made their mark on the Mille Miglia. When the demand for small sports cars diminished, Ermini switched to building special bodies but when business in these also slumped, he closed the business in 1962.

Ermini cars can often be seen competing in races for historic cars in Italy. This is Roberto Rosa's car at the Monza circuit.

An 1,100 cc Ermini engine with twin overhead
camshafts and double twin Weber carburettors.

Excalibur

Excalibur is probably the longest running of the
makers of neo-classic cars. The marque was
founded by the renowned designer Brooks
Stevens who was responsible for designing the
Jeep Station Car in 1948 among other projects.
In 1964, with his two sons, he built a car that
closely resembled the Mercedes SSK of the
1920s.

The car was built on a Studebaker chassis but
had a Corvette V-8 engine. The cars were continuously improved and were constantly being
joined by new models, such as the "Mercedes
540K". Soon after Stevens and his sons sold the
business, it became bankrupt.

This Ermini took part in the 1991 Mille Miglia for
classic cars. The cars is powered by a Fiat 1100 engine
with twin overhead camshafts and twin sparking plus
per cylinder, giving 94 bhp at 6,000 rpm.

Few car companies have become bankrupt and
re-emerged as frequently as Excalibur. Currently,
the business belongs to a German second-hand
car dealer, Udo Geitlinger and his son Jens.
Brook Stevens died on January 4, 1995, aged 83.

Excalibur sports cars

COUNTRY OF ORIGIN
USA

Excalibur SSK

YEARS IN PRODUCTION
1964–1966

NUMBER MADE
Unknown

A 1952 Ermini 1100 with a body by Motto of Turin.

SPECIAL REMARKS
The first Excaliburs had a 5,351 cc V-8 engine by
Studebaker that delivered 355 SAE at 5,800 rpm.

An Excalibur as Brooks Stevens built them.

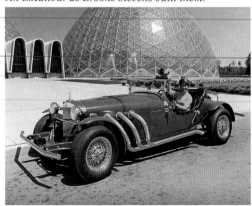

COUNTRY OF ORIGIN
Italy

YEARS IN PRODUCTION
1948–1962

NUMBER MADE
Not known

SPECIAL REMARKS
It is almost impossible to provide technical
details about Ermini engines because each was
individually crafted to deliver the power output
desired by the customer.

Facel Vega

The combination of American engineering and European body style is nothing new, bringing together the reliability and solidity of American cars with the dash and flair of European designers. Jensen already adopted these principles before the World War II, and Italian designers subsequently became strong in this field. In France, Jean Daninos attempted the same with Facel Vega. The word Facel is an acronym from Forges et Ateliers de Construction d'Eure et de Loire SA, which was the name of a company which had made tools for the aircraft industry since 1938 and which post-war had made bodies for Simca, Ford, and Panhard.

In 1954, when most of the French manufacturers had dropped luxury sports cars, Facel Vega moved in to this field. The first model, the Vega, had a 4.7 litre De Soto Firedome V-8 engine and a 2 + 2 body.

The car was superbly finished, with Daninos using stainless steel instead of chrome. The chassis was formed from 3 in (9 cm) diameter tube and was as strong as a small truck. The cars were continuously improved but unfortunately this made them yet more expensive, which made selling them more difficult. A Facel Vega cost three times as much as a Citroën DS 19, which was considered expensive in its day. The cars had a further disadvantage. Many regarded them as of mixed parentage.

Compared with Jaguar, Ferrari, Maserati, or Mercedes, which all built their own engines, Daninos scavenged parts from anywhere and used American engines. To overcome this image, Daninos had a French motor built by Pont à Mousson. This was theoretically a fine 1.6 litre

The HK 500 was the most successful Facel Vega, with 490 being sold.

four-cylinder with twin overhead camshafts but in reality the engine had many teething problems and the stream of customer's guarantee claims took the company to the verge of bankruptcy. Installation of Volvo, Austin-Healey, and BMW engines did not reverse the situation and Facel Vega disappeared from the market in 1964.

Facel sports cars

COUNTRY OF ORIGIN
France

Facel Vega FV 1

YEARS IN PRODUCTION
1954–1955

NUMBER MADE
46

SPECIAL REMARKS
The first Facels also had a Chrysler V-8 engine of 4,768 cc, developing 203 bhp at 4,400 rpm.

Facel Vega FV-2

YEARS IN PRODUCTION
1955–1956

NUMBER MADE
103

SPECIAL REMARKS
When customers wanted more power, the Facel Vega FV 2 was equipped with a 5,407 cc V-8 engine that developed 250 bhp at 4,600 rpm, making the car capable of speeds in excess of 125 mph (200 km/hour).

Facel Vega FV-3 en 4

YEARS IN PRODUCTION
1956–1957

NUMBER MADE
205

SPECIAL REMARKS
The FV 3 and FV 4 had a 4,940 cc V-8 engine that delivered 253 bhp at 4,600 rpm.

Facel Vega HK-500

YEARS IN PRODUCTION
1958–1961

NUMBER MADE
490

Daninos happily used stainless steel instead of chrome.

The exhausts were incorporated into the rear bumper.

SPECIAL REMARKS
The HK 500 was the highest volume seller Facel. It had a 5,907 cc V-8 engine that developed 360 bhp at 5,200 rpm.

Facel II

YEARS IN PRODUCTION
1962–1964

NUMBER MADE
184

SPECIAL REMARKS
The Facel II was the replacement for the HK 500. It had a 6,286 cc Chrysler V-8 engine that developed no less than 390 bhp at 5,500 rpm.

Facelia

YEARS IN PRODUCTION
1960–1962

NUMBER MADE
1.210

SPECIAL REMARKS
The sales figures demonstrate that there was demand for a smaller Facel. The Facelia was available as a coupé or convertible and had a

The replacement for the HK 500 was the Facel II, with a 6.3 litre Chrysler V-8 engine that delivered 390 SAE to the rear wheels. It was available with a four-speed manual gearbox or automatic transmission.

A lower end Facel? The Facelia had a genuine French engine with twin camshafts and a top speed of 116 mph (186 km/hour) and was fitted with disc brakes all round.

four-cylinder 1,647 cc French engine that delivered 115 bhp at 6,400 rpm.

Facel III

YEARS IN PRODUCTION
1963–1964

NUMBER MADE
619

SPECIAL REMARKS
When the customers and Daninos himself were dissatisfied with the engine in the Facelia, Facel installed a four-cylinder Volvo engine to create the Facel III. The 1,780 cc motor delivered 108 bhp.

Many enthusiasts feel that the Facel III is the most attractive creation from the Facel stable.

Facel 6

YEARS IN PRODUCTION
1964

NUMBER MADE
42

SPECIAL REMARKS
The Facel 6 was created by installing a 2,860 cc Austin-Healey six-cylinder engine in a Facel III. The driver now had more than 150 bhp available at 5,250 rpm.

Falcon

Peter Pellandine's firm, Falcon Shells, made its early money producing attractive reinforced polyester body shells for pre-war Ford Tens or Ford Populars. The renowned designer Len Terry, who did a great deal of work for Lotus, Surtees, and BRM, also worked for a time for Falcon Shells and he developed a chassis that formed the basis for a series of sports cars which now often race in historical car races.

Pete Ecury's Falcon Caribbean on the Mugello circuit in Italy. Behind him a Lister (left), Jaguar, and an Osca Formula Junior (right) can be seen.

Fourteen were made of the car illustrated, mainly with tuned Ford Anglia engines but Austin Sprite and Coventry Climax four-cylinder engines were also used. The car shown has a 1.5 litre MGA engine.

Falcon sports cars

COUNTRY OF ORIGIN
Great Britain

Falcon Caribbean

YEARS IN PRODUCTION
1957–1963

NUMBER MADE
Unknown

SPECIAL REMARKS
The Caribbean was the best seller among Falcon cars. It was available ready-to-run or as a kit. The customers found their own engines, which were usually four-cylinder units from Ford.

Felber

Willy Felber studied machine tool technology but his love was cars. After selling machine tools for several years, he opened a garage at Morges, near Lausanne and quickly became a dealer for Ferrari, Rolls-Royce, and Lotus.

In 1974, Felber started to build his own cars, or more accurately, adapted them to his personal tastes. He though nothing of stripping down a Ferrari 330 GTC in order to build a car like a Lotus Seven on its chassis. He took his creations to the Geneva Salon and managed to sell them too. He chopped the roofs off Lancias and put different front ends on Buick Skylarks, which he sold (13 of them) as a Felber Pacha. Felber quickly discovered the interest in customised Range Rovers and put beds in more than thirty of them, and equipped them with hydraulically operated timber body guards, sliding roofs, refrigerators, and other unusual equipment.

Up to 1981, Felber built or converted more than 150 cars and although he and his son-in-law now

This is how Enzo Ferrari's first car could have looked but this is actually a Felber.

The Felber Ferrari that started life as a 330 GTC.

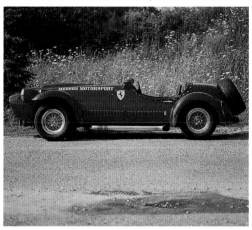

takes it easier as dealers for Alfa Romeo, Subaru, and Maserati, there is always the chances that he will busy himself with the tin snips once more.

Felber sports cars

COUNTRY OF ORIGIN
Switzerland

SPECIAL REMARKS
Swiss garage owner Felber did more than convert cars. He did not flinch to strip down a virtually brand new Ferrari in order to fit it with a body of his own design.

Ferrari

Enzo Ferrari and his cars really need no introduction. Ferrari is to sports cars what Bugatti was before World War II and Rolls-Royce still are among luxury cars. The first car built by Ferrari did not carry his name because Alfa Romeo had barred him from using it on a sports car. The car was an Auto Avia 815 (8 for eight cylinders and 15 because it was a 1.5 litre engine). The car appeared in 1940 but did not have much success.
The history really begins in 1945 when Enzo Ferrari gave his old friend, Gioachinno Colombo, instructions to build a racing car. The

result was seen for the first time on May 11, 1947 on the Piacenza circuit. The open sports car had a 1.5 litre V-12 engine that was dubbed 125 S by Ferrari (12 x 125 = 1500). The engine was subsequently bored out to form the 166, 195, and 212 alongside power horses such as the 340 and 375 Mille Miglia that had 4.1 and 4.5 litre engines and power in excess of 300 bhp. The line of models is long but this book only includes those models that were intended for road use.
In 1954, the cubic capacity had grown to 2,953 cc and the series were designated 250 GT, which remain the best known Ferraris. The 250 GT made both Ferrari and many drivers famous. The cars were also available as an impressive 2 + 2 – the 250 GTE.

There were wonderful convertibles such as the California, or dangerously fast racing cars, such as the 250 GT SWB (short wheel base). The 275 GT followed and then the 330 GT. Finally(for the time being), the last sports car with a front-mounted engine was the 365 GTB4 Daytona. The six cylinder Dinos became very famous. These were the predecessors to the 308, 328, and the Mondial that then had a V-8 engine. The long list of Ferraris continues to grow.

The Type 125 was the first Ferrari to bear his name. It was designed solely for racing so really does not belong in this book!

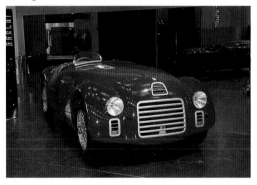

Pininfarina provided almost all the bodies for the road-going Ferraris. When Pinanfarina had no spare capacity, the work was farmed out so that this car is signed by Pinanfarina but is actually built by Carrozzeria Boano.

The last of the Mohicans: the final (for the moment) GT with a front-mounted engine is the 365 GTB4, better known as the Daytona.

The first production car was the Type 166. This 1950 coupé has a body by Vignale.

Ferrari sports cars

COUNTRY OF ORIGIN
Italy

Ferrari 166

YEARS IN PRODUCTION
1947–1950

NUMBER MADE
39

SPECIAL REMARKS
The Type 166 was the first Ferrari for every day use. The car was available in "Sport" and the more powerful "Inter" versions. The 1,995 cc V-12 engine was designed by Gioachinno Colombo and developed 95 bhp at 6,000 rpm in the Sport or 140 bhp at 7,000 rpm in the Inter.

Ferrari 195

YEARS IN PRODUCTION
1950–1952

NUMBER MADE
27

SPECIAL REMARKS
After the 166 engine was bored out, the Type 195 was created with a 2,341 cc engine that developed 130 bhp at 6,000 rpm. Most of the Ferrari 195 Inters were fitted with Ghia bodies.

Ferrari 212

YEARS IN PRODUCTION
1951–1952

NUMBER MADE
80

SPECIAL REMARKS
The next step was the 212, now with a 2,562 cc engine that developed 150–170 bhp. The more powerful engine was fitted in the 212 Export that had a shorter wheelbase than the 212 Inter.

The majority of early Ferraris such as this 212 were fitted with Ghia bodies.

The 212 engine with twin overhead camshafts and triple twin Weber carburettors.

Ferrari 340 America

YEARS IN PRODUCTION
1951–1955

NUMBER MADE
22

SPECIAL REMARKS
The 340 America was a first-class car for driving long distances. Its 4,101 cc engine provided 280 bhp. Variants on this theme were the 342 (6 made), and 375 America (13 made), with 230 and 300 bhp respectively. These cars, like the 375 Mille Miglia (5 made) were only available to order.

Ferrari 250 GT Europa

YEARS IN PRODUCTION
1953–1954

NUMBER MADE
38

SPECIAL REMARKS
The 250 GT Europa was descended from the 250 Mille Miglia. The cars were given this name following the outright victory of the 1952 race. The 250 MM was built mainly for people who wished to race the car (31 were sold). The Europa was the road-going version.

Ferrari Superamerica

YEARS IN PRODUCTION
1956–1964

NUMBER MADE
82

SPECIAL REMARKS
The 82 Superamericas sold can be divided into 35 type 410 and 47 type 410. These cars too were only available to order.

The 400 Superamerica was made between 1959–1964. It was made specially to order.

Ghia built this bizarre coupé on a 410 Superamerica chassis. The car was developed as a concept car for shows but found an American buyer.

Ferrari Superfast

YEARS IN PRODUCTION
1964–1966

NUMBER MADE
37

SPECIAL REMARKS
The 500 Superfast was introduced at the Geneva Salon in 1964. This expensive car had a 4,961 cc V-12 engine that developed 400 bhp at 6,500 rpm.

Ferrari 250 GT

YEARS IN PRODUCTION
1956–1960

NUMBER MADE
480

SPECIAL REMARKS
Ferrari started "mass production" with the 250 GT series.
The bodies of the two-seater coupés were designed by Pininfarina but the first 130 were made by Carrozzeria Boana and Ellena.

Ferrari 250 GT cabriolet

YEARS IN PRODUCTION
1959–1962

NUMBER MADE
241

SPECIAL REMARKS
Since many of the clients for Ferrari lived in California, it was not long before Pinanfarina designed an open-topped version of the 250 GT coupé.

The Ferrari 250 GT Tour de France. The body of this car is also designed by Pinanfarina and built by Scaglietti.

Ferrari Tour de France

YEARS IN PRODUCTION
1955–1959

NUMBER MADE
84

SPECIAL REMARKS
Ferrari has had a number of models which could be used for going to the shops as well as for racing on the track and the 250 GT Tour de France was such an example. The aluminium body was designed by Pininfarina and made by Scaglietti.

Ferrari 250 GT SWB

YEARS IN PRODUCTION
1959–1962

NUMBER MADE
175

SPECIAL REMARKS
One of the finest all-round Ferraris was the 250 GT SWB. This Berlinetta was built on a shorter

The 250 GT SWB for short wheelbase was a racing car that could just about be driven on the open road.

wheelbase chassis than the Tour de France. The car was designed by Pininfarina and made by Scaglietti, partially in steel. Of the 175 that were made, 82 were solely intended as racing cars.

Ferrari 250 GT California

YEARS IN PRODUCTION
1957–1962

NUMBER MADE
104

SPECIAL REMARKS
The open version of the Tour de France and SWB was known as the California. The cars had more powerful engines than used in the normal convertibles.

The open version of the Tour de France and SWB was known as the California.

Ferrari 250 GT Lusso

YEARS IN PRODUCTION
1962–1964

NUMBER MADE
350

A 250 GT Lusso, which was the deluxe version of the SWB, outside the Maranello works.

The "ordinary" family was also borne in mind with the first 2 + 2 production car – a 250 GTE.

One of the best Ferraris for daily motoring was the 330 GTC introduced at Geneva in March 1966.

SPECIAL REMARKS
The 250 GT Lusso Berlinetta was designed for those who desired a fast SWB but wanted more comfort. Its 2,953 cc V-12 engine delivered 240 bhp to the wheels at 7,500 rpm, which was enough to reach 137 mph (220 km/hour).

Ferrari 250 GTE 2+2

YEARS IN PRODUCTION
1960–1963

NUMBER MADE
1,000

SPECIAL REMARKS
For those who wanted a Ferrari as a family car, Pinanfarina designed the 250 GTE four-seater coupé. The final 50 were sold as Ferrari 330 America models and were equipped with a new 4 litre engine.

Ferrari 330 GT 2+2

YEARS IN PRODUCTION
1963–1967

NUMBER MADE
1,080

SPECIAL REMARKS
The 4 litre engine that was installed in the final 50 GTEs was the power for the new 2 + 2. These cars, which had a top speed of 125 mph (200 km/hour) initially had an electrically operated overdrive but were later equipped with five-speed gearboxes.

Ferrari 330 GTC/GTS

YEARS IN PRODUCTION
1960–1968 and 1966–1968

NUMBER MADE
600 and 100

SPECIAL REMARKS
These are superb coupés and convertibles with 4 litre V-12 engines that developed 300 bhp at 7,000 rpm, with independent suspension all round and a transverse axle. These 125 mph (200 km/hour) cars were ideal for long journeys.

Ferrari 275 GTB/GTS

YEARS IN PRODUCTION
1964–1966

NUMBER MADE
460 and 200

SPECIAL REMARKS
When the 250 GT series had been around for more than ten years, the engine was bored out and developed to 3,285 cc. The Berlinetta (hard top) and Spyder (convertible) cars had 260 bhp at 7,000 rpm under their aluminium cylinder head.

Ferrari 275 GTB4/GTB4S

YEARS IN PRODUCTION
1966–1968

NUMBER MADE
350 and 10

SPECIAL REMARKS
The 275 GT was shown at the 1966 Paris Motor Show with four camshafts instead of two. A year later this was followed by the open version, the 275 GTB4S that was built following a request from the North American importer. It is now known as the NART Spyder (North American Racing Team).

Ferrari 365 GT 2+2

YEARS IN PRODUCTION
1967–1971

NUMBER MADE
800

The 275 GTB was supplied with both twin and quad overhead camshafts.

SPECIAL REMARKS
The capacity of the V-12 engine had grown to 4,390 cc by 1967. This engine was installed in a 2 + 2 to create a luxury car that had air-conditioning, power steering, and electrically operated side windows as standard.

Ferrari 365 GTC/GTS

YEARS IN PRODUCTION
1968–1970 and 1969

NUMBER MADE
150 and 20

SPECIAL REMARKS
Body styles of the GTC and GTS were very similar to those of the 330 GTC and GTS but with the installation of a 4.4 litre engine the 365 GTC and the 365 GTS convertible were created.

Ferrari 365 GT4 2+2

YEARS IN PRODUCTION
1972–1976

NUMBER MADE
524

SPECIAL REMARKS
The production of the 365 GT 2 + 2 ended in the spring of 1971 but it was not until the autumn of the following year before there was a replacement 2 + 2 available. The new car had a quadruple overhead camshaft on a 4.390 cc engine that developed 340 bhp at 7,000 rpm.

Ferrari 365 GTB4/GTS4

YEARS IN PRODUCTION
1968–1973 and 1971-1973

NUMBER MADE
1,300 and 123

SPECIAL REMARKS
The final (for now) Ferrari Berlinettas and Spyders with V-12 engines were the 365 GTB4 and GTS4, that are better known as Daytonas. These cars can be raced at Le Mans or taken on holiday.

Ferrari 365 GTC4

YEARS IN PRODUCTION
1971–1972

NUMBER MADE
500

SPECIAL REMARKS
The 365 GTC4 that was shown at Geneva in 1971 was really a Daytona for someone who really had no interest in racing. The factory offered it as a 2 + 2 but only very small children could be carried in the rear.

Ferrari 365 GT California

YEARS IN PRODUCTION
1966–1967

NUMBER MADE
14

SPECIAL REMARKS

The 365 GT California was one of those cars that was only made to order. The car was different to its predecessors and it was clear that the Pininfarina designers had incorporated all their special ideas into the car.

Dino 206

YEARS IN PRODUCTION
1966–1969

NUMBER MADE
150

SPECIAL REMARKS
The engine, which was transverse to the rear axle of the Dino 206 delivered 180 bhp through a transaxle, which was very good for a 1,987 cc V-6. This engine was also used in the Fiat Dino, but was conventionally front mounted. The Dino 206 had no Ferrari badge and was sold as a Dino, not a Ferrari.

The Dino 206 and 246 started a new era with a V-6 tranverse-mounted engine in front of the rear axle.

Dino 246 GT/GTS

YEARS IN PRODUCTION
1969–1974 and 1972–1974

NUMBER MADE
2,609 and 1,274

SPECIAL REMARKS
When the 2 litre V-6 engine of the Dino was rebored to 2,418 cc, the Dino 246 was created, with the figures indicating a 2.4 litre engine of six cylinders.
The GTS appeared in 1974 but was not a true convertible but a "Targa".

Dino 308 GT4 2+2

YEARS IN PRODUCTION
1974–1980

NUMBER MADE
2,826

Bertone only worked on the body of a limited number of Ferraris. The 308 GT4 was one of those exceptions. The commission was a difficult one: Ferrari wanted a small coupé with space for four persons but still wanted a rear-mounted transverse V-8 engine.

SPECIAL REMARKS
Ferrari started a new era in 1974 with V-8 engines for "saloon" cars. Carrozzeria Bertone had the hot potato of designing a 2 + 2 with a rear-engined V-8. This model too was known as a Dino until 1978 when it became a Ferrari.

Fiat

Fiat was more active in motor racing at the beginning of the twentieth century than these days. A Fiat won the Cogno de Ventoux hill climb in 1905 at a speed of 100 mph (160 km/hour) with a 16.2 litre engine. In 1907, Nazzaro and Lancia drove into first and second places in the Targa Florio with a 28/40 HP. The same year, lawyer Carlo Cavalli designed the Grand Prix car in which Nazarro won the French Grand Prix. After World War II Fiats were rarely encountered on racing circuits even though the company usually had one or two sportive products in its range, such as the 1100 S which was a direct descendant of the 508 C Mille Miglia which won its class in the 1938 Mille Miglia. There were also 114 sports cars with a V-8 engine plus a long line of sporting coupés and convertibles that were based on standard factory models. Exceptions to this were the Dino and the X1/9 which were built as sports cars. The Dino had the Ferrari V-6 Dino engine mounted conventionally up front while the X1/9 had a four-cylinder engined mounted in front of the rear axle beneath a body that clearly displays Bertone lines.

The 1100S of 1947 was an improved version of the pre-war 508 C Mille Miglia.

Fiat sold four times more coupés of the Dino than convertibles of the total 6,000 that were sold.

The body of the 1200/1500 convertible was designed and built by Pininfarina.

Lothar Moll won his class in the 1997 Italia à Zandvoort race in this Fiat 128 Coupé at an average speed of 101 km/hour (63.12 mph)

Fiat sports cars

COUNTRY OF ORIGIN
Italy

Fiat 1100S

YEARS IN PRODUCTION
1947–1950

NUMBER MADE
401

SPECIAL REMARKS
The 1100S was the first sports car that Fiat brought on the market after the war. The body was made of aluminium but the two-seater was very spartan.

Fiat 8V

YEARS IN PRODUCTION
1952–1954

NUMBER MADE
114

SPECIAL REMARKS
The 8V was probably more of an experiment that a planned production car. It was the first Fiat with all-round independent suspension. The car had a 1,996 cc V-8 engine that delivered 105 bhp at 6,000 rpm.

Luggage space behind the bucket seats and a 70 litre tank for long distance races.

The standard version of the 1,290 cc engine in the 128 Sport delivered 75 bhp which gave a top speed in excess of 100 mph (160 km/hour).

No-one can explain why Fiat made a sports car with a V-8 engine. It was a complete failure.

Fiat 1100 Spider

YEARS IN PRODUCTION
1955–1959

NUMBER MADE
3,393

SPECIAL REMARKS
The first 1,030 Spyders that were built on the running gear of the Fiat 1100 had the 1100 TV engine of 1,089 cc and 50 bhp at 5,400 rpm. When Fiat introduced the 1200 series, the Spyder got the 1,221 cc engine that gave it 52 bhp at 5,200 rpm.

Fiat 1200 Cabriolet

YEARS IN PRODUCTION
1959–1963

NUMBER MADE
Approx. 15,000

SPECIAL REMARKS
Fiat introduced a new 1200 convertible in 1959,

The 1200 convertible was based on the Fiat 1100 TV running gear.

designed by Pininfarina. The mechanical details: a 1,221 cc four-cylinder engine delivering 58 bhp at 5,300 rpm, with a four-speed gearbox and four drum brakes.

Fiat 1500/1600S cabriolet

YEARS IN PRODUCTION
1960–1965

NUMBER MADE
Unknown

SPECIAL REMARKS
The body was from the 1200 but the four-cylinder engine now had twin overhead camshafts and a capacity of 1,491 cc, developing 80 bhp at 6,000 rpm. In 1962 this engine was bored out to 1,568 cc to create the 1600S with 100 bhp and a top speed of 109 mph (175 km/hour).

The Maseratis brothers built a twin cam engine for the 1600 coupé.

The body of the 2300S was designed by Ghia.

Fiat 2300S Coupé

YEARS IN PRODUCTION
1961–1968

NUMBER MADE
Unknown

SPECIAL REMARKS
Most Fiats had a Pininfarina body but the 2300S was an exception with a 2 + 2 body designed by Ghia. The car had a top speed of 119 mph (190 km/hour) with its 2,279 cc six-cylinder engine that developed either 136 or 150 bhp at 5,600 rpm. The car had all-round disc brakes.

Fiat 850 Coupé en Spider

YEARS IN PRODUCTION
1965–1971 and 1965–1972

NUMBER MADE
342,873 and 124,600

SPECIAL REMARKS
Almost half a million of these quick cars were made but you rarely see them any more. The body of the coupé was designed and built by Fiat while the convertible came from Bertone. When Fiat stopped making the convertible, Bertone went on building it for a time under its own name.

Fiat 124 Coupé en Spider

YEARS IN PRODUCTION
1967–1972 and 1966–1982

NUMBER MADE
279,672 and 151,710

SPECIAL REMARKS
The four-seater body of the coupé was developed by Fiat while the convertible came from the Pininfarina factory. This car body builder continued to build the car under the name Spydereuropa up to September 1985. At that time more than 200,000 of the convertibles had been sold, with about 170,000 of them going to

The 850 convertible had a body by Carrozzeria Bertone. The coupé was built at Fiat.

America. There was also the Abarth 124 Rally (see Abarth).

Fiat Dino Coupé en Spider

YEARS IN PRODUCTION
1966–1972 and 1967–1972

NUMBER MADE
6,068 and 1,583

SPECIAL REMARKS
The Fiat Dino had the same engine as the Dino by Ferrari but the engine was longitudinally front-mounted in the Fiat. The 2 litre then 2.4 litre V-6 engine had sufficient power (160 then 180 bhp) for top speeds of 125 and 131 mph (200 and 210 km/hour).

Fiat 130 Coupé

YEARS IN PRODUCTION
1971–1977

NUMBER MADE
4,491

The Dino initially had a 2 litre then 2.4 litre engine.

SPECIAL REMARKS
The 130 coupé was an excellent successor to the 2300S. Both cars were ideal for long journeys, offering a great deal of comfort and were equipped for those times with everything the driver could possibly wish for. The 2,866 cc V-6 engine was subsequently uprated to 3,235 cc with power of 140 and 165 bhp.

Fiat 128 Sport

YEARS IN PRODUCTION
1971–1979

NUMBER MADE
330,897

The Fiat 128 Sport; the sports car for the ordinary man.

The X1/9 was unmistakably a Bertone design.

SPECIAL REMARKS

The Fiat 128 Sport was a delightful car but it was not rare. It was an early "hot hatch" or hatchback and succeeded the 850 coupé. The 1,116 or 1,290 cc engines delivered 64 or 74 bhp at 6,600 rpm.

Fiat X1/9

YEARS IN PRODUCTION
1972–1989

NUMBER MADE
141,108

SPECIAL REMARKS

The Fiat X1/9 was a two-seater with a body that was typically by Bertone. The 1,290 or 1,498 cc four-cylinder engines was mounted in front of the rear axle which delivered 75 and 85 bhp to give top speeds of 106–112 mph (170–180 km/hour). The car had a removable "Targa" roof. Bertone continued to build the car from September 1981 to the end of 1988 under their own name.

The man behind the Mustang was Lee Iacocca. This son of an Italian immigrant studied engineering and joined Ford immediately after World War II where he rose through a number of departments to become a vice-president. Iacocca saw a future for small sports cars for four persons. "What father wants to leave the children at home?" The result was the Ford Mustang which was shown for the first time at the World Show in New York on April 13, 1964. Ford mounted a huge publicity campaign for the car costing at least $10 million but the money was a good investment as the subsequent production figures attest. At least 100,000 Mustangs were sold in the first four months after its launch.

These are the sales figures for the Ford Mustang in the first twelve years.

1964	121.538	1970	190.727
1965	559.451	1971	149.678
1966	607.568	1972	125.093
1967	472.121	1973	134.867
1968	317.404	1974	385.993
1969	299.824	1975	188.575

Ford USA

The second largest of the big three in Detroit has also built sports cars. Henry Ford built his first racing car – the famous "999" – in 1902. The company has made its money though for "ordinary" cars and racing cars were the exception. Ford in England built competitive versions of the Mustang and the GT 40 based on American ideas and the Ford Thunderbird quickly grew into a marque of its own (see Thunderbird).

Eventually the small 2 + 2 Mustang became a large car with a powerful engine but now the young man for whom it was intended could not afford it because of high insurance premiums.

The Boss was the most powerful Mustang in 1971 with a 7-litre V-8 engine giving 380 SAE at 5,600 rpm.

The Mustang Mach 1 of 1973.

The 266 bhp V-8 engine of the Mustang Mach 1.

With so many horsepower under the "hood" or bonnet, premiums in excess of $1,000 were demanded for persons under 25 who lived in cities. This was twice the cost of insuring a European sports car. Something had to change. The result was the Mustang II of 1974 which was almost 20 in (50 cm) shorter, 4 in (10 cm) narrower, and 1 in (2.5 cm) lower than its 1973 big brother. The car could fit in the garage now and had a 2.8 litre V-6 engine from the European Capri. The insurance premiums were now affordable. Whether the enthusiast liked the new Mustang is another issue but the car fitted well into Ford's philosophy of building cars that make money.

Ford USA sports cars

COUNTRY OF ORIGIN
USA

Ford Mustang 1964

YEARS IN PRODUCTION
1964

NUMBER MADE
121,538

SPECIAL REMARKS
The Mustang could be ordered with either a V-6 or V-8 engine. The smaller engine was 3,273 cc delivering 122 bhp at 4,400 rpm while the standard V-8 was 4,728 cc and developed 203 bhp at 4,400 rpm.

Ford Shelby Mustang GT 500

YEARS IN PRODUCTION
1967–1969

The Mustang had only just been launched in 1964 when it was already being tipped to win the Indianapolis 500.

"What father wants to leave the children at home?" A 1967 convertible.

The enthusiast's Mustang: the Shelby GT 500 KR (King of the Road). A total of 14,368 Shelby Mustangs were built between 1964 and 1970.

Carroll Shelby conjured a true racing car from the Mustang. The GT 350 R developed 350 bhp.

With its length of 175 in (444 cm) the Mustang II would fit in the garage.

NUMBER MADE
4,123

SPECIAL REMARKS
The GT 500 shared a body with the GT 350. The difference was the engine. The V-8 engine of the 500 was 7,003 cc while the GT 350 had a "mere" 4,728 cc.

their noses up at the Mustang II, it sold extremely well. The final 134,867 "big" Mustangs were sold in 1973.

An early Mustang II "fastback".

Ford Mustang II, 1974

YEARS IN PRODUCTION
1974

NUMBER MADE
385,993

SPECIAL REMARKS
Although the true Mustang enthusiasts turned

Ford Europe

When Henry Ford II decided he wanted to win Le Mans, he tried to buy Ferrari. He almost succeeded but Enzo Ferrari changed his mind at the last moment. The only other option was for Ford to build a European car, firstly to win Le Mans and secondly to show Ferrari that Ford did not need them. This led to the birth of the Ford GT 40.

The cars were made in Britain and they had to have all the teething problems ironed out of them before they could achieve victory at Le Mans. The car was known as a GT 40 because it was 40 in (102 cm) high. The first victory was followed by others and Ferrari were forced to watch Ford's success. All three Ford GT 40s had retired in 1964 and the first three places were taken by Ferrari and there was no success for Ford the following year when six GT 40s were forced to retire and the first three places were once again reserved for the cars from Modena. But by then Ford turned the corner.

Ford sent thirteen GT 40s to Le Mans in 1966 and although ten failed to go the distance, the other three came first, second, and third. Ford took first and fourth the following year and the race was won by a GT 40 in 1968 and 1969. Ford

had proved that its British colleagues could build fine cars. The British were very ingenious and even managed to make a racing car using a side-valved Ford Anglia engine. Such cars can still be seen competing in races for historic cars. It is no surprise therefore that the Capri was turned into something other than an ordinary car. When the 2 + 2 coupé was introduced in 1968 it resembled a smaller Mustang with a long bonnet and short rear end. The Capris were made in Britain and Germany and were introduced from the outset with a range of different engines. The smallest was a four-cylinder 1,300 cc giving 50 bhp while the largest in Britain was a 3-litre V-6 that developed 140 bhp. With a turbocharger this could be easily taken up to 450 bhp.

In the autumn of 1962 Ford introduced the Ford Cortina as a replacement for the Ford Consul (some markets called them the Consul Cortina). The car was available in two-door and four door variants and surprisingly also as a virtual competition car.

The Lotus Cortina Mk I looked like the other two-door Cortinas but had a twin-cam 1,558 cc engine with head and bottom end significantly converted by Lotus. Twin Weber carburettors ensured the right mixture and when tuned properly, the engine developed 106 bhp at 5,500 rpm.

Two GT 40s during the Le Mans 24 hour race. Number 2 was the car of McLaren/Donohue which came fourth, number 57 of Hawkins/Bucknum retired after 17 hours.

Another quick car from the Ford stable was the Escort which also made a first-class competition car. The Escort started its life as a small family saloon in 1968 with a choice of engines ranging from 1,098–1,558 cc, the latter being with twin camshafts, delivering at least 117 bhp.

Ford Europe sports cars

COUNTRY OF ORIGIN
Great Britain

Ford GT 40

YEARS IN PRODUCTION
1966–1972

NUMBER MADE
31 road cars

SPECIAL REMARKS
A number of the GT 40s made were detuned for road use but they were not really suitable as road cars.
The engine was mounted in front of the rear axle in the centre of the car and was 4,727 cc developing 335 bhp at 6,250 rpm.

Of the 107 GT 40s that were built, 31 were destined for road use.

Ford Capri

YEARS IN PRODUCTION
1968–1987

NUMBER MADE
Unknown

SPECIAL REMARKS
The Capri was a smaller version of Iacocca's Mustang with a long bonnet, small passenger compartment that had space for two adults and two children.

A German Ford Capri – a sportive 2 + 2.

A Capri driven by Toine Hezemans racing at Zandvoort in 1974 in the German Touring Car Championship.

This 1971 3-litre Capri still regularly runs in historic car races.

Ford Cortina

YEARS IN PRODUCTION
1962–1982

NUMBER MADE
Not known

The archetypal wolf in sheep's clothing. A Lotus Cortina.

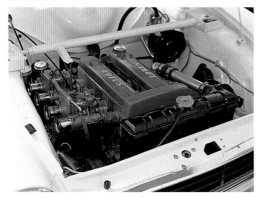

The Lotus engine with twin overhead camshafts and double twin Webers.

SPECIAL REMARKS
The 1.6 litre engine of the Lotus-Cortina was significantly developed by Lotus. It was given a head with twin overhead camshafts and double twin Weber carburettors to develop 106 bhp at 5,500 rpm. The top speed was 106 mph (170 km/hour) and to stop safely at such a speed the front wheels had disc brakes.

Ford Escort

YEARS IN PRODUCTION
1968–

NUMBER MADE
Unknown

SPECIAL REMARKS
The Ford Escort Twin Cam of 1968 had ample power right from its birth. The Lotus developed engine delivered 117 SAE at 6,000 rpm. For those who wanted more power, the engine could be provided with fuel injection.

A Zakspeed tuned Escort takes a corner in Zandvoort in 1975.

Frazer Nash

Archibald Goodman Frazer Nash was born in 1899 and he began to make motor sport cars in 1924. These were tough trials cars that performed well in this difficult branch of motor sport. Frazer Nash did not earn much from his hobby and so he was forced in 1926 to sell the company to H.J. Aldington's AFN. AFN built Frazer-Nash cars (which acquired a hyphen in the process) in small numbers and the marque re-appeared after World War II with a Bristol engine which in reality was a modified BMW 328 engine. The activity remained marginal given the small numbers involved.

A Frazer-Nash Le Mans Replica of 1948 seen competing in the Mille Miglia for veteran cars.

Frazer-Nash sports cars

COUNTRY OF ORIGIN
Great Britain

Frazer-Nash Le Mans

YEARS IN PRODUCTION
1950–1953

NUMBER MADE
33

SPECIAL REMARKS
AFN built several sports cars with the name "High Speed" in 1948 but after one of them came third at Le Mans in 1949, the name was changed to Le Mans Replica. The cars were powered by a Bristol engine.

Frazer-Nash Mille Miglia

YEARS IN PRODUCTION
1950–1952

NUMBER MADE
11

SPECIAL REMARKS
The Frazer-Nash Mille Miglia was merely a Le Mans Replica with a streamlined body that slightly resembled the Jaguar XK120.

Frazer-Nash Targa Florio

YEARS IN PRODUCTION
1952–1954

NUMBER MADE
13

A 1949 Frazer-Nash Mille Miglia during a race at the Nürburgring in 1981.

SPECIAL REMARKS
Franco Cortese won the Targa Florio in 1951 with a Frazer-Nash, beating a Ferrari and Maserati. This was reason enough to name the Mille Miglia as a Targa Florio.

Frazer-Nash Le Mans Coupé

YEARS IN PRODUCTION
1953–1956

NUMBER MADE
9

SPECIAL REMARKS
By changing a Targa Florio into a coupé, the Le Mans Coupé was created. This car also had the 1,971 cc Bristol engine that developed 111 bhp at 5,250 rpm.

When a "High Speed" came third at Le Mans in 1949, AFN sold the car as the Le Mans Replica.

Gatsonides

Maurice Gatsonides was born in Java in 1911. He was one of the few Dutch car makers in the post-war Netherlands. The racing and rally driver had planned his first car during the war and took his Gatford to various events in 1946. It is not possible to speak of production cars because his total output was a mere eight cars. The last Gatso was delivered in 1951.

Gatsonides sports cars

COUNTRY OF ORIGIN
The Netherlands

Gatso

YEARS IN PRODUCTION
1946–1951

NUMBER MADE
8

SPECIAL REMARKS
"Maus" Gatsonides built his first cars with Ford or Mercury V-8 engines. These were first-class touring cars, which Gatsonides drove in rallies. The car known in his home country as the "platje" or crab was built for the then new Zandvoort circuit.

The smallest and best-known Gatso was known as "the crab". It had a Fiat engine. This car was restored in 1991.

The Maigret author Georges Simenon bought this Ghia Assimmetrica at the Geneva Salon.

Ghia

Carrozzeria Ghia is one of the oldest specialist car body builders in Italy. Giacinto Ghia was born in Turin in 1887 and started building sporting bodies for cars back in 1915. His factory was destroyed by Allied bombing in 1943 and Ghia could not come to terms with this loss and died on February 21 1944. Much has happened at the factory on the Via da Montefelto in Turin since that time. People have worked there who have become famous such as Ditta Boana, Tom Tjaarda, and Giorgietto Giugiaro. They designed and built cars that still remain some of the prettiest ever created. Ghia attempted to bring out a car under its own name from time to time, such as the Ghia L 6.4 as a successor to the Dual Ghia. Only twenty-six of these cars were sold.

Ghia exhibited the Ghia 1500 GT at the Turin motor show in 1962. This was a speedy-looking car based on a shorter version of the Fiat 1500 chassis. This was followed the next year by the Ghia 230 S with the Fiat 2300 engine. The Ghia 450 SS was a superb concept car designed by Giugiaro that was built in small numbers in 1967.

Ghia is now a part of the Ford Motor Company. It was acquired by Ford as part settlement from De Tomaso of the Pantera debacle (q.v.).

Ghia sports cars

COUNTRY OF ORIGIN
Italy

Ghia Assimmetrica

YEARS IN PRODUCTION
1960–1962

NUMBER MADE
Unknown

SPECIAL REMARKS
After Virgil Exner got Ghia to build the Chrysler XNR in 1960, the Plymouth Asimmetrica, a descendant from this concept car was created. The two-seater car was built on a Valiant chassis of 193 in (489 cm). It was powered by a six-cylinder engine.

Ghia L 6.4

YEARS IN PRODUCTION
1961–1963

NUMBER MADE
26

SPECIAL REMARKS
This 210 in (533 cm) long Ghia had a Chrysler V-8 engine of 6.4 litre (hence the name) which delivered 340 SAE.

The automatic transmission was a "Torque-Flite" automatic box from Chrysler. Theoretically, the car was capable of 140 mph (225 km/hour).

Ghia 1500 GT

YEARS IN PRODUCTION
1962–1967

NUMBER MADE
Approx. 925

SPECIAL REMARKS
The Ghia 1500 GT was built on the Fiat 1500 chassis with the wheelbase reduced from 99 in (242 cm) to 92 in (235 cm). The four cylinder engine provided 84 bhp at 5,200 rpm. This was enough to take the car to a top speed of 106 mph (170 km/hour).

Ghia G 230 S

YEARS IN PRODUCTION
1963

NUMBER MADE
Unknown

SPECIAL REMARKS
The Ghia G 230 S was first exhibited at the 1963 Turin show. It was a fine "fast-back" coupé that

The L 6.4 was an Italian car with American mechanical parts from Chrysler. The model was designed for the US market but was also sold in Europe by Ghia.

The 1500 GT was a fast 112 mph (180 km/hour) 2-seater.

Maggiorelli and Magior won their class in the 1950 Mille Miglia with this Giannini 750.

was built on a tubular chassis and powered by a six-cylinder Fiat 2300 engine.

Ghia 450 SS

YEARS IN PRODUCTION
1965–1967

NUMBER MADE
12

SPECIAL REMARKS
Ghia built the 450 SS as a 2 + 2 coupé and as a convertible, using parts from the Plymouth Barracuda S.
The V-8 engine was 4.5 litres and provided 238 SAE.

Giannini

The name Giannini is almost unknown outside the circle of car enthusiasts. In Italy the name is mentioned in the same breath as Abarth and Stanguellini. The brothers Attilio and Dominico Giannini started their garage business in Rome in 1920. They were dealers for Italia cars and converted and tuned engines for enthusiasts. A car prepared by them won its class in the first Mille Miglia in 1927.
The brothers turned the diminutive Fiat 500 Topolino into little racing cars. After World War II these cars were once again the foundation of

Giannini built the 850 Grand Prix in 1968. The car was also sold as the Abarth Scorpion.

their business. Giannini also built their own engines with twin camshafts from 1949. These engines were not just made for their own use but also supplied to their competitors (see Giaur, Gilco, and Stanga) and they were extremely good even when asked to work hard throughout a 1,000 mile (1,600 km) race A Giannini won its class in the 1950 Mille Miglia at an average speed of 63.375 mph (101.397 km/hour).

After 1954, the Giannini company's most successful venture was making special bodies for Fiat cars. The engines were also tweaked a little. Quite a number of Formula Junior cars were built, equipped with either Fiat or Lancia engines but these cars were too heavy to win races.

Giannini are famous for their versions of the Fiat Nuova 500 which were converted and tuned in a number of ways. It was still possible in 1997 to order such Fiats from Giannini.

Giannini were famous for their special versions of the Fiat 500. The car continues to be sold at the end of the Twentieth century.

Giannini sports cars

COUNTRY OF ORIGIN
Italy

Giannini 500

YEARS IN PRODUCTION
1957–present day

NUMBER MADE
Unknown

SPECIAL REMARKS
Many Italian motor enterprises have made money by converting and tuning the Fiat 500. Giannini offered the little car with no fewer than eight different engines: the smallest is a 390 cc delivering 16.5 bhp at 5,000 rpm and the largest if a 625 cc giving 32 bhp at 5,800 rpm.

Giaur

Bernardo Taraschi built sports and racing cars under the Urania name in 1947. In common with others, Taraschi used Fiat parts but he also experimented with twin-cylinder BMW motorcycle engines. In 1950 he founded a new company together with the Giannini brothers (q.v.), known as Giaur.

The letters GIA are from Giannini and the UR from Urania. Taraschi was a successful driver with Giaur, winning his class in a race in Bari but his richest rewards were in the Mille Miglia where he won his class four times.

After things had been quiet with the company for some time, the sons of Attilio Giannini,

Bernardo Taraschi drove the Giaurs to much success. This is a 750 cc car of 1950.

This Giaur 750 broke a number of World records at the Monthléry circuit in 1956. The top speed was 148.125 mph (237 km/hour), aided by a Rootes

Ruggero and Antonio, made an effort to breathe new life into the company. They built a new 987 cc engine and mounted it in a Lotus 23 chassis to win the 1000 cc class of the Italian championship three years in a row. The brothers made a renewed effort with a 1,600 cc V-8 engine in 1966 but this time without success.

Giaur sports cars

COUNTRY OF ORIGIN
Italy

Giaur 750

YEARS IN PRODUCTION
1950–unknown

NUMBER MADE
Unknown

A Giaur 750 photographed during the 1997 Mille Miglia.

SPECIAL REMARKS
The Giaurs could be bought with a choice of engines but mostly of 750 cc capacity. The power unit was usually a Giannini, Fiat, or four-cylinder Crosley for the American market.

Gilbern

Gilbern was founded by Giles Smith and Bernard Friese, each lending the first parts of their first names to form the company name. The business, based in Wales until it closed down in 1973, marketed spacious sports cars as kits or ready-to-run vehicles. The exception to this policy was the Gilbern Invader of which 600 were solely delivered as completed cars between 1969 and 1973.

The start of the Gilbern adventure was in 1959 and in contrast to many other small marques, Gilbern had a great deal of success and this can be seen from the production figures. In common with their competitors, Gilberns were constructed with many bought in mechanical parts. The chassis was built by Gilbern and the client could have their engine of choice mounted on it.

The Invader was Gilbern's best seller but it could not prevent the company from going under.

Gilbern sports cars

COUNTRY OF ORIGIN
Great Britain (Wales)

Gilbern GT

YEARS IN PRODUCTION
1959–1966

NUMBER MADE
Approx. 400

SPECIAL REMARKS
The front suspension of the GT was from an Austin A35, the gearbox from an MG, and the rear axle from BMC. The client chose their own engine.

Gilbern Genie

YEARS IN PRODUCTION
1967–1969

NUMBER MADE
197

SPECIAL REMARKS
The Genie was equipped as standard with disc brakes and these were quite essential because the car was usually supplied with a highly-tuned 3 litre engine.

Gilbern Invader

YEARS IN PRODUCTION
1969–1974

NUMBER MADE
Approx. 600

SPECIAL REMARKS
The Invader was also available with an automatic gearbox and there was a sports car version in the range. After 1972, the rear axle was from the Ford Taunus (the German equivalent of the Cortina) and the front suspension from a Cortina.

1972/1973 Gilbern Invader Mk III.

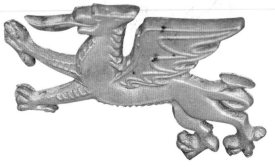

Gilco

Gilberto Colombo attempted to earn his living by building small sports cars but this was not easy to do. Most of his parts were purchased from Fiat but because he wanted his cars to compete in the 750 cc class, he used Giannini brothers engines. These smaller engined cars were built from 1948–1952 and then subsequently Combo built his cars with larger Fiat, Alfa Romeo, or Lancia engines.

This Gilco 750 is a regular entrant in the present day Mille Miglia.

The cockpit of a Gilco 750.

COUNTRY OF ORIGIN
Italy

SPECIAL REMARKS
Combo installed a great variety of engines in his Gilco cars. Cars of his with Alfa Romeo, Ferrari, Maserati, Stanguellini, and Nardi engines have become renowned.

Ginetta

The four brothers Bob, Douglas, Ivor, and Trevor Walkett had an engineering consultancy before they started to make low priced sports cars in 1957. The first prototype from their Woodbridge works had something of the Lotus 6 about it. Once friends of the brothers had seen the car, the first orders rolled in. Most of the cars were sold as kits. Such a Ginetta kit cost a mere £156 in 1958.

The most successful Ginetta was the G4 which was first seen at the London Racing Car Show. The G4 could be supplied with any four-cylinder Ford engine. The body, like all Ginettas, was of glass-fibre reinforced polyes-

The Gilco was a "real man's car" with no roof or any creature comforts.

The Ginetta G16 was an open-topped G12.

Ginetta sports cars

COUNTRY OF ORIGIN
Great Britain

Ginetta G2

YEARS IN PRODUCTION
1957–1960

NUMBER MADE
Approx. 100

SPECIAL REMARKS
The G2 was mainly offered with the four-cylinder Ford Anglia engine.

Ginetta G3

YEARS IN PRODUCTION
1960–1962

NUMBER MADE
Approx. 60

SPECIAL REMARKS
The G3 was an improved G2. The car was also sold as a kit and enthusiasts could also order just the glass-reinforced polyester body shell.

Ginetta G4 en G5

YEARS IN PRODUCTION
1961–present day

NUMBER MADE
More than 500

SPECIAL REMARKS
The four-cylinder Ford Anglia engine of the G4 was 997 cc. The G5 is identical but is supplied with a 1.5 litre engine that develops 90 bhp at 6,000 rpm. This car can achieve straight line speeds in excess of 125 mph (200 km/hour).

Most Ginetta G4s had a Ford engine.

ter. The company moved in 1962 to larger premises in Witham. The G5 with a Ford Cortina engine grew out of the G4, the G6 was made for the German market with a DKW engine and the G7 had a trans-axle. The G8 and G9 were prototype Formula 2 and 3 racing cars.
The G10 of 1965 had a Ford V-8 engine and was intended for the US market. The G11 had the same body as the G10 but with an MG engine while the 1966 G12 was merely a circuit prepared G4 with a centre-mounted engine. The G13 was never developed and the G14 got no further than the drawing board. The Hillman Imp engine was fitted in the G15. This car was sold as a kit for £799 and the G16 was a G15 with a more powerful engine. The next model, the G17 was a single-seater racing car for Formula 4 and the G19 was a similar car but for Formula 3. The G20 was never built. In 1970, the G21 appeared, being an enlarged G15. The company is still going and these days sells the G27 with a Ford Pinto engine.

The Ginetta G4 can often be seen participating in races for historical cars.

Ginetta G10

YEARS IN PRODUCTION
1965–1968

NUMBER MADE
6

SPECIAL REMARKS
The G10 was built with a 4,728 cc Ford V-8 because American customers had more faith in engines from Detroit than European motors.

Ginetta G11

YEARS IN PRODUCTION
1965

NUMBER MADE
12

SPECIAL REMARKS
The G11 was mainly intended for the home and European market. There was an MG engine under the bonnet, otherwise it was identical to a G10.

Ginetta G15

YEARS IN PRODUCTION
1968–1974

NUMBER MADE
More than 800

SPECIAL REMARKS
When purchase tax on cars was replaced with Value Added Tax in 1973 the advantage of a kit car disappeared. G15 models sold after this date were delivered as completed cars.

Ginetta G21

YEARS IN PRODUCTION
1970–1978

NUMBER MADE
150

SPECIAL REMARKS
Ginetta attempted to break into the middle-sized sports car market with the G21, which was supplied with a choice of two engines: the Ford 3 litre V-6 or four-cylinder 1,725 cc Sunbeam that developed 79 bhp at 5,200 rpm.

Glas

In common with many other Germans, Hans Glas was extremely successful in the rebuilding Germany economy after World War II. This economic miracle worker turned a company building agricultural machinery into a car maker. Glas quickly realised that the demand from the new Federal Republic of Germany for cheap cars would be enormous. His production capability enabled him to supply more than 200,000 Goggomobils and from this little car the Glas was created, first with a 600, then a 700, and subsequently with a 992 cc engine. Once the engine had grown to a 1,300 cc, the Glas was turned into a sports car but the company's fortunes had turned. By the late 1960s, most Germans could afford a larger car and did not want to be seen in a Goggomobil. Glas's response was to put the larger engine in a medium-sized car but this was not successful. His potential customers still chose a different marque. Hans Glas was forced to sell his company to BMW in 1966. BMW built a couple of new models with BMW engines.

The body of the Glas 1300 and 1700 GT were designed and built in Italy by Piero Frua.

Glas sports cars

COUNTRY OF ORIGIN
Germany (Federal Republic)

Glas 1300 GT/1700 GT

YEARS IN PRODUCTION
1964–1967 and 1965–1967

NUMBER MADE
3,760 and 1,802

SPECIAL REMARKS
The Glas 1300 GT was available as a coupé or convertible. The 1.3 litre engine delivered 85 bhp but more power was provided for those who wanted it with the 1.7 litre 105 bhp engine.

Glas/BMW 1600GT

YEARS IN PRODUCTION
1967–1968

NUMBER MADE
1,002

SPECIAL REMARKS
BMW continued to build the 1600 GT for a year following their take-over of Hans Glas's business but the cars then had 1,573 cc four-cylinder BMW engines which developed 105 bhp at 6,000 rpm which gave the car a top speed of 115 mph (185 km/hour).

Glas/BMW V8

YEARS IN PRODUCTION
1966–1968 and 1969

NUMBER MADE
300 and 71

The Glas V-8 had a motor formed from two 1,300 cc four-cylinder engines. Once BMW took over this was replaced by a BMW engine.

SPECIAL REMARKS
Glas attempted to move into the market for more expensive cars but this was the end of his business. His products could not compete with their opponents. This was a shame because the V-8 with its 2,580 cc engine and 150 bhp was a fine car. The final versions of this car had a 2,982 cc BMW V-8 engine.

Gordini

Amadeo Gordini was born in Italy in 1899 but moved to France when he was young so it was in Paris that he established a garage when he was twenty-five. He had learned his trade at the age of eleven in the garage of none other than Edoardo Weber (later to become famous for his carburettors) and when he started work with Isotta-Fraschini in 1913, his immediate boss was Alfieri Maserati.
He quickly specialised in France in the conversion and tuning of engines. His cars regularly won prizes but motor racing is expensive and he sought financial support from Simca. Simca agreed on condition that he used as many Simca

Gordini had a lot of success with his cars in the 750 cc class. This is a 1952 car.

It rained almost continuously during the 1991 Mille Miglia – not quite the weather for an open Gordini.

This Gordini 20S of 1954 is in the Schlumpf museum. It has a 1,987 cc six-cylinder engine.

parts in his car as possible. Hence it was a Simca-Gordini that came seventeenth in 1937 in the Le Mans 24 hour race.

Although a stray bomb destroyed Gordini's workshop on the Boulevard Victor in Paris, Gordini was able to win his first post-war race on September 9, 1945.

Simca continued to support Gordini, resulting in some impressive cars: many of them single-seaters but also sports cars. The money from Simca enabled him to employ good drivers such as Jean-Pierre Wimille who was regarded as the best driver in the world at that time but also Prince Bira, Trintignant, and later also Fangio all drove for Gordini. Eventually Gordini cars were unable to compete with the opposition. Because Simca had no engines with twin overhead camshafts, Gordini was not permitted to use them. This was just one of many handicaps. Gordini attempted to get back to winning in 1950 by installing a 4.5 litre V-12 engine but Simca did not approve and withdrew their support. Gordini now struggled financially and new smaller engines were developed with which he was able to win races now and then but the golden era had passed. By 1956 the money ran out and "Le Socier" as the French called him was forced to sell his last cars to the Schlumpf brothers. Gordini worked for a time as a consultant for Renault, who were glad to use his famous name on their cars. Gordini died on May 25, 1979 but his cars live on, among other places in the Schlumpf museum in Mulhouse.

Gordini sports cars

COUNTRY OF ORIGIN
France

Gordini-Renault R8

YEARS IN PRODUCTION
1964–1966

NUMBER MADE
Unknown

Renault 8 Gordini car can still be encountered on the track.

Gordini did excellent work for Renault. The 1,108 cc engine of the Renault 8 developed 46 SAE while the Gordini R8 produced 95 bhp at 6,500 rpm.

Gordon-Keeble

Back in 1960, John Gordon was relatively unknown when he showed a prototype car at the Geneva Salon in the hope of finding a backer. Jim Keeble saw something in the proposals and invested his money, and so Gordon-Keeble was born. The car had a body designed by the 21-year-old Giugiaro who then worked for Bertone. The first car had an aluminium body but the production cars had glass-fibre reinforced polyester body shells. The engine was from a Chevrolet Corvette and the rear-axle was a complex De Dion affair. The car had all-round disc brakes which was not yet a matter of course at that time and the car cost a mere £2,798. Because this cost did not actually cover the production costs, Gordon was forced to quit the business in 1965. Keeble continued without him,

The typical Bertone lines of the Gordon-Keeble.

The front end with its quad headlights conjures up the Ferrari 330 GT of 1964.

Abarth used a scorpion, Ferrari a prancing horse, Lamborghini chose a bull as its marque emblem but Gordon-Keeble used a tortoise!

trying to sell the car for £4,058 as a Keeble but this did not succeed either. A total of 99 cars were sold but the demise of the business in 1967 was inevitable.

Gordon-Keeble sports cars

COUNTRY OF ORIGIN
Great Britain

Gordon-Keeble

YEARS IN PRODUCTION
1964–1967

NUMBER MADE
99

SPECIAL REMARKS
The Gordon-Keeble was powered by the 5,354 cc V-8 engine from the Chevrolet Corvette and had an expensive De Dion rear axle. The engine delivered 300 bhp and produced a top speed of 144 mph (230 km/hour).

GSM

The South African firm of Glassport Motor Company in Belleville was established by Bon van Niekerk and Vester de Wit. In addition to tuning kits, the company also made sports cars that were sold under the name Dart. The company moved into the British market in 1960 to sell the car as the GSM Delta but the

project failed and the company was declared bankrupt within a year. The South African production continued however, and a fine 2 + 2 known as the Flamingo was launched in 1963. This had the engine from the German-made Ford Taunus inside its polyester body shell. The Dart/Delta continued to be built but the South African end of the business closed down too in 1965.

GSM sports cars

COUNTRY OF ORIGIN
South Africa

GSM Dart 1500

YEARS IN PRODUCTION
1956–1965

NUMBER MADE
Unknown

SPECIAL REMARKS
The Dart 1500 engine specification is: four-cylinders in line, four-stroke, overhead valves, 1,498 cc, 8.5:1 compression ratio, 85 bhp at 5,600 rpm.

GSM-Delta

YEARS IN PRODUCTION
1960–1965

NUMBER MADE
35

SPECIAL REMARKS
The Delta was available with either a 997 or 1,498 cc Ford engine. Tuned, the engines developed either (997 cc) 72 bhp at 7,000 rpm or (1,498 cc) 116 bhp at 8,000 rpm. This gave top speeds of 112 mph (180 km/hour) or 125 mph (200 km/hour).

GSM Flamingo

YEARS IN PRODUCTION
1962–1965

SPECIAL REMARKS
The Flamingo was GSM's first and last coupé model. It was a fine 2 + 2 with the 1.7 litre engine from the German made Ford Taunus.

A 1961 GSM Delta. Beneath the bonnet was a Ford 1,197 cc engine.

Hansa:
see Borgward

Healey

One of the persons who have created automobile history is Donald Healey. He was a driver who won rallies such as the Monte Carlo, technical director with car makers Triumph, and also built cars under his own name. In addition to these, there were also the Austin-Healeys, Nash-Healeys, and Jensen-Healeys.

At the age of 48 in 1946, Healey began cautiously to build touring and sports cars bearing his own name. The major mechanical elements were bought in, such as the engine, gearbox, and

The Duncan bodied Healey was a primitive car that was not really suitable for road use.

Four Healey chassis were given bodies by Karosserie Beutler in Switzerland in 1948–1949.

The Beutler Healey was a two-seater with space behind the leather seats.

Healey Silverstones can regularly be admired running on the track in historic races. These two are duelling on the Silverstone circuit.

rear axle. The superb front suspension used for his Silverstone was made by him. The first Healeys were made using parts from pre-war Rileys. Later, Healey used the Alvis six-cylinder engine in his cars. Healey made his own cars from October 1946 to November 1951. He had made a total of 633 of them.

Healey sports cars

COUNTRY OF ORIGIN
Great Britain

Healey 2.4 litre

YEARS IN PRODUCTION
1946–1950

NUMBER MADE
188

SPECIAL REMARKS
Healey used the 2.4 litre Riley engine in his sports cars. The convertibles were given the name Westland (87 built) and the coupés were Elliots (101 of them).

Count Johnny Lurani won his class in the 1948 Mille Miglia in an Elliot. Thirty-nine of the cars had bodies by Duncan.

Healey-Sportsmobile

YEARS IN PRODUCTION
1947–1949

NUMBER MADE
23

SPECIAL REMARKS
The Sportsmobile was not a success. The car was technically as good as the other Healeys but this convertible did not have any appeal.

Healey-Silverstone

YEARS IN PRODUCTION
1949–1951

NUMBER MADE
105

Healey's most successful car that he built himself was the Silverstone.

The Riley engine of the Silverstone had high-mounted but not overhead twin camshafts.

The complex front suspension of the Healey Silverstone.

SPECIAL REMARKS
The Healey Silverstone was a magnificent car. It is built these days as a replica and you can drive to work in it or race it on the track. The "motorcycle" mudguards and the headlights could easily be removed and the windscreen could be recessed into the body.

Healey-Tickford

YEARS IN PRODUCTION
1951–1954

NUMBER MADE
224

SPECIAL REMARKS
From 1951, Healey installed Alvis engines in his cars including the Tickford. These were 2,993 cc six-cylinder engines that developed 107 bhp at 4,200 rpm.

Healey-Abbott

YEARS IN PRODUCTION
1951–1954

NUMBER MADE
77

SPECIAL REMARKS
The Abbott was built for those who wanted a Tickford but in a convertible version. It was a 2 + 2 and when the hood was down, the rear passengers had no view.

Healey-G-Type

YEARS IN PRODUCTION
1951–1954

NUMBER MADE
25

SPECIAL REMARKS
The G-type was in reality a Nash-Healey (see Nash) but with an Alvis six-cylinder engine and a four-speed gearbox instead of a three-speed box.

Hillman

The Hillman name disappeared in 1976 which was a shame considering that the company had built cars since 1907 which had included some famous sports cars before World War II. The post war output was mainly down-to-earth family saloons but with the occasional convertible or a two-door coupé version of a four-door saloon. The Imp was Hillman's opposition to the Mini of the British Motor Corporation. Hillman was still owned by the Rootes Brothers, William and Reginald when the Imp was launched but they sold out to Chrysler in 1964. With the mini, the engine was mounted trans-

The Imp is fun to race.

The road-holding has its boundaries.

Fortunately the Imp is strongly built.

versely at the front. With the Imp it was fitted at the rear. This did nothing to improve road-holding. In spite of this, Imps were widely raced and can still be seen competing in races for cars that are long in the tooth. The factory supplied the Imp in three versions: a 42 bhp 875 cc engine, the 55 bhp Sport or 65 bhp Rally that had the larger 998 cc four-cylinder engine.

Hillman sports cars

COUNTRY OF ORIGIN
Great Britain

Hillman Imp

YEARS IN PRODUCTION
1963–1976

NUMBER MADE
Approx. 440,000

SPECIAL REMARKS
Hillman did not scrimp technically with the Imp because both the engine and gearbox were cast in aluminium alloy

Honda

When Soichiro Honda had become the world's biggest maker of motorcycles (the company probably still is) his company started to make cars. In the 1950s and 60s, the Japanese built small

cars that were cheap mainly because they were more suited to Japan's small roads. Another reason is that Japanese are on average quite small and hence when the first Japanese cars were exported to Europe and America they were too small for the average Westerner. The Honda sports cars were equally the same.

When the S500 was marketed it was initially intended solely for Japan, Once the cylinders were enlarged in 1962 to 606 cc, Honda attempted to sell the car in Europe. Although rather small, the car has a number of very interesting technical features. The technology owed much to Honda's background as a motorcycle manufacturer and the rear wheels were actually chain driven.

The four-cylinder engine had twin overhead camshafts, four carburettors, and produced power of 57 bhp. Enthusiasts were not concerned that this power was available at 8,500 rpm. Initially the S500 was only available as a convertible but from August 1965 it was also available as a coupé. The S800 celebrated its arrival in Europe in Paris. Its power was 70 bhp at 8,000 rpm from its 791 cc engine.

Honda sports cars

COUNTRY OF ORIGIN
Japan

The Honda S600 was a marvellous little sports car for small people.

The Honda S600.

Honda S600

YEARS IN PRODUCTION
1962–1966

NUMBER MADE
13,084

SPECIAL REMARKS
The Honda S600 was technically extremely interesting. It was clearly designed by a motorcycle manufacturer.

The interior of the Honda S600.

The four-cylinder engine of the S600.

Honda S800

YEARS IN PRODUCTION
1966–1970

NUMBER MADE
13,084

SPECIAL REMARKS
The little S800 had a top speed of more than 100 mph (160 km/hour). This was quite an achievement for a 791 cc engine.

Racing with an S800. The 70 bhp engine took the car in excess of 100 mph (160 km/hour).

HRG

HRG never became a big car maker but British enthusiasts speak respectfully about the 197 cars built by the three friends E. Halford, G. Robins, and H. Godfrey. They started making cars in 1935 and finished in 1966 but only a few prototypes were experimented with from 1956 onwards.

The pre-war cars were quite basic, consisting of little more than an engine and two seats on four wheels but the British enthusiasts loved them for driving in trials at week-ends and to work during the week.

HRG occasionally built a more road-going model but these were never as successful. After World War II, HRG re-appeared with the trusty 1500 developed before the war but once motorists got to know the MGs, Triumphs, and Austin-Healeys, the demand for these rather primitive and spartan cars diminished.

The 1500 was the best selling HRG. It was introduced in 1940 and remained in the range until 1956 when even the died-in-the-wool enthusiast found it a bit old-

HRG sports cars

COUNTRY OF ORIGIN
Great Britain

HRG Aero

YEARS IN PRODUCTION
1945–1949

NUMBER MADE
45

SPECIAL REMARKS
The HRG was never a cheap car. In 1948 the enthusiast was asked to pay £850 plus £236 purchase tax for the 1500 Sports two-seater. The car gave the owner lots of fun for his money.
The four cylinder engine had an overhead camshaft and delivered 61 bhp at 4,800 rpm. This could take the car to 100 mph (160 km/hour).

Hudson

Hudson suffered the same problem after World War II as Nash: it was almost impossible to sell the cars. The company decided in 1954 to merge with the American Motors Company. Hudson moved from Detroit to Kenosha in Wisconsin, where the Nash factory was located. The final Hudson rolled of the line in 1957. The company started building cars in 1909.

Hudson built some fine cars. The 1948 Hudsons were at 62 in (159 cm) lower than their competitors and hence many stock car prizes went to Hudson drivers.

Hudson sports cars

COUNTRY OF ORIGIN
USA

Hudson Jet Italia

YEARS IN PRODUCTION
1954

NUMBER MADE
26

SPECIAL REMARKS
The final Hudsons made in Detroit were the Jet Italias which were built by Touring of Milan in Italy for financial reasons. Hudson shipped the rolling chassis of the Jet to Italy and received the finished car back.

The Hudson Jet Italia was a marvellous 2 + 2 with a 3,310 cc six-cylinder engine that gave 115 bhp at 4,000 rpm.

HWM

Hersham & Walton Motors or HWM was founded in 1946 by the drivers George Abecassis and John Heath. They became agents for Alta sports cars and started to build their own specials with Alta and, later, Jaguar engines. HWM cars were made for hill climb, daily use, and track and their Formula 3 cars were feared by the competition. In addition to the owners themselves, drivers such as Paul Frère, Stirling Moss, Peter Collins, and Lance Macklin raced for HWM.
The company did not manage to sell many cars and when John Heath was killed in a crash in the 1956 Mille Miglia it was the end for the company.

HWM sports cars

COUNTRY OF ORIGIN
Great Britain

HWM-Jaguar

YEARS IN PRODUCTION
1952–1956

NUMBER MADE
Unknown

SPECIAL REMARKS
HWM started making cars with Alta engines but the customers preferred alternatives and cars were even delivered with Cadillac V-8 motors. The most popular choice was the Jaguar XK120 engine.
The true enthusiasts wanted Jaguar D-type engines with which Phil Scragg won his division of the 1959 Hill Climb Championship.

This was the most successful HWM in 1958. A six-cylinder Jaguar D-type engine throbbed beneath the bonnet.

Abecassis had many victories in this 1956 HWM-Jaguar. The car stand still be seen on the circuits.

A 1955 HWM-Jaguar photographed at rest during the 1997 Mille Miglia.

Innocenti

Innocenti Societa Generale per l'Industria Metallurgica e Meccanica became world famous for their Lambretta scooters but the company aspired to greater things and started assembling BMC cars in 1960. The factory built the Austin A40, the Morris 1100 but most of all the famous Mini. The business was taken over in 1972 by British Leyland and then sold in 1979 to Alejandro de Tomaso (q.v.). Under De Tomaso, the company built the Innocenti Mini and later the Maserati Biturbos. The factory was closed down by De Tomaso in 1993 after he had sold much of the business to Fiat.

The Innocenti 950 had a 42 bhp, 948 cc engine. After the engine had been increased to 1,098 cc in 1963, it developed 55 bhp at 5,400 rpm.

Innocenti sports cars

COUNTRY OF ORIGIN
Italy

Innocenti 950

YEARS IN PRODUCTION
1961–1970

NUMBER MADE
Approx. 17,500

SPECIAL REMARKS
The body was designed at Ghia by Tom Tjaarda and shown at the Turin motor show in 1960. The 950 convertible was based on the Austin-Healey Sprite running gear.
A coupé version of this car was introduced in 1967 and the convertible was taken out of production.

Intermeccanica

Frank Reisner was a Hungarian with an American passport, living in Italy. Reisner built sports cars with big engines at Moncalieri near Turin. Although his company was known as Intermeccanica, his first cars were sold under the name Italia.
Reisner's interests extended beyond Intermeccanica and he also had shareholdings in small companies that built the Omega, Griffith, and Apollo sports cars. His importer for Germany was Erich Bitter and when Bitter became dissatisfied with the cars supplied from Italy, he began making his own cars (see Bitter).

The first Italias were only available as two-seater convertibles.

Reisner returned to California in 1975 where he built replicas of the Porsche Speedster.

Intermeccanica sports cars

COUNTRY OF ORIGIN
Italy

Intermeccanica Italia

YEARS IN PRODUCTION
1966–1970

The Italia was also a good-looking coupé. It was designed by Franco Scaglione.

The final Intermeccanica was the Indra.

NUMBER MADE
Approx. 1,000

SPECIAL REMARKS
For the first three years Reisner only built convertible models of the Italia. These were then followed by a small number of coupés. Franco Scaglione designed the body. Beneath the bonnet was the 5,766 cc V-8 engine from the Ford Mustang.

Intermeccanica Indra

YEARS IN PRODUCTION
1971–1973

NUMBER MADE
Unknown

SPECIAL REMARKS
Reisner exhibited a new model at the Geneva Salon in 1971. It was the Indra based on a shortened Opel Diplomat chassis. The car, which was at first solely available as a convertible but later also as a coupé, had a 2,784 cc six-cylinder Opel engine or a V-8 engine of either 5,354 or 5,733 cc.

Iso Rivolta

When Commendatore Renzo Rivolta had earned enough from motorcycles and the Isetta bubble cars (he sold the design to BMW, who made

them for many years), he turned to making sports cars. His cars were based on a well-established concept: Italian flair for body design and indestructible American mechanical parts. Renzo Rivolta died in 1966 and the business was taken over by his son Piero who at 26 had ambitious plans but too little experience. This combination brought the company into difficulties. He was forced to shut the factory in 1974 but rumours surfaced some years later that he intended to start up again.

Iso Rivolta sports cars

COUNTRY OF ORIGIN
Italy

The best of the Iso cars: the Grifo 7 Litri

Iso Rivolta

YEARS IN PRODUCTION
1961–1970

NUMBER MADE
797

SPECIAL REMARKS
Rivolta chose the right people for his first car. The chassis was designed by Giotti Bizzarini, the body by Bertone, and the V-8 engine was the 5,354 cc Chevrolet Corvette.

Iso Grifo

YEARS IN PRODUCTION
1963–1974

NUMBER MADE
494

SPECIAL REMARKS
The Grifo was built on a shorter version of the Rivolta chassis. It was a true two-seater. The first 414 cars had the 304 bhp 5.3 litre V-8 engine but the other 90 were fitted with a 6,996 cc V-8. The 406 bhp at 5,200 rpm of the "7 litri" was more than an answer to Ferrari to which they had no response.

Iso Lele

YEARS IN PRODUCTION
1969–1974

NUMBER MADE
317

SPECIAL REMARKS
Bertone designed the body for the successor to the Rivolta. The Lele was more sleek and had a more powerful 5,733 cc V-8 engine that produced 355 bhp. The car was supplied as standard with a five-speed gearbox and automatic transmission was available as an option.

The Iso Lele was not successful but this had nothing to do with the quality of the car.

Jaguar

The Jaguar story is well known. William Lyons founded Swallow Sidecars in Blackpool in 1922 to make sidecars for motorcycles. The business expanded into making special car bodies for Austin Sevens and other small cars in 1927. The first car of his own design was introduced in 1931.

It was a two-door car using parts from the Standard Motor Company and was known as SS 1. The letters represented Swallow Sidecars but after the war Lyons did not want to use the Swallow name anymore and he named his cars after one of his pre-war models – the Jaguar. Lyons success lay in building superb cars at a low cost. The SS 1 was a case in point. It was a marvellous sporting coupé with a long bonnet with a small 2-litre side-valve engine. Even the XK120, one of the prettiest cars of the 1940s and 1950s, was reasonably priced and cost about half the price of comparable cars at that time.

William Lyons took an XK120 to the London Motor show to attract attention to the new MkV saloon being launched but the public only had eyes for the beautiful sports car. Many British car makers have recruited the help of Italian designers for the bodies of their cars but Jaguar

did not do so. In his time, Lyons himself kept his personal finger on the pulse and led by example. History shows how well he did this.

Jaguar sports cars

COUNTRY OF ORIGIN
Great Britain

Jaguar XK120

YEARS IN PRODUCTION
1948–1954

NUMBER MADE
12,055

SPECIAL REMARKS
The XK120 was built in three models: as

The bonnet of the Jaguar E-type – this is a Series 1 – was half the length of the car.

The dashboard of the XK120 is simple but effective.

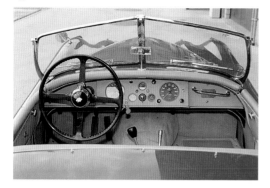

The XK120 engine is the origin of today's XK engine.

The successor to the XK 140 was the 150 with a less spectacular body. The windscreen was now one piece

Jaguar XK140

YEARS IN PRODUCTION
1954–1957

NUMBER MADE
9,051

SPECIAL REMARKS
Careful study is needed to tell an XK140 apart from the 120. The 140 has heavier bumpers and fewer bars in its grill. The 3,442 cc engine produced 190 or 213 bhp. There were still the same three versions: roadster (3,354), convertible (2,889), and coupé (2,808).

Jaguar XK150

YEARS IN PRODUCTION
1957–1961

NUMBER MADE
9,398

SPECIAL REMARKS
The successor to the XK140 had a more powerful engine. The significance of 150 is the top speed of

roadster (7,612), as convertible with real side windows in the doors (1,765), and as a coupé (2,678). The six-cylinder engine had twin camshafts producing 160 bhp at 5,000 rpm. The roadster was available as an optional extra with an engine that developed 180 bhp at 5,300 rpm.

The XK120 roadster had a soft-top that barely kept out the elements and virtually n-one ever attached the side flaps.

The XK140 can be recognised by the heavier bumpers. In many European countries, this car cost more than a Porsche convertible.

150 mph (240 km/hour). Again three types were built: 2,265 roadsters, 2,671 convertibles, and 4,462 coupés. There was also a Roadster S with a 265 bhp engine in place of the 190 bhp standard engine.

Jaguar E-Type Series 1

YEARS IN PRODUCTION
1961–1964

NUMBER MADE
15,496

SPECIAL REMARKS
In common with the XK120, the E-type was a lot of car for its money. In 1961, the car costs slightly more than half the cost of the cheapest Ferrari and even ten per cent less the small Lotus Elite. The car now had a 3.7 litre engine giving 265 bhp at 5,500 rpm. Slightly more than half of the cars made were convertibles.

Jaguar E-Type Series 1.5

YEARS IN PRODUCTION
1964–1968

NUMBER MADE
22,916

SPECIAL REMARKS
The only difference in the successor to the Series I was beneath the bonnet. The engine remained rated at 265 bhp but was now 4,235 cc. A new model 2 + 2 coupé appeared in 1966, of which 5,598 were made.

Jaguar E-Type Series 2

YEARS IN PRODUCTION
1968–1971

The E-type was also available as a 2 + 2 coupé from 1966. This is a Series 2 car.

NUMBER MADE
18,808

SPECIAL REMARKS
It goes without saying that most Jaguar E-types went to America where they were called XKE. When the safety and environmental regulations in the United States were made more onerous, the engine had to be adapted and had two instead of three carburettors.

Jaguar E-Type Series 3

YEARS IN PRODUCTION
1971–1975

NUMBER MADE
15,287

SPECIAL REMARKS
The final E-type was certainly the best in technical terms. Beneath its long bonnet was a 5,343 cc V-12 engine that provided 276 bhp at 5,850 rpm with two overhead camshafts (one per head) and four carburettors. The top speed of the E-type Series 3 was 150 mph (240 km/hour) and it accelerated from 0–60 in 6 seconds (0–100 km/hour in 6.4 seconds). The car was truly a technological wonder.

The Series 3 was only available as a 2 + 2 coupé or as a convertible. Both models were on the same long wheelbase.

A Series 3 E-type during restoration.

Jensen

The company run by brothers Richard and Alan Jensen was a specialist car body builder in the 1920s. In 1939 the Jensen brothers introduced a car bearing their own name and immediately the war was over, they resumed activities. The company built fine, stately cars that could hold their own with Bentley and the Austin Princess but they also built sporting convertibles and coupés. They also built bodies for their competitors, such as the Volvo P 1800. Jensen were also known for the Jensen-Healey. By 1976 their was too little interest in the company's products and the business was wound up.

Jensen sports cars

COUNTRY OF ORIGIN
Great Britain

Four-wheel drive and a longer wheelbase were the characteristics of the Jensen Interceptor FF. The car was also distinguished by the double air vents in the front wings.

The radiator "grill" was really a flap that was thermostatically controlled and opened automatically when the engine was hot and closed when cold.

Jensen 541

YEARS IN PRODUCTION
1955–1960

NUMBER MADE
419

SPECIAL REMARKS
The Jensen 541 was much admired at the 1953 London Motor Show. The polyester body was quite new at the time and the flap which automatically opened and closed when the car was hot or cold was also intriguing. The six-cylinder Austin engine was uprated from 130 to 152 bhp in 1957 and put in the 541 R models.

The engine was easily accessible in the Jensen 541.

The Jensen 541 was the first production car to be equipped with all-round disc brakes. The six-cylinder Austin engine was 3,993 cc.

Jensen 541 S

YEARS IN PRODUCTION
1961–1963

NUMBER MADE
127

SPECIAL REMARKS
The successor to the 541 R was the 541 S, which was slightly wider and longer although the shape

The Jensen 541 S was the same shape as the 541 R but was slightly longer and wider.

of the car was virtually unaltered. The thermostatically operated flap had disappeared and been replaced by a conventional radiator grill.

Jensen CV-8

YEARS IN PRODUCTION
1962–1966

NUMBER MADE
499

SPECIAL REMARKS
The four-seater CV-8 also had a polyester body but with a Chrysler 6,276 cc V-8 engine that developed 305 bhp at 4,600 rpm.
With its top speed of 140 mph (225 km/hour) the car was ideally suited to covering long fast journeys.

Jensen Interceptor

YEARS IN PRODUCTION
1967–1976

The biggest selling Jensen was the Interceptor. Of the standard model, 6,175 were sold and 320 of the special 4 X 4 version. Only 232 were sold of the very luxurious SP with its 7.2 litre engine.

NUMBER MADE
6,727

SPECIAL REMARKS
The body of the Interceptor was designed in 1967 by Carrozzeria Vignale. There was also a four-wheel drive model using the Ferguson Formula (FF) of which 320 were made and 267 convertibles were sold with 6,276 or 7,212 cc Chrysler V-8 engines.

Jensen-Healey

YEARS IN PRODUCTION
1972–1976

NUMBER MADE
10,926

SPECIAL REMARKS
Donald Healey provided both Austin and Jensen with sports cars that sold well, making his partnership with Jensen successful. The engine was a Lotus twin-cam four-cylinder 1,973 cc developing 142 bhp at 6,500 rpm.

Jensen GT

YEARS IN PRODUCTION
1975–1976

NUMBER MADE
473

SPECIAL REMARKS
There have always been enthusiasts for a fast estate car.
Jensen built one by putting a new body on the Jensen-Healey running gear to create a 2 + 2 with lots of room in the back that was accessible via the rear hatched door.

Jowett

Jowett always did things differently than the competition. The brothers Benjamin and William Jowett used horizontally-opposed twin engines as long ago as 1906 and they continued to stick to their principles when others used four or six-cylinders in line and they continued to do so in 1946.

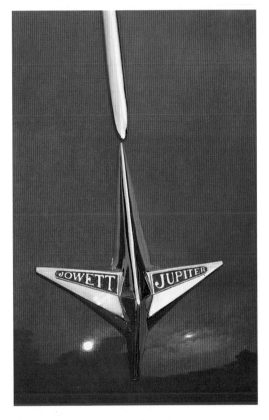

Jowetts were also sold as rolling chassis. Various specialist car body builders made use of them and hence Beutler made this 1951 sporting convertible in Switzerland.

The Jowett Javelin had a four-cylinder horizontally-opposed engine mounted ahead of the front axle. The sporting version, the Jowett Jupiter was introduced at the 1949 London Motor Show. This two-seater weighed 1,540 lb (700 kg) and since the 1,485 cc engine produced 60 bhp at 4,500 rpm, the top speed was quite high. The tubular chassis of the Jupiter was developed by Professor Robert Eberan von Eberhorst who also worked on the Auto Union racing cars.

In other respects, the quality of the Jowett cars was not high and they were only bought by the British because they did not have to wait for delivery. Once the waiting lists disappeared with their competitors, Jowett became bankrupt.

Jowett sports cars

COUNTRY OF ORIGIN
Great Britain

Jowett Jupiter

YEARS IN PRODUCTION
1950–1954

NUMBER MADE
899

The Jowett Jupiter dashboard. Note the steering column-mounted gear lever.

SPECIAL REMARKS
Although the Jupiter had little to offer on the track in its contemporary days, they are now often seen on circuits competing in races for historical cars.

The Jowett Jupiter was only built with right-hand steering.

Kaiser Darrin

Henry Kaiser made a great deal of money building Liberty ships for the US Navy (building a complete warship in four and a half days). Joseph Frazer had worked for Willys (the maker of the Jeep) and when the two of them met, they decided to make a Kaiser-Frazer car. The company's sports car was the Kaiser Darrin, designed by Howard "Dutch" Darrin on the basis of Kaiser's Henry J chassis. When Kaiser withdrew the car in 1954, Darrin continued by buying 100 Kaiser-Darrin bodies which he fitted with Cadillac V-8 engines.

A point of interest with the Darrin was its sliding doors.

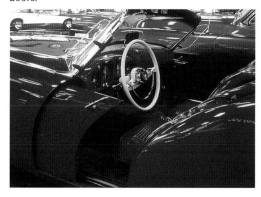

About the only place one can see a Kaiser-Darrin today is in an American motor museum.

NUMBER MADE
435

SPECIAL REMARKS
Once "Dutch" Darrin took over production of the sports car bearing his name, he installed a Cadillac engine which could also be fitted with a McCulloch turbocharger as an option.

Kaiser-Darrin sports cars

COUNTRY OF ORIGIN
USA

Kaiser-Darrin

YEARS IN PRODUCTION
1954–1955

The Kaiser-Darrin was originally sold with a Willys Jeep 2,638 cc six-cylinder engine.

Kieft

The history of Kieft cars is short but complicated. After Cyril Kieft built his first Formula 3 car in 1950, the company changed hands three times and finally became bankrupt in 1960. The Formula 3 car was the basis for about 650 sports cars that were sold in varying stages of build from kit to finished car.

The speedometer is the least important instrument in a sports car.

A 1953 Kieft-Bristol with a 1,971 cc six-cylinder engine beneath its aluminium bonnet.

There are bigger children's pedal-cars than the 104 in (265 cm) long Kleinschnittger.

Kieft sports cars

COUNTRY OF ORIGIN
Great Britain

Kieft-Bristol

YEARS IN PRODUCTION
1953–1955

NUMBER MADE
Unknown

SPECIAL REMARKS
Kieft used a variety of engines. The customer could choose from MG, Coventry-Climax, Bristol, and even American De Soto engines.

Kleinschnittger

In the immediate post-war years there were very few sports cars in Germany or the rest of Europe. The MG was being built in England but this was unaffordable for post-war Germans and Porsche too were very expensive. Consequently Germans at that time were not too proud to park a Kleinschnittger outside their home, even though the cars was extremely basic. It had no starter

motor but a recoil start using a rope like lawn mowers or outboard motors and there was no battery or reverse gear. To turn the car around meant lifting the back of the car and pulling it around.

Kleinschnittger sports cars

COUNTRY OF ORIGIN
Germany

Kleinschnittger

YEARS IN PRODUCTION
1950–1957

NUMBER MADE
2,980

SPECIAL REMARKS
The Kleinschnittger look fast but its 122 cc engine only took it to a top speed of 44 mph (70 km/hour). A 246 cc engined version appeared in 1956 with 15 bhp and a top speed of 62 mph (100 km/hour).

There was a 122 cc/6 bhp single-cylinder two-stroke engine and 20 litre fuel tank beneath the bonnet.

Lagonda

Pre-war Lagondas were undoubtedly sports cars but it is debatable whether the post-war cars were still true sports cars. The 2.6 litre engine in the synonymous car was a six-cylinder with twin overhead camshafts designed by W.O. Bentley in 1939. The engine was uprated in 1952 to 3 litres and climb in power to 142 bhp at 5,000 rpm.

Lagonda sports cars

COUNTRY OF ORIGIN
Great Britain

Lagonda 2.6 litre

YEARS IN PRODUCTION
1947–1953

NUMBER MADE
550 (all models)

SPECIAL REMARKS
The top speed of 94 mph (150 km/hour) was quite outstanding in 1947. The 2,6 litre Lagonda achieved this with ease thanks to its six-cylinder engine that readily produced 106 bhp at 5,000 rpm.

The 2.6 litre Lagonda as built 1947–1953.

A number of fine convertible models were based on the basis of the Lagonda 3 litre. This is a 3-position drophead coupé of 1953.

The dashboard of the 3 litre Lagonda. The hand of the tachometer turns anti-clockwise.

Lagonda 3 Litre

YEARS IN PRODUCTION
1953–1958

NUMBER MADE
Unknown

SPECIAL REMARKS
Sales improved slightly after HRH Prince Philip bought one of them. The car was extremely expensive, equating to the cost of about eight Volkswagen Beetles.

Lamborghini

Ferruccio Lamborghini was born on April 28, 1916, the son of a rich farmer and he was conveyed to his funeral on February 20, 1993 by a farm cart towed behind a tractor. It had been his last wish to be transported to his burial behind one of the vehicles made by his company and he chose a tractor. When Lamborghini had

made a great deal of money from building tractors, hydraulic tools, and air conditioning equipment, he put some of his money into building super-cars. One of his motives was to show Ferrari that he could do it better and to an extent he achieved this. The first Lamborghinis made the Ferraris of the day resemble Model-T Fords in comparison. The Ferraris had fixed rear axles and drum brakes while the Lamborghinis had independent suspension and disc brakes on all four wheels. To be fair, Lamborghini had done little more than lay his money down and give the orders but the same was equally true of Ferrari.

The first Lamborghini was the technical accomplishment of Giotto Bizzarini, Gianpaolo Dalara, and Paolo Stanzani, with a body designed by Franco Scaglione. The 350 GTV prototype was succeeded by the production version and a complete series of successful cars. The energy crisis and other major problems brought the company into difficulties several times and Ferruccio decided enough was enough and sold the car business to people who very nearly finished the marque off. After the car company had passed through several sets of hands on the verge of criminality, the business was bought by President Suharto of Indonesia for his son Hutomo.

Carrozzeria Zagato built two of these coupés on the basis of the 350 GT.

The business is still owned by Suharto and the family is rich enough for the business to continue in existence.

Lamborghini sports cars

COUNTRY OF ORIGIN
Italy

Lamborghini 350GT

YEARS IN PRODUCTION
1963–1966

NUMBER MADE
143

Bertone built the Miura convertible which was introduced at the 1968 Brussels Motor Show.

This is what the prototype of the 350GT looked like. The car was dubbed the 350GTV with V for veloce or speed.

The looks of the 400GT were very similar to the 350GT but with twin headlights to comply with American regulations.

The first Lamborghini sports car, the 350GT could put Ferrari to shame.

The imposing dashboard of the 400GT.

Lamborghini Islero en Islero S

PRODUCTIEJAREN
1968-1970

NUMBER MADE
125 and 100

SPECIAL REMARKS
The Islero and its quicker version the S had slightly more room for the children in the back

The Islero body was designed and built by Marazzi.

SPECIAL REMARKS
The Lamborghini 350GT had everything a Ferrari owner could wish for: an aluminium body containing a 3,463 cc V-12 engine of 270 bhp at 6,500 rpm, with four camshafts, six twin Weber carburettors, a five-speed gearbox, all-round independent suspension and disc brakes on all wheels. The final 23 cars of this type had a 4 litre engine.

Lamborghini 400GT

YEARS IN PRODUCTION
1966–1968

NUMBER MADE
247

SPECIAL REMARKS
The successor to the 350GT had a bigger engine and more spacious coupé body, now in steel, by Carrozzeria Touring.

The 3,929 cc/320 bhp at 6,500 rpm engine gave a top speed of 162 mph (260 km/hour).

Bertone's concept car the Marzal became the Espada in 1968.

The engine of Bob Wallace's car. The sound of fuel being sucked into the jets is deafening.

then the 400GT but was otherwise mechanically very similar. The body was designed and built by Marazzi.

Lamborghini Espada

YEARS IN PRODUCTION
1968–1978

NUMBER MADE
1,217

SPECIAL REMARKS
The Espada was sold for ten years as the first two four-seater Lamborghini. This time the design was by Bertone who was responsible for designing and building virtually all the Lamborghini models from then on. The car was mechanically identical to the 400GT and had a top speed of 156 mph (250 km/hour).

Lamborghini Jarama en Jarama S

YEARS IN PRODUCTION
1970–1978

NUMBER MADE
177 and 150

Bob Wallace built this Jarama S for himself when he was an engineer at Lamborghini.

The superbly finished interior of the Jarama. This is an example from the first series.

SPECIAL REMARKS
The Jarama appeared in the market as a 2 + 2, after the Islero. Bertone designed the body but it was still built by Marazzi. The Jarama S was introduced in 1973 with a 260 bhp engine instead of the earlier 250 bhp motor.

Lamborghini Miura, S en SV

YEARS IN PRODUCTION
1967–1973

The Lamborghini Miura was an impressive car.

The Miura with engine and luggage compartments open.

The engine of the Miura produced 350–385 bhp which gave top speeds of around 187 mph (300

NUMBER MADE
474, 140 and 150

SPECIAL REMARKS
The Miura, which the works knew as the P400, was the first really eye-catching Lamborghini. The car extremely fascinating in 1967 and still gets looked at thirty years later. The body was by Bertone and the Miura had a rear-mounted V-12 engine that was transversely mounted in front of the back axle. The "S" version appeared in 1969 with a 370 bhp engine instead of the original 350 bhp and the "SV" came along in 1971 with its 385 bhp rocket of an engine.

YEARS IN PRODUCTION
1973–1982

NUMBER MADE
150 and 466

SPECIAL REMARKS
The Miura was exceptional but Bertone's Countach was a real flight of fantasy. The suffix "LP" stands for Longitudinale Posteriore" or "longitudinally rear-mounted". The 4 litre engine was now mounted lengthways in front of the rear

Lamborghini Countach LP 400 en S

The Lamborghini Countach 400 S still looks impressive today.

This is what the LP 500 prototype of the Countach looked like. Marcello Gandini designed the car when he worked at Bertone.

The interior of the Urraco was sober and business-like.

The doors of the Countach needed a high garage roof.

Lamborghini Urraco

YEARS IN PRODUCTION
1975–1979

NUMBER MADE
776

SPECIAL REMARKS
The Urraco was intended to compete with the Porsche and Dino by Ferrari. The 2 + 2 was designed by Bertone. The car was powered by a rear-mounted V-8 engine. There were three versions: the P200 with 1,994 cc/182 bhp, the P250 with 2,463 cc/220 bhp, and P300 with 2,996 cc/265 bhp at 7,000 rpm. The first version was made specially for the Italian market the P300 for America.

axle and delivered up to 385 bhp at 8,000 rpm. The "S" had wider wheels and improved suspension. The Countach was still sold in 1997, in an improved version.

Lancia

Vincenzo Lancia (1881–1937) at first earned a living as a book-keeper but then became a driver for Fiat and went on to build cars. He made his first sports car in 1906 which was quickly dubbed "scaringly quick". The Lancia company has been responsible for major technical advances such as their Lambda which had a monocoque shell as early as 1924, brakes on all four wheels, and a V-4 engine with an overhead camshaft.

The Lamborghini Urraco or "Bull" had to compete with the Porsche 911 and Dino by Ferrari but failed in its efforts.

Lancia has always been involved with motor sport. The company prepared rally cars but has also been involved in Grand Prix racing indeed its involvement with motor racing almost broke the company. To avoid bankruptcy, the motor sport activity was sold to Ferrari. Fangio became World Champion in 1956 in a "Lancia" of the Ferrari team. Since its Grand Prix racing debacle, Lancia has had mixed fortunes. Some fine cars were built

The Lancia B20 is still welcomed on the track today. This one is taking a corner at Monza in a race for veterans.

Once again, Zagato produced competition cars. This Flaminia is seen on the Mugello circuit.

and world championships have been won – especially in rallying – but there were repeated financial troubles, resulting in Fiat taking the company over in 1969. Lancia lost their independence and were forced to develop mass-produced products yet in spite of this, Lancia has retained its good name.

Tom Tjaarda designed this Fulvia which was built by Vignale. Note the large aerofoil above the boot lid.

Lancia sports cars

COUNTRY OF ORIGIN
Italy

Lancia Aurelia GT

YEARS IN PRODUCTION
1951–1958

NUMBER MADE
3,871

SPECIAL REMARKS
The GT, which appeared in 1950, was the sporting version of the Aurelia saloon. The car was designed by the renowned Vittorio Jano and had a 1,991 but later 2,451 cc V-6 engine and a gearbox that was incorporated into the differential. The Aurelia GT had a body by Pininfarina and was suitable for both daily use and competitive motor sport.

The Aurelia GT – this is a B20 with a 1,991 cc V6 engine delivering 80 bhp at 5,000 rpm – was designed by Pininfarina. This model was widely used in club races but also competed at Le Mans and the Mille Miglia.

Lancia Aurelia Spyder and Aurelia America

YEARS IN PRODUCTION
1955–1956 and 1956–1958

Pininfarina's B24 Spyder was both comfortable and fast, making it an outstanding car for long journeys.

The Aurelia America can be recognised by the pano-ramic windscreen and unusually-shaped bumpers.

NUMBER MADE
240 and 521

SPECIAL REMARKS
Spurred on by his success with the Aurelia GT, Pininfarina designed an open version which was sold in the showrooms as the Aurelia B24 Spyder. The motor sport version was the America which can be recognised by its panoramic windscreen.

This car was designed for sunny climates and racing and hence the side windows had to be clamped in place as with older MGs.

Lancia Appia

YEARS IN PRODUCTION
1953–1963

NUMBER MADE
Unknown

SPECIAL REMARKS
The Lancia Appia sold well and remained in production for ten years with about 100,000 being made.
It is not surprising then that a number of the specialist car body builders used the car as a basis for specials, some of which were made in series, others were just one-offs. The 1,090 cc engine was V-4 unit.

Lancia Appia Zagato

YEARS IN PRODUCTION
1956–1963

NUMBER MADE
406

SPECIAL REMARKS
After Zagato had shown their creation to Lancia, the car maker decided to include the car in their

The first 50 Appia Zagato cars were all different from each other. They were really sales proto-types.

range. The car was available to rally drivers and upcoming racing drivers as a Lancia Appia Zagato GT.
The engine developed 60 bhp at 4,900 rpm and had a top speed of 94 mph (150 km/hour).

Lancia Appia Vignale

YEARS IN PRODUCTION
1956–1963

NUMBER MADE
583

SPECIAL REMARKS
Vignale sold its convertible by the same means as Zagato, through the Lancia dealer network.

In contrast with the Zagato that had an aluminium body shell, the Vignale model was built of steel.

This convertible by Vignale is built on an Appia chassis with a 99 in (251 cm) wheelbase. The overall length was 162 in (413 cm).

Touring of Milan built two-seater coupés on a shortened Flaminia chassis. From 1963 onwards, these had a 2,775 cc engine.

Designs by Zagato always had something extraordinary about them, so that you puzzled over whether it was good-looking or ugly. The unusual feature in their Flavia was the rear side

The convertible by Touring of Milan was little more than a coupé with a soft-top. km/hour).

Pininfarina was responsible for the body of the Flavia coupé.

Lancia Flaminia

YEARS IN PRODUCTION
1957–1970

NUMBER MADE
Unknown

SPECIAL REMARKS
Lancia aimed itself at the market for prestige cars with the Flaminia. These were exceptionally good-looking cars, whether the saloon, coupé, or the convertible. The V-6 engine grew during its lifetime from 2,451 cc to 2,775 cc and the power increased from 102 to 152 bhp. Pininfarina built 5,284 four-seater saloons, Touring built 2,018 two-seater coupés and 847 convertibles, and Zagato built 593 sporting coupés.

Lancia Flavia

YEARS IN PRODUCTION
1963–1974

NUMBER MADE
Unknown

SPECIAL REMARKS
Professor Antonio Fessa was behind the first front-wheel drive Lancia. His four-cylinder horizontally-opposed engine was 1,488 cc, subsequently 1,800 cc, and finally 1,991 cc.
Pininfarina built 26,084 2 + 2 coupés between 1962–1973 and Lancia built 628 competition coupés between 1963–1967. Other specialist car body makers also provided variations on the Flavia theme.

Lancia Fulvia Coupé en HF

YEARS IN PRODUCTION
1963–1972

NUMBER MADE
134,035 and 6,419

SPECIAL REMARKS
The two-seater coupé version of the Lancia Fulvia saloon appeared two years after Lancia had introduced their new saloon in 1963. The two-seater, which was this time designed and built by Lancia, was a great success and the works team were European champions three times and World champions twice.

Lancia proved with the Fulvia coupé that they could design attractive car bodies that sold well.

The Fulvia HF engine was 1,584 cc and developed 114 bhp at 6,500 rpm, with its overhead cams per cylinder and double twin Weber carburettors.

Lancia Fulvia Zagato

YEARS IN PRODUCTION
1965–1972

NUMBER MADE
7,102

The Lancia Fulvia Sport Zagato had a two-persons body of unitary construction made of aluminium.

The dashboard of the Fulvia coupé.

SPECIAL REMARKS
The Zagato version of the Fulvia was so successfully sold that the small body works just north of Milan could barely keep pace with demand. At first the 1,298 cc V-4 engine developed 101 bhp, then the motor was increased to 1,584 cc in 1969, developing 130 bhp and giving top speeds of 109–115 mph (175–185 km/hour).

Lancia Stratos

YEARS IN PRODUCTION
1972–1974

NUMBER MADE
492

SPECIAL REMARKS
Bertone is renowned for their unusual designs. The proposal for the Stratos was shown to Lancia in 1970 who bought the design and commissioned Bertone in 1972 to build the car in a somewhat amended form.
The Stratos was an excellent successor to the Fulvia HF and delivered a whole string of competition successes.

Bertone's Stratos concept car was really only intended as an eye-catcher for exhibitions.

With only minor modification to the Stratos proto-type, a very quick rally car was created that was almost invincible.

The factory version of the Beta coupé had a 132 in (235 cm) wheelbase instead of the standard one of 140 in (254 cm). It could be supplied with a Volumex turbo.

Lancia Beta

YEARS IN PRODUCTION
1972–1981

NUMBER MADE
Unknown

SPECIAL REMARKS
Pininfarina designed a coupé based on a shortened version of the Beta underframe of

Sports cars were nothing new for Lancia but not with the success of the Beta HPE of which 71,258 were sold.

It is clear that the Beta Monte Carlo originated from Pininfarina because it had similar lines to a Ferrari coupé designed by the company.

The engine was mounted in front of the rear axle.

In contrast with the pre-war 14 hp, the post-war model had independent front suspension.

1906–1960 is worthy of a wider reputation. Lea Francis specialised in making sports cars in the 1920s but after World War II they mainly produced saloons, estates, and the occasional convertible. When the company launched the Lynx sports car in 1960 it went broke. An attempt was made to restart Lea Francis in 1990 but this failed.

Lea Francis sports cars

COUNTRY OF ORIGIN
Great Britain

Lea Francis 14 hp

YEARS IN PRODUCTION
1947–1949

NUMBER MADE
129

SPECIAL REMARKS
In 1947, Lea Francis re-introduced the 14 hp Sports that had been made before the war. The car had a 1,767 cc four-cylinder overhead valve engine that developed 65 bhp.

which 111,801 were sold. The Spyder was less popular with 9,390 being sold, perhaps because it was a Targa rather than a true convertible. More interesting models were the Beta HPE sports car which sold 71,258 and the Monte Carlo which was like a miniature version of a Ferrari coupé with transverse mounted engine in front of the rear axle. This model sold 7,595 examples.

Lea Francis

The name Lea-Francis is probably unknown outside of Britain and this is a great shame because the company which built cars from

The front windscreen could be pushed down flat to make way for two small semi-circular "Brooklands" racing windshields.

The Ligier JS2 could reach 150 mph (240 km/hour) with its 195 bhp at 5,500 rpm engine.

Ligier

When Guy Ligier who had been a regular member of the French national team finished playing rugby, he turned to motor sport – first as a driver, and then as a constructor of Formula One cars. With his lack of success in Grand Prix racing, he also dabbled in producing electric vehicles which can still be found running around the streets of Paris. Ligier made just one sports car: the JS2. The initials stood for Jo Schlesser, a friend of Ligier who was killed during the 1968 French Grand Prix while driving a Honda.

Ligier sports cars

COUNTRY OF ORIGIN
France

Ligier JS2

YEARS IN PRODUCTION
1971–1977

NUMBER MADE
150

SPECIAL REMARKS
The initial Ligier JS2 cars had a V-6 Ford engine mounted in front of the rear axle but this was quickly replaced by the Citroën-Maserati V-6.

Lister

Brian Lister showed off his first sports car in 1954 and when this was sold, he made a couple more. Archie Scott-Brown won eleven races in

1957 in a Lister and he broke the lap record on virtually every circuit on which he appeared. Scott Brown was killed while racing on the Spa circuit in 1959 and this upset Lister so much that he decided to turn his back on motor sport but in the 1980s his name was attached by WP Automotive to new Lister-Jaguar motor-sport cars, based on the XJS. The Lister Storm was built in 1991 to compete at Le Mans and the original Lister-Jaguar was also recreated.

Listers are perhaps even more admired now than in their day and can be seen regularly in races for veterans.

Lister sports cars

COUNTRY OF ORIGIN
Great Britain

Jaguar engines are very reliable but Ben Hulsman proves here they can blow.

Frank Costin designed this aerodynamic body for the 1959 Lister-Jaguar.

Lister-Jaguar

YEARS IN PRODUCTION
1958–present time

NUMBER MADE
54

SPECIAL REMARKS
Drivers such as Stirling Moss and Jim Clark drove Listers in the late 1950s. Most of these cars were powered by the engines from Jaguar C and D types. The other engines were Chevrolet Corvette, Maserati, or Bristol.

LMX-Sirex

Michel Liprandi and Giovanni Mandelli introduced their LMX alongside the Turin motor show in 1968. The car was not inside the exhibition hall because the pair did not have enough money for a stand. The coupé had a body designed by Franco Scaglione, a German Ford engine, and the front suspension from a Ford Zodiac. After the partners ceased in business in 1973, their car was made and sold by the Samas company as a Sirex LMS but after a year this company too was forced to finish.

Beneath the bulge on the bonnet of the LMX is a Ford V-6 engine from the German Ford Taunus 20M TS that delivers 126 bhp.

LMX sports cars

COUNTRY OF ORIGIN
Italy

LMX-Sirex

YEARS IN PRODUCTION
1968–1974

NUMBER MADE
50 and 20

SPECIAL REMARKS
Although customers had their own choice of engine, the LMX was generally fitted with turbocharged 2.3 litre V-6 engine from the German Ford Taunus that produced almost 200 bhp.

The body of the two-seater was designed by the well-known Franco Scaglione who was also responsible for designing the Lamborghini 350 GTV, the Intermeccanica, Arnolt-Bristol, and the Alfa Romeo SS.

Lola

There is no branch of motor sport on four wheels for which Eric Broadley's Lola has not built cars. Lola has produced everything from club racers to cars for the Indianapolis 500, and Formulae 1, 2, and 3. At the end of the seventies, Lola was the largest constructor of racing cars in the world. Their most famous cars were the T70 and the Mk 6, the latter of which was the basis for the Ford GT40 (see Ford). Lola cars were generally not intended for the open road but an exception was first Lola with which Broadley began his career. The Mk 1 can be driven on road or track.

Lola sports cars

COUNTRY OF ORIGIN
Great Britain

Lola Mk 1

YEARS IN PRODUCTION
1958–1963

A Lola Mk 1 on the circuit at Zolder in Belgium.

The body shell of a Mk 1 can easily be removed from the chassis, making access easy for maintenance.

The Lola Mk 1 was an open two-seater which was generally powered by a 1,100 cc Coventry-Climax engine.

Lotus

The name of a car marque is usually that of a constructor as with Ferrari, Bugatti, Horch, or Porsche. An exception to this rule is Lotus which is not derived from its founder Colin Chapman.

As a young engineering student Chapman designed his first sports car

A Lotus Seven is a car for the true enthusiast who requires no comfort, no springs, just pure motor sport.

on a kitchen table. Colin's wife Hazel thought it so attractive that she convinced her husband to build a few of the cars. This led to the foundation of the Lotus Engineering Company.

Lotus supplied cars as kits for the do-it-yourself builder, sports cars for the open road and track,

The Lotus Elan, like this S4 was never intended for use on track.

The Lotus Seven, with a 1,498 cc Cosworth engine weight 1,034 lb (470 kg) and can reach 100 mph (160 km/hour).

The Elite finally got power-assisted disc brakes in 1962.

There was a soft-top for the Lotus Seven but it does not offer much protection.

The road-holding of the Elite was so good that it was difficult to get them to spin or roll.

but also racing cars for the various formulas. Lotus had considerable success in both Grand Prix racing and the lower formulas with a very long list of victories.

tomers could choose between a kit or ready-to-run car. After about 3,000 had been sold, Colin Chapman sold the rights in the Seven to Caterham Cars (q.v.).

Lotus sports cars

COUNTRY OF ORIGIN
Great Britain

Lotus Seven

YEARS IN PRODUCTION
1957–current day (see Caterham)

NUMBER MADE
Unknown

SPECIAL REMARKS
The first cars made by Colin Chapman were sold as a Lotus VI but production did not really get under way until the Seven appeared. The cus-

An Elan, driven by Phil van der Lof, son of the famous driver and car collector Dries van der Lof, takes a corner on the Zandvoort circuit.

The interior of the Lotus Elan S4 with a great deal of leather and wood.

Lotus Elite

YEARS IN PRODUCTION
1958–1963

NUMBER MADE
988

SPECIAL REMARKS
The Elite was a marvellous car that was amazingly quick because it only weighed 1,150 lb (575 kg) and had a 1.2 litre Coventry-Climax engine that with its 76 bhp at 6,100 was really overpowered. The body was made of glass-fibre reinforced polyester but this proved to be a disadvantage after a few years when the bodies began to crack easily.

Lotus Elan

YEARS IN PRODUCTION
1962–1973

NUMBER MADE
9,150

SPECIAL REMARKS
The Elan was almost a mass-production product

The Elan + 2 had enough room for two (small) children in the back.

for Lotus. It could be purchased as a kit car or ready-to-run. This car too had a reinforced polyester body although this time mounted on a central tube instead of a floor pan. There were four different series of the Elan which were continuously improved and from 1965, the Series 3 included a coupé.

The Lotus Europa was intended to be the ordinary man's sports car but its Cosworth engine made it far too expensive.

The Lotus Elite S1 resembled the Volvo and Scimitar sports estate cars.

NUMBER MADE
2,398

SPECIAL REMARKS
The Elite S1 had nothing in common with its illustrious predecessor. On the contrary, it was scarcely a sports car with its 2 + 2 body looking more like an estate car. The 1,973 cc engine was a Jensen-Healey with a cylinder head with four valves per cylinder that delivered 162 bhp.

Lotus Elan +2

YEARS IN PRODUCTION
1969–1974

NUMBER MADE
3.300

SPECIAL REMARKS
As the name implies, the Elan + 2 was a 2+2 coupé that was not intended for motor sport. The car even provided a measure of comfort and had a fine wooden dashboard.
The 'S' version had two fog-lights and wheels with Rudge knave-plates. The Elan 130 had a 126 bhp Lotus engine and five-speed Lotus gearbox.

Lotus Eclat S1

YEARS IN PRODUCTION
1975–1980

NUMBER MADE
1,299

SPECIAL REMARKS
The Eclat, which was launched in October 1975 at the London Motor Show, was in reality an Elite S1 with a "normal" rear end. There was still space for four persons provided those in the back were not taller than 4 ft 7 in (140 cm). The car was otherwise identical to the Elite S1 and had the same power unit.

The Eclat S1 was in reality an Elite S1 with a "normal" rear end.

Lotus Europa

YEARS IN PRODUCTION
1966-1975

NUMBER MADE
9.230

SPECIAL REMARKS
The Europa was designed by Ron Hickman although the concept was Colin Chapman's who wanted to make an inexpensive fast sports car.

The first examples had Renault R16 engines but later cars had a twin-cam Ford Cosworth four-cylinder engine.

Lotus Elite S1

YEARS IN PRODUCTION
1974–1980

Mandarini

Marcos

There were scores of small firms building sports cars in Italy in the 1940s and 1950s. They mainly had two things in common: they used converted and tuned 500 or 1,100 cc Fiat engines (depending on the class for which the car was intended) and their names ended in "..ini".

Mandarini was just one more of these firms. Their cars took part in the Mille Miglia but it is impossible to say which years because in those days these specials were all entered as Fiats.

The Marcos name was created by taking the MAR from Jem Marsh and the COS from Frank Costin.
Jem Marsh was a well-known dealer in car parts and accessories and Frank Costin (see Costin-Nathan) had just left de Havilland, the aircraft manufacturer.

The Marcos company was set-up in 1959 with the purpose of building sports cars as kits to save the purchaser 33 per cent tax on the sale. Costin had built gliders for the RAF and it is therefore not surprising that the new Marcos was constructed in wood. Even the chassis was largely made of hardwood. The first models, known as Marcos GT Xylon, were ugly as sin but very quick. The partners did not co-operate very long and Costin soon left the business. Marcos went bust in 1971 but the company was subsequently started up again and now produces several hundred cars each year.

Mandarini sports cars

COUNTRY OF ORIGIN
Italy

Mandarini

YEARS IN PRODUCTION
1955–unknown

NUMBER MADE
Unknown

SPECIAL REMARKS
The Mandarini was one of many Fiat specials. The car was first made in 1955 and had a Fiat 1100 engine.

The customer had a choice between a five-speed gear box or a four-speed with electrically-operated overdrive in 1964.

This Mandarini can still regularly be seen racing successfully in competitions for historical cars.

The Mini Marcos got a hatch-back rear door in 1975.

The 1.6 litre Ford engine is easily accessible.

Marcos sports cars

COUNTRY OF ORIGIN
Great Britain

Marcos GT

YEARS IN PRODUCTION
1964–1969

NUMBER MADE
405

Historic car racing: a Marcos GT 1600 slipstreams a Ginetta G4.

Marcos introduced a model in 1964 that would be built for many years. The car had a glass-fibre reinforced polyester body on a wooden chassis with a four-cylinder Ford engine of 1,498, 1,599 or 1,650 cc. As an alternative a Volvo 1,778 engine could be chosen.

Marcos 3 litre

YEARS IN PRODUCTION
1969–1972 and 1981–present day

NUMBER MADE
361

SPECIAL REMARKS
Marcos cars finally got a steel chassis in 1969 and the bodies were also slightly improved. The engines of this model were from the Volvo 164, Triumph TR6, or a Ford V-6. The car went back into production again in 1981 and currently is sold with a Rover V-8 engine.

The original Marcos 3 litre had a top speed of 119 mph (190 km/hour) which was fast in those days for a car you could drive to work

The sun-roof was an optional extra but the specially customised paint work had to be arranged by the

175

The Mantis was not a success. The failure of the Mantis broke Marcos.

Marcos Mantis

YEARS IN PRODUCTION
1970–1971

NUMBER MADE
32

SPECIAL REMARKS
Marsh was bankrupted by this model in 1971. Although the quality of the car was first-class, people did not like the design. It was designed by Dennis Adams and was powered by a 2,498 cc Triumph TR6 engine that delivered 143 bhp at 5,700 rpm.

Marcos Mini

YEARS IN PRODUCTION
1965–1981

NUMBER MADE
Approx. 1,200

SPECIAL REMARKS
There was little argument about it, few people

The Mini Marcos is probably one of the ugliest cars ever to hit the road. This example from the third series has wind-up windows in the doors.

Even the spare wheel had to be put into the car via the side doors.

liked the look of the Mini Marcos. Beneath the polyester body of unitary construction was an Austin Mini engine. When Marcos went bust in 1971, Rob Walker purchased the rights and built a further five hundred or so Marcos Minis.

Maserati

Ferrari is perhaps the best-known name but Maserati has the longest history.
The brothers Carlo, Bindo, Alfieri, Ettore, and Ernesto Maserati started building racing cars in 1926 and managed to do so for eleven years before finances forced them to sell out to the industrialist Omar Orsi.
The contract of the sale stipulated that the brothers must work for Orsi for a further ten years. When this period was completed in 1947, the brothers started a new company, naming their new marque Osca (q.v.).
After the war Orsi recognised that little money was to be made from motor racing so he developed the A61500 coupé, which was launched at the Geneva Salon. The car had a Pininfarina body and shortly after its introduction the engine was uprated to 2 litres and in 1954 it got a new cylinder head with twin overhead camshafts. The car was sold in small quantity up to 1957. In that year Maserati launched its 3500 GT which formed the basis

Things became more successful with the 3500 GT. Most of the cars made had bodies by Touring of Milan.

for all the future six-cylinder engines. This car was very successful and was sold for some years. The works had had access for some time to a 5-litre V-8 engine from the 450 S racing car. This engine was adapted for installation in the 5000 GT, the first of which was built specially for the Shah of Persia. Subsequent high points in the Maserati story are the Quattroporte or four-door car with a V-8 engine, the Mexico, Ghibli Khamsin, and the Indy. Each of these cars was powered by the same V-8 engine with four camshafts. As a counterpart to the Dino by Ferrari, there was the Maserati Bora with its V-8 engine and smaller version, the Merak with a V-6 engine.

Orsi sold most of the shares to Citroën in 1968 (see Citroën for SM Citroën-Maserati). When the French allowed the company to be declared bankrupt in 1975, the company was bought from the receivers by De Tomaso who built his own models with a Maserati engine and amazed the automotive world with his Biturbo. Chrysler ordered Maserati to make a couple of Chryslers for the US market in 1984 to be sold as "made by Maserati".

Chrysler invested $35 million in the business but withdrew from Modena four years later when

The factory probably made no more than 125 Ghibli Spyders but today there are about 300 in existence!

De Tomaso sold 49 per cent of the Maserati shares to Fiat who decided in 1997 to merge Maserati with Ferrari.

Maserati sports cars

COUNTRY OF ORIGIN
Italy

Maserati A6

YEARS IN PRODUCTION
1947–1953

NUMBER MADE
137

SPECIAL REMARKS
The first road cars made by Maserati had 1,488 cc engines that developed 65 bhp at 4,800 rpm. When 60 of them had been sold, the A6G2000 was introduced with a 2 litre engine of which 79 were sold, 63 of which had twin camshafts.

This 1951 A6G2000 had a Pininfarina body. This car is now in the United States but continues to bear its original European number plates.

The firm of Frua were responsible for the sporting body of this A6G.

Maserati 3500 GT/GTI

YEARS IN PRODUCTION
1958–1964

NUMBER MADE
2,223

SPECIAL REMARKS
The first 1,980 Maserati 3500 GTs were almost all provided with coupé bodies by Touring of Milan. Vignale developed a convertible version

Carrozzeria Touring still made aluminium bodies for the 3500 GT and GTI.

The twin ignition leads on the 3500 GT engine betray the engines racing car origins.

The open-topped version of the 3500 GTI was built by Vignale. The car had a wheelbase reduced from 102 in (260 cm) to 98 in (250 cm).

A Maserati Sebring in Modena. The man with his hand on the wing is Ermanno Cozza, and the three people opposite the right-hand door are Maria Teresa de Filipis, Luigi Villoresi, and Ir. Giulio Alfieri.

of the GT and 242 were sold. The six-cylinder engine delivered 220 bhp with triple twin carburettors and 235 bhp with fuel injection.

Maserati Sebring

YEARS IN PRODUCTION
1962–1966

NUMBER MADE
446

SPECIAL REMARKS
Vignale also built a coupé on the shorter convertible chassis. This was sold as the Maserati Sebring. The first 348 of these cars had a 3.5 litre engine while the remainder had 3.7 litre six-cylinder motors that delivered 245 bhp at 5,500 rpm. All the engines were equipped with fuel injection.

Maserati Mistral

YEARS IN PRODUCTION
1963–1970

NUMBER MADE
948

The gigantic rear window was also the hatch-back third door.

SPECIAL REMARKS

Frua followed on from Vignale with the creation of a new model, the Mistral. This two-seater with a top speed of 156 mph (250 km/hour) had a classical six-cylinder 4 litre engine that delivered 255 bhp. Of the total made, 120 were sold as convertibles. The Mistral was the final version of this class of car.

Maserati 5000 GT

YEARS IN PRODUCTION
1959–1964

NUMBER MADE
32

SPECIAL REMARKS

The 5000 GT was only made to order. The customer ordered a chassis and had the body built by one of the well-known Italian car body specialists. Allemano built most of them (21), followed by Touring (4). The others were built by Pininfarina, Bertone, Monterosa, Michelotti, Ghia, and Frua.

The Shah of Persia was the first customer for the 5000 GT. The car was built according to his instructions.

Maserati Mexico

YEARS IN PRODUCTION
1966–1968

NUMBER MADE
250

SPECIAL REMARKS

The 2 + 2 Maserati Mexico had a V-8 engine that was at first available as a 4.2 litre and then after 1968 as a 4.7 litre. This new car was built by Carrozzeria Vignale.

The Mexico was the successor to the 5000 GT. Its body was built by Vignale.

Maserati Ghibli

SPECIAL REMARKS

Many car enthusiasts believe that the Ghibli was one of the best looking cars ever to come out of Italy and the designer Giugiaro also agreed that the car was his best work. Only 125 left the line as convertibles.

The number of convertibles has subsequently grown significantly though with owners having the roof removed. The first Ghiblis had a 4.7 litre

Many find the Maserati Ghibli the finest Italian car ever made.

All the Maserati V-8 engines at that time had four overhead camshafts and four twin Weber carburettors.

The 2 + 2 Indy had a body of unitary construction designed by Vignale.

V-8 engine that developed 330 bhp but this increased after 1970 to 4.9 litres with power of 355 bhp at 5,500 rpm.

Maserati Indy

YEARS IN PRODUCTION
1969–1974

NUMBER MADE
1,136

SPECIAL REMARKS
The Indy was a four-seater coupé designed by Vignale for the Turin Motor Show of 1968. The car was supplied with three different V-8 engines: 4.2, 4.7, or 4.9 litres.

Maserati Khamsin

YEARS IN PRODUCTION
1974–1982

NUMBER MADE
421

SPECIAL REMARKS
Bertone was unable to do much work for Maserati because they were the main supplier to Lamborghini. Despite this, the Khamsin 2 + 2,

The Khamsin was a strange mixture with a Bertone body, Maserati V-8 engine, and incorporation of Citroën technology.

with room for two small children, originated with Bertone. The car was powered by a Maserati V-8 engine and had a host of technical innovation from Citroën.

Maserati Bora

YEARS IN PRODUCTION
1971–1978

NUMBER MADE
495

SPECIAL REMARKS
The 1971 Geneva motor show saw a new Maserati with a V-8 engine that was a complete sensation. The car, the Maserati Bora, had its 4.7 litre V-8 mounted in the middle of the car and developed 310 bhp at 6,000 rpm, making it capable of a top speed of 175 mph (280 km/hour).
The body was designed by Giugiaro who was the proprietor and managing director at that time of Ital Design.

When centrally-positioned engines became popular, Ir. Alfieri mounted a Maserati V-8 admidships in a Bora. The body was by Ital Design (Giugiaro) and the brakes were by Citroën.

Maserati Merak

YEARS IN PRODUCTION
1972–1978

NUMBER MADE
1,466

SPECIAL REMARKS
A year after the Bora had been introduced, a smaller version of the car was shown at Geneva. The new car, known as the Merak, looked identical but was powered by the V-6 engine used in the Citroën Maserati.
The factory had a substantial supply of these engines.

The Maserati Merak closely resembled the Maserati Bora but was crammed full of Citroën mechanical parts. Its engine was identical to the one used in the Citroën-Maserati

Matra

Matra was founded in the south of France in 1941 as Méchanique Aviation Traction. Once the war was over, the company was principally engaged in the development of French aerospace activities with the company building Ariane rockets as well as sports and racing cars.

Matra made the polyester bodies for the Djet of René Bonnet (q.v.). When this company went bust in 1964, Matra took the company over. At first the production of the Djet was continued but this was followed by the M530, the Bagheera, and a whole series of racing cars for Formulae 1, 2, and 3. The car division of Matra was sold to Simca in 1969, bringing the marque within the Chrysler empire.

L'ÉPOPÉE

Matra sports cars

COUNTRY OF ORIGIN
France

Matra Bonnet Djet

YEARS IN PRODUCTION
1964–1968

NUMBER MADE
1,681

SPECIAL REMARKS
Matra continued producing the Bonnet Djet, perhaps more successfully than the original factory (see Bonnet). The 1966 models were sold as Matra Djet 5 and at the end of 1966 this became Jet 6 without the "D". This model had a 1,255 cc engine instead of the 1,108 cc motor.

Matra M 530

YEARS IN PRODUCTION
1967–1973

The Matra M 530 was available in several versions. The LX was the deluxe model with a roof that could be removed in two sections.

NUMBER MADE
9,609

SPECIAL REMARKS
The M 530 was largely similar to the Jet but was powered by a Ford Taunus 17-M engine in front of the rear axle. When Simca took over Matra in 1969 the car changed its name to Matra-Simca 530.

Matra-Simca Bagheera

YEARS IN PRODUCTION
1964–1968

NUMBER MADE
47,802

SPECIAL REMARKS
The Bagheera was a polyester body-shelled coupé with space for three on the front seat and was a quite interesting and unusual car. The 1,294 cc four-cylinder Simca engine was mounted behind the front seat. The combination of 84 bhp at 6,000 rpm and the weight of 1,947 lb (885 kg) gave a top speed of 115 mph (185 km/hour).

The Matra-Simca Bagheera was designed by Philippe Guédon. When Simca was sold to PSA in 1979, the car continued to be made as the Talbot-Matra Bagheera.

McLaren

The New Zealander Bruce McLaren was a famous racing driver and became the youngest driver to win a Grand Prix (he was only 22 years old). Since then his name has become famous through the highly successful McLaren Formula One team but he has also built sports cars that were very successful. Only one road-going McLaren sports car – the M6GT– which was based on a CanAm car, was built by him during his life. Only a small number of these cars were built and McLaren never had the chance to develop the car because he was killed at age 33 on June 2, 1970 on the circuit at Goodwood. His name lives on in the McLaren FI super-car considered by many to be the best road car ever made.

McLaren sports cars

COUNTRY OF ORIGIN
Great Britain

McLaren M6GT

YEARS IN PRODUCTION
1969–1970

NUMBER MADE
Unknown

SPECIAL REMARKS
The McLaren M6GT was the forerunner of the new breed of super-cars that appeared on the scene in the 1990s from Porsche, Ferrari, Bugatti, and of course McLaren. The car had a highly-tuned 5,735 cc Chevrolet V-8 engine producing 400 bhp. It was more or less a racing car for the open road.

Although the McLaren M6GT was designed as a road car, it was really more at home on the track.

Mercedes

Mercedes-Benz, or to be more precise Daimler-Benz, has been involved in motor sport and building both sports and racing cars since its earliest days. There were classic cars such as the extremely fast SSK and SSKL cars with which Rudolf Caracciola shot right through the field, quite apart from the Silber Pfeile Grand Prix cars that were built on Hitler's orders and with state financial help. He ordered them to win every race they entered and in this they succeeded. Mercedes-Benz Grand Prix cars were allowed back into Grand Prix racing in 1951 and once again they won almost everything, including World championships for Juan Fangio in 1954 and 1955. Soon after this the Stuttgart factory began to make fine sports cars once again. The 300 SL and 300 SLR are prime examples of their

Because the window openings were small and there was no air condition, the Gullwing could become extremely hot.

The 2,195 cc six-cylinder engine of the 220 S delivered 106 bhp at 5,200 rpm in 1957. The 3.102 lb (1,410 kg) had a top speed of 100 mph (160 km/hour).

In total, 314 of the Mercedes 300 coupé were built. Of these 216 had carburettors and 98 had fuel injection.

The 300 SL Roadster is a car for sunny days.

The 170 S was the last Mercedes-Benz with a four-cylinder side-valve engine.

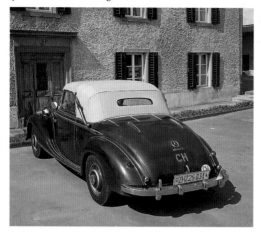

art. These cars also managed to amass victories in the Le Mans 24 hour race, the murderous Carrera Panamerica, and the 1,000 mile (1,600 km) Mille Miglia. Mercedes-Benz also made sports cars for the wider public with models such as the 190 SL, the 300 S, and the 230, 250, and 280 SL cars.

The marque is also well known for its sporting coupés and convertibles that were based on their highly successful saloon cars.

Mercedes-Benz sports cars

COUNTRY OF ORIGIN
Germany

Mercedes-Benz 170 S convertible

YEARS IN PRODUCTION
1949–1952

NUMBER MADE
2,433

The dashboard of the 170 S convertible. In the centre is the Becker radio specially made for Mercedes.

SPECIAL REMARKS
The first post-war convertibles were the model 170 which was available in two versions: "A" a two-seater (830 built) and "B" a four-seater. The power unit was a four-cylinder 1,767 cc side-valve engine that delivered 52 bhp at 4,000 rpm.

Mercedes 220 cabriolet/coupé

YEARS IN PRODUCTION
1951–1955

NUMBER MADE
2,275 and 85

SPECIAL REMARKS
The 220 was presented to the International Automobile Association in April 1951. The car had a completely new body and two versions were also available of this type: a convertible (1,278 built) and a coupé. The six-cylinder overhead-valve engine had a capacity of 2,195 cc giving 80 bhp at 4,850 rpm.

The D220, seen here in the convertible version, had a new bridging body.

Mercedes 220 cabriolet/coupé

YEARS IN PRODUCTION
1956–1960

The 220 S coupé was sold as a 2 + 2 but there was not much room for back seat passengers.

NUMBER MADE
1,942 and 3,429

SPECIAL REMARKS
An entirely new 220 convertible appeared in July 1956, followed in October by the coupé version. The cars no longer had separate chassis but bodies of unitary construction, which made them much lighter and more economical to run.

Mercedes 190 SL

YEARS IN PRODUCTION
1955–1963

NUMBER MADE
25,881

SPECIAL REMARKS
The 190 SL quickly gained a bad reputation in Germany because the car was so popular with "women of loose morals". This is a shame since this was a car of real quality. The 1,897 cc four-cylinder engine produced 105 bhp at 5,700 rpm.

The 190 SL was a smaller and cheaper version of the 300 SL Roadster.

The interior of the 190 SL was luxuriously trimmed with leather and had a very comprehensive dashboard.

The six cylinder engine of the 220 SE was uprated to 2,281 cc for the 230 SL and the engines were further increased to 2,496 cc in 1966 and 2,778 cc in 1968.

Although it got a bigger engine, the body of the convertible remained the same.

The interior trim was superb and once more of leather.

Mercedes 230/250/280 SL

YEARS IN PRODUCTION
1963–1971

NUMBER MADE
19,831, 5,186, and 23,885

SPECIAL REMARKS
The successor to the 190 SL was the 230 SL. The striking point of the range was the hardtop which quickly got the nickname "pagoda". The engine capacity was increased and the power rose from 150 to 170 bhp at 5,750 rpm.

Mercedes 300 S cabriolet/coupé

YEARS IN PRODUCTION
1951–1955

NUMBER MADE
344 and 216

SPECIAL REMARKS
The 300 S is one of the best looking cars to emerge from Europe in the 1950s. The car was available in both convertible and coupé form. The 2,996 cc six-cylinder engine with triple carburettors delivered 150 bhp. The follow on 300 SC was built from 1955–1958 and had fuel injection, now delivering 175 bhp at 5,400 rpm. Of the SC, 102 convertibles and 98 coupés were built.

A Mercedes-Benz 300 C weighed 3,872 lb (1,760 kg) but with its engine delivering 150 bhp at 5,000 rpm, could reach 112 mph (180 km/hour).

The 300 S still had a column gear change. In those days only racing cars had a tachometer.

Mercedes 300 SL en 300 SL 'Gullwing'

YEARS IN PRODUCTION
1954–1957

NUMBER MADE
1,400

SPECIAL REMARKS
Mercedes brought out a the new 300 SL sports car in 1952. The famous "Gullwing", which got its name from the way the doors lifted upwards to resemble a seagull's wings, was developed from the 300 SL which had a 2,996 cc six-cylinder engine providing 215 bhp at 5,800 rpm.

Mercedes 300 SL Roadster

YEARS IN PRODUCTION
1957–1963

NUMBER MADE
1,858

SPECIAL REMARKS
Most of the customers for the 300 SL lived in California and Mercedes-Benz received more and more complaints from customers about the high temperatures in the "Gullwing". Mercedes responded by changing the "Gullwing" into a roadster.

The motor sport version and prototypes of the 300 SL Gullwing had "wings" instead of doors.

Can you see the shape of a gull's wing?

Lots of chrome and leather yet they could not find a good place for the radio.

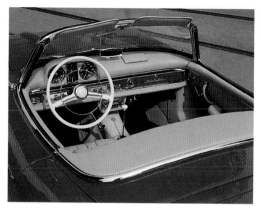

Mercedes 280/350/450 SL convertible

YEARS IN PRODUCTION
1974–1980

NUMBER MADE
25,436, 15,304, and 66,298

SPECIAL REMARKS
Customers continually wanted more power so Mercedes-Benz built ever bigger engines but the bodies remained unchanged. The difference with older models, in addition to the bigger engines, was a higher price.

The 280, 350, and 450 SL were also available as a coupé. Of the coupé versions 10,666, 13,925, and 31,739 were sold of the respective models.

Mercury

Ford launched its new brand Mercury name in 1938 to compete with the Buick and Oldsmobile marques of General Motors which were good sellers. Even after the war, the Mercury was a better quality car than a Ford.

The Montego Cyclone was the finest sporting car available from Mercury. He had a fixed differential, Hurst gearbox, 7-litre V-8 engine providing 204 bhp at 4,400 rpm; top speed more than 125 mph (200 km/hour).

For the first two years, the Mercury Cougar was only available as a coupé.

When the Ford Mustang was introduced in 1964, Mercury dealers were at a definite disadvantage compared with their Ford colleagues. At that time the Mercury brand did not have any sports cars in its range. This was corrected three years later with the launch of the Mercury Cougar. The Cougar proved to be a good competitor for the Mustang.

The car was only available with a V-8 engine but the customer could choose from a wide range of models, although for the first two years there was only a fixed-head coupé. The first convertible was added in 1969. The Mercury Cougar is still built, although today's version looks considerable less sportive than its predecessors.

Mercury sports cars

COUNTRY OF ORIGIN
USA

The size of the 1971 Montego placed it in the gap between the "small" Comet and large Marquis.

The Cougar customer could choose in 1970 from three engines: 5,769 cc/253 or 304 bhp, and 7,003 cc/340 bhp.

Few open-topped Cougars were wanted in 1971. Only 59,424 coupés were sold but even fewer convertibles at 3,440.

Once again, only a fixed-head coupé was available of the Cougar in 1974 but there was a choice of four different V-8 engines ranging from 5.8–7.5 litres.

Mercury Cougar

YEARS IN PRODUCTION
1967–present day

NUMBER MADE
Unknown

SPECIAL REMARKS
The 1967 Cougar was far more luxurious than the Mustang of the same year. The Cougar had retractable headlights which gave the car a special look. In spite of this, Mercury sold "only" 123,672 Cougars against almost half a million Ford Mustangs that year.

Messerschmitt

A number of German aircraft manufacturers switched over to making cars after World War II. One of these was Ernst Heinkel who had built jet fighters as well the famous bombers. Other famous constructors from the era included Fritz Fend and Willy Messerschmitt. Fend developed a cheap car that he intended for the many war wounded in Germany at that time but Willy Messerschmitt built in great volume for people who found an ordinary car too expensive but who did not want to ride a motorcycle. Most of the cars were three-wheelers with two at the front and one behind but some had two wheels close together at the back. A sports car version known as the Tiger appeared in 1958 although strictly speaking this was not a Messerschmitt because Willy Messerschmitt had sold the business to Fritz Fend.

The Tiger was known as FMR. This two-seater was powered by a single-cylinder two-stroke engine of 173 or 191 cc. The successor, known as the TG 500 sports car, had a twin-cylinder 493 cc engine that delivered 19.5 bhp at 5,000 rpm. This car was reintroduced to the market in 1990.

Fend wanted to call his sports car Tiger but Krupp owned the rights to this name so it got initials instead.

The TG 500 was also available as an open-topped car without canopy or side windows.

The Tiger was sold in 1990 as a replica but with a Mini-Cooper engine and costing DM 36,500. The proud owner in this photo has an original TG 500.

Messerschmitt sports cars

COUNTRY OF ORIGIN
Germany

Messerschmitt TG 500

YEARS IN PRODUCTION
1958–1961

NUMBER MADE
Approx. 320

SPECIAL REMARKS
It was clear to see that the Messerschmitts were designed by aircraft manufacturers. They looked like aircraft without wings. The small three wheelers were relatively fast at 56 mph (90 km/hour) but the TG 500 could reach 78 mph (125 km/hour).

MG

Cecil Kimber (1888–1944) was workshop foreman in a garage owned by William Morris in Oxford when he built his own special in a corner of the garage during his spare time. The car proved to be very successful and he decided in 1923 to produce more of them. He founded MG in 1924 with the initials being derived from Morris Garage. The cars were built from Morris parts which made them cheap to maintain. The MG could be compared with the Model-T Ford: Henry Ford

The MG TC was in reality a pre-war TB with a new gearbox. This was the car that started the sports car boom in the United States.

brought mobility to the masses and MG made it possible for many people to be able to afford a sports car. The company was taken over by Morris Motors in 1935 and became part of British Motor Corporation in 1952 and in turn part of British Leyland in 1968.

Many Americans came to know the small, agile, and fast MG sports cars during World War II and when production resumed after the war the United States was the largest market. In those days the Americans bought everything the British could make. The spartan T series was quickly replaced with the superb MGA, which was the first British sports car to sell more than 100,000. This was followed later by the MGB of which hundreds of thousands were made. With the Americans remaining such loyal customers it is not surprising that MGs were adapted to the wishes and taste of the United States. These demands grew ever higher though and eventually the severe regulations had dire effects on the wonderful cars. Great heavy bumpers spoiled the lines of these sports cars which now

A true enthusiast would probably fasten two spare wheels on his petrol tank.

had environmentally-friendly engines but lacked performance.
By 1979 the MG had become unsaleable and production was halted. The marque came back to the market in 1996.

MG sports cars

COUNTRY OF ORIGIN
Great Britain

MG TC

YEARS IN PRODUCTION
1945–1949

NUMBER MADE
10,002

SPECIAL REMARKS
Immediately after the war, production of the pre-war MG TB was restarted but the car now had an improved gearbox and was designated MG TC.
The car can be recognised by its 19 in (48 cm) tall but thin wheels and the 13 gallons (60 litres) capacity fuel tank attached to its rear.

All the MG TCs were built with right-hand drive.

The MG TD; modern engineering and smaller wheels.

The dashboard of the TD was a neater arrangement.

MG TD

YEARS IN PRODUCTION
1950–1953

NUMBER MADE
29,664

SPECIAL REMARKS
The successor to the TC had very similar looks but in reality the car now had independent front suspension, which improved road-holding. Spoked wheels were now only available as an optional extra and the 15 in (38 cm) wheels were now more normal.

MG TF 1250/TF 1500

YEARS IN PRODUCTION
1953–1954

NUMBER MADE
6,200 and 3,400

SPECIAL REMARKS
The TF had only a passing resemblance through the door shape with its predecessors but was

The final T series cars were the TF which got a 1.5 litre engine in 1954 but they could still not hold their own against Healeys and Triumphs.

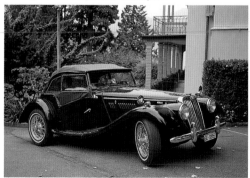

entirely modernised. The final 3,400 had 1.5 litre engines under their bonnets that provided 64 bhp at 6,400 rpm.

MGA roadster

YEARS IN PRODUCTION
1955–1962

NUMBER MADE
Unknown

SPECIAL REMARKS
MG entered a new era with the MGA and the days of the pre-war MGs were now forgotten. The MGA was designed by Sydney Enevers and was an immediate success. Until 1959 the car was powered by a 1,489 cc engine and then by a 1,588 cc engine.
The Mk II from 1961 had a more powerful 1,622 engine.

The modern styling brought a new era to MG. Now they could compete with their rivals.

The cockpit of the MGA. The round black knob beside the loudspeaker is the horn button.

The MGA's first engine was 1,489 cc but grew eventually to 1,622 cc and from 68–90 bhp.

The coupé version of the MGA was much higher than that of the roadster but for this it had real door handles on the outside and wind up windows.

MGA Coupé

YEARS IN PRODUCTION
1956–1962

NUMBER MADE
Unknown

SPECIAL REMARKS
The coupé was technically identical to the roadster but its price was substantially higher. The cost of spoked wheels instead of the standard pressed steel ones could also add considerably to the basic price of the car.

MGA Twin Cam

YEARS IN PRODUCTION
1958–1960

NUMBER MADE
2,111

SPECIAL REMARKS
The MGA Twin Cam had an engine with twin overhead camshafts but this version was not very successful. The engine proved to be very unreliable unless kept carefully in tune. The outward appearance of the car was characterised by the Rudge nave plates on the wheels. This MGA had all-round disc brakes.

The rear window of the coupé was made up of three elements.

The MGA Twin Cam. The roadsters had no door handles on the outside. To open a door if the hood was up required pushing a window aside in order to pull the door release cord on the inside.

MG lost is good name for reliability with the Twin Cam because the engine proved to be unreliable.

MGB Roadster

YEARS IN PRODUCTION
1962–1980

NUMBER MADE
387,259

Once MG switched over to a unitary body construction the MGB was born. This early model has chrome bumpers.

MG had always mounted the body on a separate chassis but the MGB changed to monocoque construction. The car was more luxurious in its appointment with wind-up windows in the doors. The four-cylinder 1,798 cc delivered 95 bhp at 5,400.

MGB GT

YEARS IN PRODUCTION
1965–1980

NUMBER MADE
125,621

SPECIAL REMARKS
Three years after the "B" was introduced, the MGB GT was launched. This car had an improved five bearing engine with considerably better engine life, although the performance remained the same. The GT had a "third door" lift-up hatched back end.

Sporting drivers tend to prefer an open car which is a shame because the MGB GT has a number of definite advantages.

MGC

YEARS IN PRODUCTION
1967–1969

NUMBER MADE
8,999

SPECIAL REMARKS
When the MG engineering experts could drag no more out of the four-cylinder engine they created a 2,912 cc six cylinder that produced 145 bhp. The model was dubbed MGC and about half of them were made as open roadsters. The front wheels did not have disc brakes.

MGB GT V8

YEARS IN PRODUCTION
1973–1976

The MGB GT V-8 were in a class of their own.

The classic MG: hood down and the wind in your hair.

NUMBER MADE
2,591

SPECIAL REMARKS
The GT V-8 was first created by garage owner Ken Costello who put a Rover V-8 engine in his own MG in 1970. MG was so pleased with the car that they adopted the idea. The 3,528 cc V-8 developed 137 bhp at 5,000 rpm. Today this car has a class all of its own in races for historic cars.

MG Midget

YEARS IN PRODUCTION
1961–1979

NUMBER MADE
226,427

SPECIAL REMARKS
This small MG was made on the same production line as the Austin-Healey Sprite. The only differences were the radiator grille and badge. When the Austin-Healey ceased production in 1971, the Midget remained for a further eight years.

The first Midgets were somewhat primitive, having clip on side windows and no door handles.

Monterosa

Giorgio Sargiotti laid the foundations for his car body company, Carrozzeria Monterosa, in January 1946, at the village of Moncalieri on the outskirts of industrial Turin.

The business slowly developed a speciality for building special car bodies. Repairing dented bodywork was pushed increasingly into the background as Sargiotti dreamt of building his own cars. In common with most specialist car makers in Italy, Sargiotti used Fiat parts. His first models were based on the running gear of a Fiat 600. The Monterosa 600 was available in three versions: a 2 + 2 sports coupé, a standard saloon, and luxury saloon. The last of these three had an over-abundance of chromium plate. The sports coupé could be bought with an uprated engine. Sargiotti turned to either Abarth or Stanguellini for this work.

A four-cylinder 633 cc engine giving 19 bhp at 4,600 rpm was fitted in the rear of the Monterosa 600.

Monterosa sports cars

COUNTRY OF ORIGIN
Italy

Monterosa 600

YEARS IN PRODUCTION
1959–1961

NUMBER MADE
Unknown

SPECIAL REMARKS
Carrozzeria Monterosa has built special bodies for many cars. The company attempted to launch a new car of their own with the Monterosa 600 but this was only partially successful.

This car was not called a Monteverdi but just an MBM. The engine was developed by Osca and the wheels originate from Cooper.

Monteverdi

Peter Monteverdi was a famous racing driver who had won many races in a Fiat, Porsche, or Ferrari when he decided in 1959 to build his own racing car.
The car was primarily destined for Formula Junior. Monteverdi called his creation MBM (Monteverdi Basel Motors) and the car performed well.
Two years later he developed a Porsche engined Grand Prix car but following a bad experience with it he switched over to sports cars and sporting tourers.
His first cars were powered by Osca engines and then later principally by big Chrysler V-8 engines. This Swiss builder showed a new model at the Geneva Salon each year between 1969 and 1980. These were mainly fast coupés and convertibles but also off-road vehicles and even a prototype four-door Range Rover which is still built by Land Rover. Its is difficult to say how many cars Peter Monteverdi has built because the man, who now lives in Morocco, will not say.

The final examples, which were principally research vehicles, exited his workshop in 1980. Monteverdi had a small stand at the Geneva show in 1992 where he exhibited a pale purple sports car known as the Hai F1 of which, according to him, five have been sold.

Monteverdi sports cars

COUNTRY OF ORIGIN
Switzerland

Monteverdi MBM Sport

YEARS IN PRODUCTION
1961

NUMBER MADE
Unknown

SPECIAL REMARKS
The MBM Sport was built using mechanical parts from Osca. The 1,092 cc engine developed 100 bhp at 7,500 rpm.

Monteverdi High Speed 375

YEARS IN PRODUCTION
1967–1977

The open-topped version of the Monteverdi High Speed was the Palm Beach.
The V-8 engine had power enough for a top speed of 156 mph (250 km/hour).

The High Speed 375 L, with "L" for luxury, was a spacious and very fast 2 + 2. The body was initially by Frua and later from Fissore.

NUMBER MADE
Unknown

SPECIAL REMARKS
The convertible version of the High Speed 375 was known as the Palm Beach. The car had a 7,206 cc Chrysler V-8 engine that developed 380 to 402 bhp.

Monteverdi Hai 450 SS

YEARS IN PRODUCTION
1970–1973

NUMBER MADE
Unknown

SPECIAL REMARKS
Monteverdi gambled on a mid-engined sports car with the Hai. Behind the bucket seats was a 6,974 cc V-8 engine that delivered 450 bhp at 5,000 rpm.

Monteverdi Sierra

The Sierra Convertible was the last sporting car to go into production with Monteverdi.

The Monteverdi Sierra dashboard.

YEARS IN PRODUCTION
1977–1978

NUMBER MADE
Unknown

SPECIAL REMARKS
The Monteverdi Sierra was introduced at the Geneva motor show in 1977. A year later a four-seater Sierra Convertible was launched. The motor was once again a Chrysler V-8 but this time a 5,898 cc one that developed 190 bhp at 4,000 rpm.

Moretti

Giovanni Moretti started his own business in 1925 when he was 21 years old. The business was situated at Via Monginevro 280 in Turin and it was here that he built his first motorcycle. Before World War II, Moretti had already moved on to motorised three-wheeler delivery vans but when he restarted after the war, he started to

Moretti built his own engines, even for the smallest cars. This sports car has a four-cylinder 612 cc engine that develops 20 bhp at 4,250 rpm.

The "750" made Moretti world famous. The four-cylinder engine was only 748 cc yet developed 58 bhp due to its twin camshafts.

Moretti sports cars

COUNTRY OF ORIGIN
Italy

Moretti 600

YEARS IN PRODUCTION
1949–1953

NUMBER MADE
Unknown

Morgan

build sports cars. In contrast to most of the other special car builders in Italy who used Fiat or Lancia parts, Moretti made his own. He was not scared of building engines with overhead camshafts and his engines made him world famous. The four cylinder engines of 750 cc developed 27 to 58 bhp.

By the 1960s customers were more interested in factory built cars than hand-made ones, however good they were, and Moretti specialised more and more in adapting car bodies and development of his own bodies. By 1970, the Moretti firm solely appeared in the telephone directory as a car body specialist and this work is still carried out.

A hood or side windows were unnecessary luxuries. There was also only one door.

The Morgan car marque was founded at the beginning of the twentieth century by H.F.S. Morgan. Morgan was always known by those perhaps close enough to him to know his first name as "HFS". HFS went to Crystal Palace Engineering College and was an engineering draughtsman for the Great Western Railway, drawing locomotives for seven years. In 1906 he set-up his own garage and it was here that he developed the Morgan three-wheeler. A Peugeot air-cooled engine was placed between the two front wheels, driving the rear wheels by a chain. The three-wheeler car was continuously improved but its outward appearance changed little so that some forty years after introduction it was virtually unchanged. In 1950, the car was powered by a four-cylinder water-cooled Ford Anglia engine.

Most pre-war three-wheelers had air-cooled engines which stood exposed between the front wheels. The F4 was more sophisticated.

Morgan drivers fix their cases to the luggage rack.

Morgan built a true sports car on four wheels in 1936 and this car too remained in production unchanged for a long time. Beneath the hand-crafted body of course there were technical improvements.

Pre 1952 cars were mainly powered by Coventry Climax Plus Four engines. Then Morgans used the Standard Vanguard engine and after 1954, the Triumph TR series motors and the Ford Anglia 105E. The Plus Eight was launched in 1968 with a Rover V-8. This car is still available today with a 3.9 litre engine which produced 190 bhp and a top speed of more than 125 mph.

Morgan sports cars

COUNTRY OF ORIGIN
Great Britain

Morgan Super

YEARS IN PRODUCTION
1934–1952

NUMBER MADE
632 (from 1945–1950)

All the three-wheelers were solely right-hand drive.

SPECIAL REMARKS
Morgan has built over 40,000 three-wheelers but the last one, the Super, came off the production line in 1952. The Super was a four-seater F4. Customers could choose between a 993 cc or 1,172 cc Ford engine.

Morgan Flat Rad

YEARS IN PRODUCTION
1936–1950

NUMBER MADE
2,252 (from 1945–1952)

SPECIAL REMARKS
The nickname is derived from the flat radiator with which this model was delivered even pre-war. The car was sold as both a two-seater and four-seater version. The 4/4 had a small 1,267 cc Standard Ten engine that produced 41 bhp. The Plus 4 was powered by a 2,088 cc Standard Vanguard engine.

A 1950 Morgan 4/4. The dual spare wheels were standard equipment. The top speed was about 78 mph (125 km/hour).

The dashboard of a 1967 Morgan 4/4.

Morgan enthusiasts dream of owning a Plus 8, preferably with an aluminium body. This Plus 8 was sold from 1975 onwards.

Morgan Cowled Radiator

YEARS IN PRODUCTION
1955–1982

NUMBER MADE
4,778

SPECIAL REMARKS
The revised version of the 4/4 had a rounded nose and only had enough room for two. It was produced with a 1,172 cc Ford Anglia side-valve engine, a Triumph TR3 motor, of the Ford Anglia overhead valve 105E engine

Morgan Plus 4 Plus

YEARS IN PRODUCTION
1964–1966

NUMBER MADE
26

SPECIAL REMARKS
The number made shows that this car was not successful. This was the first Morgan with a coupé body, and a plastic one to boot.
Mechanically, the car was identical to the Cowled Radiator model.

Morgan Plus 8

YEARS IN PRODUCTION
1968–present day

NUMBER MADE
More than 5,000

SPECIAL REMARKS
Morgan introduced the Plus Eight in August 1968. It was a two-seater with a superb Rover V-8 aluminium engine of 3,532 cc that developed 184 bhp at 5,200 rpm.

The car is dangerously fast because of its light weight of only 1,870 lb (850 kg).

Muntz

Frank Kurtis developed a good reputation for building competitive motor sport cars. His success with road cars was somewhat less and he was therefore glad to pass the project, including staff, tools, and factory, to Earl "Madman" Muntz.

The resulting car was known as the Muntz Jet and it was built in the small Californian town of Glendale. The 28 cars built had an aluminium body and a Cadillac 5.4 V-8 engine. The factory moved in 1950 to Evanston, Illinois, where the cars had steel bodies and Lincoln engines.

The functional dashboard of the Muntz. Note the searchlight on the extreme left which were very popular in those days.

Muntz sports cars

COUNTRY OF ORIGIN
USA

Muntz Jet

YEARS IN PRODUCTION
1949–1954

NUMBER MADE
394

SPECIAL REMARKS
"Madman" Muntz made his money dealing in second-hand cars and claimed to be the biggest second-hand car dealer in the world.

Muntz was so rich that he had his own television programmes. He also set-up a factory to make car radios. His Muntz Jet car sold for $5,000–6,000 which was a great deal of money in those days but for this money a cocktail bar and expensive Muntz radio was included.

Muntz had no more success than many before him. According to him, he lost $1,000 for every car he sold.

Nardi-Danese

Nash-Healey

Enrico Nardi was a famous racing driver before World War II who drove Ferrari's first car, the Auto Avia 815, together with Rangoni in the 1940 race that replaced the forbidden Mille Miglia. The Auto Avia 815 failed to complete the Gran Premio di Brescia because of technical problems. After the war Nardi sold conversion kits, accessories, and wooden steering wheels in partnership with Renato Danese and soon started to sell complete sports cars that were mostly constructed from Fiat parts. All manner of engines were installed in these cars. There were cars with Bertone bodies and Panhard engines, but others had Crosley, BMW, and Lancia motors.

There was even a model equipped with a Plymouth V-8 engine. Danese parted to do his own thing in 1951 and the marque became simply "Nardi".

Nardi-Danese sports cars

COUNTRY OF ORIGIN
Italy

Nardi

YEARS IN PRODUCTION
1948

NUMBER MADE
Unknown

SPECIAL REMARKS
The Nardi-Danese was built on a tubular frame with front suspension and rear axle from Fiat. Customers chose their own engines.

There are few surviving Nardi-Danese cars but occasionally one can be seen in a race for historic cars such as this 1948 example.

Donald-Healey was looking for a new market for his sports cars in 1949 when he met George Mason on board the Queen Mary while crossing the Atlantic to America. Mason was head of car makers Nash-Kelvinator.
Mason was very interested in Healey's plans for building sports cars using Nash engineering. The two men struck an accord and the Nash-Healey was born. The first cars were built on Healey Silverstone chassis and powered by 3,847 cc six-cylinder Nash engines. Donald Healey and his son Geoffrey came ninth in their class in the 1950 Mille Miglia driving a prototype and that same year Duncan Hamilton and Tony Rolt came fourth overall at Le Mans. In 1952 a Nash-Healey improved its placing at Le Mans to third. The Nash-Healey was shown in October 1950 at the London and Paris motor shows with bodies by Panelcraft that were based on designs by Healey. After 104 cars had been delivered Nash got Pininfarina to take the body under their wings and the car was given a complete facelift. From January 1952 onwards the bodies were built in Italy.

A Nash-Healey of the second series that were made in Italy.

An Italian-styled Nash-Healey roadster.

One of the first Nash-Healeys with body designed by Healey and made by Panelcraft.

The dashboard of the Nash-Healey.

Nash-Healey sports cars

A Nash-Healey came third at Le Mans in 1952, so a special series of coupés were sold as Nash-Healey Le Mans.

COUNTRY OF ORIGIN
USA

Nash-Healey

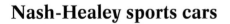

YEARS IN PRODUCTION
1950–1954

NUMBER MADE
506

SPECIAL REMARKS
Nash shipped the mechanical parts to Britain where Healey installed them to form a rolling chassis which was then shipped to Italy to receive its body. The finished car was then shipped to America.

Nissan

The first car made by Datsun was the Datsun 10, which first came off the production lines in 1932. Production only stepped up into gear though after World War II when the company was taken over by Nissan. The first new car was the Datsun DX, which was a small car closely resembling the American Crosley. Nissan gambled on its first sports car in 1952, the DC3. In reality, it was more of a sporty-looking convertible because the 860 cc engine only developed 20 bhp, barely enough to achieve a top speed of 44 mph (70 km/hour). The next sports car did not arrive until 1959. The Datsun S-211 was a four-seater with a polyester body and a 988 cc engine that gave 34 bhp. The engine in the S-211 became larger and more powerful, and this more powerful 60 bhp engine was installed in 1960 in the Fairlady that could reach 82 mph (132 km/hour). The famous 240 Z was gradually developed from the Fairlady, and its successors are still being made and sold.

The Fairlady was first sold in the Benelux countries in Europe. This 1959 Fairlady has Belgian number plates.

Nissan sports cars

COUNTRY OF ORIGIN
Japan

Datsun DC3

YEARS IN PRODUCTION
1952–1957

The 1952 Datsun Sports looked sporting but had a top speed of 44 mph (70 km/hour).

NUMBER MADE
Unknown

SPECIAL REMARKS
The DC3 was Nissan's first sports car, although it could go no faster than 44 mph (70 km/hour). The car was made with Austin A40 parts which Nissan built in Japan under licence.

Datsun S 211

YEARS IN PRODUCTION
1959–1960

NUMBER MADE
20

SPECIAL REMARKS
The S-211 had a polyester body, space for four persons, and a 988 cc 34 bhp engine. The car had a two-tone paint finish in the American style and was intended for the Japanese market.

Datsun S 212

YEARS IN PRODUCTION
1960–1961

NUMBER MADE
288

SPECIAL REMARKS
Once the engine of the S-211 was uprated to 1,189 cc, the car became the S-212. The four-cylinder motor now delivered 48 bhp at 4,800 rpm so that it can almost be regarded as a true sports car.

The Datsun SP-310 was known as the Fairlady 1600 in Japan. There was a sideways-facing third seat in the rear.

Datsun SP 310

YEARS IN PRODUCTION
1961–1966

NUMBER MADE
6,900

SPECIAL REMARKS
The public were treated to a new Nissan sports car at the 1961 Tokyo Motor Show, the Datsun SP-310. The engine of this car was 1,488 cc with power of 85 bhp.

Datsun SP 311

YEARS IN PRODUCTION
1962–1970

NUMBER MADE
49,305

SPECIAL REMARKS
The SP-311 was built to a design by the renowned Count Albrecht Goertz. Unfortunately you needed to be shorter than 5 ft 7 in (1.70 m) to fit in the car. The SP-311 had a 2-litre engine with twin camshafts.

Motor sport provided good publicity for the 240 Z. This car ran in the 1968 Monte Carlo Rally. The car was given away to a Dutch garage owner afterwards because it was cheaper than shipping the car back to Japan.

A small air spoiler proved to be valuable at high speeds.

The Datsun 240 Z became a common sight on the roads of Europe.

Datsun 240 Z

YEARS IN PRODUCTION
1969–1973

NUMBER MADE
133,953

SPECIAL REMARKS
The 240 Z brought Nissan international recognition for sports cars. The 2.4 litre six-cylinder engine produced 150 SAE at 6,000 rpm, giving a top speed of more than 125 mph (200 km/hour).

Datsun 260 Z

YEARS IN PRODUCTION
1973–1977

NUMBER MADE
349,899

SPECIAL REMARKS
The 260 Z was a 240 Z with a 2.6-litre engine. From March 1974, the car was also available as a 2 + 2 with a 12 in (30 cm) longer wheelbase.

The 195-70 VR 14 tyres of the 260 Z were much wider than the 175 SR 14 types used for the 240 Z.

NSU

Motor sport has always been important for NSU. The factory in Neckarsulm in German made cycles around the turn of the nineteenth and twentieth centuries, followed by motorcycles, and then fast sports and racing cars. The company then stopped building cars in 1906, after having built a number of racing cars with supercharged engines and concentrated on making motorcycles. Not until 1958 did another NSU car appear at a motor show, this time the Prinz, a small two-door car with an air-cooled twin-cylinder 583 cc engine that produced 20 bhp. There was then also a sports coupé. This Sport Prinz had a body by Bertone and its engine produced 30 bhp at 5,500 rpm. The most interesting model was the NSU Spider or convertible. This car has a rotary engine by Felix Wankel. Unfortunately the engine had all manner of teething problems that required considerable attention. The first truly functioning Wankel engine was developed by Mazda. A further sports car was the NSU 1000 TTS. Externally the car appeared to be a normal four-seater but it was extremely fast and unbeatable in its class.

The 1,320 lb (600 kg) NSU Sport Prinz was a two-seater with rear-mounted air-cooled twin-cylinder engine.

This was the view most competitors saw of the 1000 TTS.

NSU sports cars

COUNTRY OF ORIGIN
Germany

NSU Sport Prinz

YEARS IN PRODUCTION
1959–1967

NUMBER MADE
20,831

SPECIAL REMARKS
The talented designer, Franco Scaglione, still
worked for Bertone when he designed the body
of the Sport Prinz. The first few cars were built
in Turin but the rest were produced by Drauz in
Heilbronn.

NSU Wankel Spider

YEARS IN PRODUCTION
1964–1967

*The rotary engine by Felix Wankel was first installed
in an NSU Spider. The teething problems were never
really cured.*

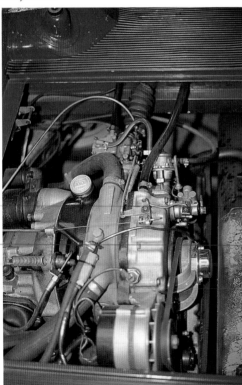

*If the NSU Spider had been sold with a normal
engine, more would certainly have been sold.*

The NSU Spider had an eight-track cartridge player.

NUMBER MADE
2,375

SPECIAL REMARKS
The low numbers produced shows how little
faith the public had in the rotary Wankel engine.
The engine was 996 cc and produced 50 bhp at
5,000 rpm.

NSU 1000 TTS

YEARS IN PRODUCTION
1967–1971

NUMBER MADE
2,404

SPECIAL REMARKS
The capacity of the TT engine was reduced from
1.2 litre to 996 cc so that the car could compete
in the 1 litre class races. The new engine was
designated TTS.

The experts eased 70 bhp at 6,150 rpm out of
the small engine to give a top speed of 100 mph
(160 km/hour).

Oldsmobile

Oldsmobile is the oldest American car maker, who celebrated their centenary in 1997. Oldsmobile were not the first car makers in the United States – that was the Duryea Brothers who had already built thirteen cars by 1896, but they went bust in 1919.

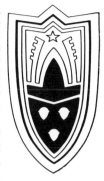

OLDSMOBILE

An Oldsmobile broke a World record in Florida with a speed of 54 mph (87 km/hour). The extremely tough Carrera Panamericana was won in an Oldsmobile Super 88 by Hershel McGriff in 1950 and Lee Petty won the first ever Daytona 500 mile race in 1959 with an Oldsmobile although the marque has made little impression on the race since. Oldsmobile mainly produced sensible family saloons but the occasional sporting model, such as the 4-4-2 has emerged from time to time.

The model number represents a four-speed gearbox, with quadruple carburettors, and twin exhaust. Another sporting model was the Toronado, which was the first mass-produced American car with front-wheel drive. The Firebird was developed as a potential rival for the Ford Thunderbird. The car was solely delivered as a convertible in 1971 but then subsequently only as a 2 + 2 coupé.

Oldsmobile sports cars

COUNTRY OF ORIGIN
USA

The Oldsmobile Starfire was introduced on January 1, 1961 as a deluxe convertible. The car was built on an "88" chassis but with a more powerful "Rocket" motor.

Oldsmobile Toronado

YEARS IN PRODUCTION
1966–1993

NUMBER MADE
Unknown

SPECIAL REMARKS
The Toronado was not only of interest for its front wheel drive but because it 385 bhp V-8 engine was the most powerful ever made by Oldsmobile.

Oldsmobile 4-4-2

YEARS IN PRODUCTION
1968–unknown

A 4-4-2 led off the field in both the 1970 and 1972 Indianapolis 500. This is a replica of the 1972 "Official Pace Car".

An Oldsmobile Hurst (new for 1968) of which 515 of the special version in silver, black, or white with gold were sold. The basis for the car was a 4-4-2 Holiday Coupe.

Rear leather, a tachometer, and polished aluminium bright-work were some of the detailed features of the Starfire.

NUMBER MADE
Unknown

SPECIAL REMARKS
The Cutlass could be bought with options in 1964 that formed the 4-4-2. By 1968, the car was sold as a separate model that appealed mainly to younger drivers.

Oldsmobile Hurst 4-4-2

YEARS IN PRODUCTION
1968

NUMBER MADE
515

SPECIAL REMARKS
George Hurst was a well-known expert in the

conversion and tuning of engines. He also produced sporting accessories. In 1968, he built a special based on the 4-4-2 Holiday Coupe and this car went into series production in limited numbers.

Oldsmobile Starfire

YEARS IN PRODUCTION
1961-1966

NUMBER MADE
Unknown

SPECIAL REMARKS
The Starfire was intended to compete with the Ford Thunderbird. A new 6,466 cc V-8 engine was developed specially for this car that delivered 336 SAE at 4,600 rpm.

The 1973 Cutlass cost $121 more in the 4-4-2 version than the standard model. For this money, the customer got a firmer suspension and go-faster body stripes.

The Opel GT was intended for the America market. The car was launched there in September 1968.

Opel

Opel was generally seen as the car for the successful business man and it took a great deal of advertising for Opel to change this image. The company has generally not produced sports cars although both coupé and convertible versions of some of their popular saloons have been produced. This is not to say that cars like the Commodore GS/E, Kadett

coupé, or Manta did not have quite some performance.

The international motor show at Frankfurt in 1965 saw the prototype of the first true Opel sports car, the Opel GT. There was no expectation by the public that this "concept" car would go into production but three years later the car was in the showrooms. The body was constructed by Chausson in Paris and painted by Brissoneau & Lotz in Creil, to the north of Paris, who were also responsible for the interior trim. The car was finally assembled by Opel in Bochum, Germany. The Opel GT was mainly aimed at the American market and when the safety and environmental regulations were tightened up, it meant the end for the car.

The Opal GT was available with 1.9 litre engine and choice of 4-speed manual gearbox or automatic transmission.

Opal sports cars

COUNTRY OF ORIGIN
Germany

Opal GT

YEARS IN PRODUCTION
1968–1973

NUMBER MADE
103,463

SPECIAL REMARKS
More than 100,000 Opel GT's were sold. Most of the cars were powered by a 1,897 cc four-cylinder engine of 90 bhp at 5,100 rpm but 3,573 had 1,078 cc engines giving 60 bhp at 5,200 rpm. Two cars were fitted with a Targa body and sold as Aero-GT.

Osca

In 1947, the Maserati brothers had fulfilled the condition of Adolfi Orso, when he bailed them out of bankruptcy and took over Maserati, that they work for Maserati for a further ten years.

Ernesto, Ettore, and Bindo decided to start up their own business once more. They moved from Modena to Bologna and set-up Osca (Officine Specializzate per la Costruzione di Automobili Fratelli Maserati SpA) and started once more on the work that had driven them to bankruptcy: building sports cars and racing cars. Their first product was the Osca MT4, a small two-seater with a four-cylinder engine of their own design. This was followed by both smaller and larger cars, coupés, and convertibles, driven by twin cam engines.

The company was particularly successful in 750 cc class racing. The car performed well in the Mille Miglia and at Le Mans. A 1.5 litre Osca won the 1954 12-hour race at the Sebring circuit. These successes led Fiat to order engines tuned by the Maserati brothers, with twin-cam heads for the 1960 Fiat 1500 Spyder. Another best seller of the company was their Osca 1600 GT with a 105 bhp four-cylinder twin-cam engine with an aluminium body by Zagato.

By 1963 the brothers, unable to continue the business because of their age, sold Osca to the leading motorcycle maker, MV Agusta, and retired from the world of motor cars.

Osca sports cars

COUNTRY OF ORIGIN
Italy

Osca MT 4

YEARS IN PRODUCTION
1948–1959

This was the first Osca, the MT4 with chassis number 1101. The car was more suitable for the track than the open road.

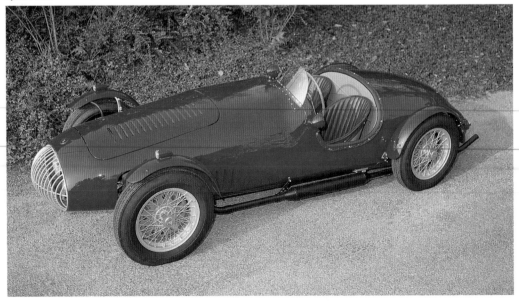

The 1,092 cc engine of the MT 4 had a single overhead camshaft and delivered 72 bhp at 6,000 rpm.

This is MT 4 chassis no. 1139, built in 1954.

NUMBER MADE
80

SPECIAL REMARKS
The MT 4 was supplied with various types of body and therefore used for a range of different purposes. It was widely used on the track but equally at home on the road.

Osca 750

YEARS IN PRODUCTION
1956–1960

NUMBER MADE

17

SPECIAL REMARKS
The Osca 750 with a 749 cc engine with twin

overhead camshafts was only approved for use on the open road in Italy. Most of the cars were bought for motor sport.

Osca 1600 GT

YEARS IN PRODUCTION
1960–1963

NUMBER MADE
127

SPECIAL REMARKS
The majority of 1600 GT cars were supplied with two-seater coupé bodies by Zagato. The firms of Fissore (19) and Boneschi (2) also built bodies for this car.

A four-cylinder engine of 749 cc with a compression ratio of 9:1 that delivered 70 bhp at 7,500 rpm powered the Osca 750, officially known as Tipo S-187.

The majority of the Osca 1600 GT bodies were in aluminium by Zagato and can re recognised by the famous "double bubble" roof.

Osi

Osi (Officine Stampaggi Industriali) was founded in 1960 as a subsidiary of Ghia to build short series of cars such as the Innocenti Spyder, the coupé versions of the Fiat 2300. Special bodies were constructed on the most diverse of chassis and running gear. The prototype Ford Osi 20M TS made its appearance in 1966. The car was shown at Geneva and the following year went into production. Ford shipped the appropriate parts from Cologne to Turin and received completed cars back. The car was slightly longer and wider than the standard Ford Taunus (the German equivalent to the Cortina) and had space for four persons.

Osi sports cars

COUNTRY OF ORIGIN
Italy/Germany

Osi 20M TS

YEARS IN PRODUCTION
1967–1968

NUMBER MADE
Approx. 3,400

SPECIAL REMARKS
When the 20M TS went into production, some 800 people worked for Osi. The car was mechanically identical to the standard German Ford Taunus TS.

The Osi sold well in Germany thanks to its combination of Italian form and German engineering.

Paganelli

Paganelli was set-up in Naples in 1948 to make sports cars. The company managed to hold its head above water against intense competition but was finally forced to throw the towel in by the mid 1950s. Most Paganelli cars were based on Lancia parts.

The number plate shows that this Paganelli may be driven on the road.

Paganelli sports cars

COUNTRY OF ORIGIN
Italy

A roof and doors were an unnecessary luxury for a Paganelli.

Paganelli-Lancia

YEARS IN PRODUCTION
1948–1955

NUMBER MADE
Unknown

SPECIAL REMARKS
In contrast with the majority of small-scale Italian car makers who used Fiat parts, Paganelli worked with Lancia.

Panhard

Panhard & Levassor were founded in Paris in 1886 by René Panhard and Emile Levassor. The Panhard works was one of the first in the world to build cars for sale. The company built racing and sports cars as well as small personal cars and limousines. Panhard were often far ahead of their time and hence in the immediate post World War II period, Panhard built cars using the Grégoire principle – one of the first proponents of front-wheel drive. Panhard also used "sliding engines" in some of their cars. One of the first Panhard's with front wheel drive was the Dyna which had a twin-cylinder air-cooled engine. The four-seater body was mainly constructed in aluminium. The engines grew in size but Panhard remained loyal to the two-cylinder principle, together with air-cooling and front-wheel drive. Charles Deutsch built sports cars that achieved a fair degree of success, especially at Le Mans, under the Panhard C-D name. The client did not need to know that these tubular chassis cars had little to do with Panhard except from the engine and gearbox.

Panhard was taken over by Citroën in 1965 and Citroën allowed Panhard to continue producing cars for a short time but eventually the end came

The Dyna Junior was a fairly spartan car. Young French men and women dreamed of owning one of these two-seaters in the way English youth dreamed of an MG TD.

for them. The final Panhard car was made in 1967.

Panhard sports cars

COUNTRY OF ORIGIN
France

Panhard Dyna Junior

YEARS IN PRODUCTION
1952–1956

NUMBER MADE
Approx. 2,000

SPECIAL REMARKS
The sports version of the Panhard Dyna was shown for the first time at the Paris Motor Show in 1952. The first models were powered by a 38 bhp engine. Later models had more power with 745 cc/40 bhp and 848 cc/42 bhp engines.

The convertible version of the Panhard Dyna. With its 848 cc twin-cylinder engine it had a top speed of 78 mph (125 km/hour).

The boot was only accessible through the small rear seat.

A four-seater 1966 Panhard 24BT, powered by the PL17 Tigre 848 cc twin-cylinder engine that produced 50 bhp at 5,750 rpm.

The well arranged dashboard of the 24BT.

Panhard 24

YEARS IN PRODUCTION
1963–1967

NUMBER MADE
23,245

SPECIAL REMARKS
The Panhard 24 was the world's most expensive twin-cylinder engine sports car. The car was based on the Panhard PL17 and was available in various versions.
The 24B and BA were four-seater saloons, the C had a shorter wheelbase and was a two-seater or 2 + 2. The BT and CT had the more powerful PL17 Tigre engine.

Panhard-CD

YEARS IN PRODUCTION
1963–1965

NUMBER MADE
160

The Panhard CD was the fastest production car ever made by Panhard. It was claimed to achieve more than 100 mph (160 km/hour).

SPECIAL REMARKS

The CD was a true sports car. It had an aerodynamic polyester body and tubular chassis. A Panhard CD won the important Le Mans Index in 1962.

The boot of the CD was surprisingly large.

The tuned 848 cc engine produced 50 bhp at 5,750 rpm to achieve 100 mph (160 km/hour).

Panther

Bob Jankel built his first car when he was just sixteen. This was a sports car that closely resembled the Lotus Seven but it was barely suitable for the road. After Jankel had worked for someone else for a few years, he decided to start up his own works and the second prototype emerged from it in 1970. It was an evocation of the famous Jaguar SS 100, of which car enthusiasts dreamed in the 1930s. Jankel's version had a passing resemblance to the SS Jaguar but with contemporary Jaguar mechanical engineering. His business went into receivership in 1980 but the new Korean owners kept him on as a director of the company.

Panther sports cars

COUNTRY OF ORIGIN
Great Britain

Panther J72

YEARS IN PRODUCTION
1972–1980

NUMBER MADE
426

SPECIAL REMARKS
The J72 represented Jankel and 1972, when the company was founded. In contrast to the glass-fibre reinforced polyester of his competitors, Jankel built aluminium bodies. In 1972, the Panter J72 cost £4,655.

Pegaso

Although Don Wilfredo Ricart was a good technical expert, Enzo Ferrari good not stand the sight of him when they worked together in the 1930s at Alfa Romeo. The Spanish engineer turned up in Barcelona in 1951, where he built super cars under the Pegaso name in the old Hispano-Suiza factory. The first car was the Z102, which was shown at Paris in 1951. The car stood out for its technical innovation, including an aluminium 2.5 litre V-8 engine with four overhead cams and four twin Weber carburettors.

The car had a De Dion-type rear axle with a five-speed gearbox mounted behind the differential. The body was from Touring of Milan who became main supplier to Pegaso. The firm managed to survive for eight years but Ricart was forced to close down in 1959, having built 112 cars.

The Panther J72 had a purely passing resemblance to a Jaguar SS 100 when seen from a distance but was much more expensive than an E-type Jaguar.

This Pegaso Z102B was known as "El Dominicano". It was owned by Rafael Trujillo, the assassinated ex-president of Haiti.

Pegaso sports cars

COUNTRY OF ORIGIN
Spain

Pegaso Z102

YEARS IN PRODUCTION
1951–1958

NUMBER MADE
Unknown

SPECIAL REMARKS
The Z102 was sold with three different engine sizes: 2.5, 2.8, and 3.2 litre. The figures for power were not published but were of the order of 175–250 bhp. In 1953, turbocharged motors were available with one or two turbochargers.

Not all the bodies were supplied by Touring of Milan. This Z102B was given a body by Pegaso themselves.

Pegaso Z 103

YEARS IN PRODUCTION
1955–1958

NUMBER MADE
Unknown

Touring of Milan built this 1953 Pegaso body.

The interior of a Z102B. Note the gear-change sequence on the gear-lever.

The Pegaso Z103 was introduced in Paris in 1955. The V-8 engines were now 3.9 or 4.8 litre but the inlets were controlled by a straight-forward centrally-positioned single camshaft. The body was once more by Touring of Milan.

Plymouth

The Plymouth mar-que was established in 1928 by Walter P. Chrysler who wanted to compete with the cheaper Fords and Chevro-lets. Up to 1955, these cars were on-ly sold with six-cylinder engines. The make sold well before the war and after World War II, the company continued the previous policy with low cost cars, mainly for the whole family. When Ford launched the Mustang in 1964, Plymouth hoped to win a share of this growing market by quickly developing a competitor for the Mustang.

The Plymouth Barracuda was in reality a Plymouth Valiant with a different front end and huge rear window. This window was the biggest that Detroit had ever installed. The first cars were powered by a 3,682 cc six-cylinder engine of 147 bhp at 4,000 rpm. When Pontiac launched their GTO, Plymouth responded with the Road Runner. This car was based on the floor pan of a Plymouth Belvedere Satellite and had a V-8 engine which delivered 395 SAE at 4,700 rpm. A special version of the Road Runner was the Super Bird which was also available as a Dodge. It stood out because of its large plastic front end and the enormous wing behind. This oddity was only made for a couple of years and it was mainly intended for NASCAR racing.

The Plymouth Barracuda had an enormous rear window, that soon acquired the nickname of "Glass-back".

Another unusual Plymouth was the Asimme-trica. Virgil Exner, who was Chrysler's head designer, got Ghia to build the XNR concept car in 1959. Two years later the car was produced in small volume.
The car was known as Asimmetrica because nothing about the car was symmetrical.

Plymouth sports cars

COUNTRY OF ORIGIN
USA

Plymouth Barracuda

YEARS IN PRODUCTION
1964–1974

NUMBER MADE
Unknown

SPECIAL REMARKS
The Barracuda was successfully launched on April 1, 1964 as a competitor for the popular Ford Mustang. The Barracuda too got a V-8 engine from 1965.

The 1973 Road Runner could reach a top speed in excess of 125 mph (200 km/hour) with its 7.2 litre V-8 engine which developed 425 SAE or 280 bhp.

Plymouth Road Runner

YEARS IN PRODUCTION
1968–1975

NUMBER MADE
Unknown

SPECIAL REMARKS
The buyer of a Road Runner could choose between a 6.3 or 7.2 litre V-8 engine with power of 335 or 425 SAE. All the cars had a four-speed manual gearbox.

Plymouth Super Bird

YEARS IN PRODUCTION
1970

NUMBER MADE
1,920

SPECIAL REMARKS
The plastic nose of the Super Bird was 19 in (48 cm) long, making the car 221 in (561 cm) long. The rear wing stuck up 25 in (64 cm) above the boot lid.

The "Glass-back" was followed by the "Wing Thing" – a Road Runner Super Bird which was a bird with an unusual tail. Plymouth claimed a top speed of almost 200 mph (320 km/hour).

The wings protruded 25 in (64 cm) above the boot lid.

The personalised paint job of this Asimmetrica was not by Ghia. The car had a six-cylinder engine from the Valiant.

Plymouth Asimmetrica

YEARS IN PRODUCTION
1961

UMBER MADE
Unknown

SPECIAL REMARKS
After the first Asimmetrica had been displayed at a number of shows, it was sold to the famous Maigret author, Georges Simenon.

Pontiac

Oakland was a make of car that formed part of General Motors. The company was founded in 1907 and merged with GM in 1909. With the creation by GM of its new make Pontiac in 1926, the end was in sight for Oakland, which finally had to make room for increased Pontiac production in 1931. Pontiac filled the market slot between the cheaper Chevrolet and more expensive Oldsmobile and was regarded before World War II as a guarantee of a reliable family car. Pontiac came under the leadership of 43 year old Simon E. "Bunkie" Knudsen in 1956, who started to develop cars that were both longer and wider but also lower to the ground and with more powerful engines. These cars were aimed at motoring enthusiasts and although they were not actually sports cars, models such as the Grand Prix regularly won club races and a Pontiac won the Daytona 500

This Grand Am of 1975 with a 170 or 200 bhp V-8 engine was not very successful. Only 8,786 were sold.

race for "production" cars with an average speed of 149 mph (239 km/hour). Knudsen's car developed 390 bhp and accelerated from 0–60 mph in about four seconds (0–100 km/hour in 4.6 seconds). Knudsen became General Manager of Chevrolet in 1961. Knudsen was succeeded by Pete Estes and later John Z. Delorean. Now Pontiac began to build true sports cars, albeit much larger cars than a Porsche or MG. Delorean's Tempest GTO was a two-door coupé with a 6.9 litre V-8 engine that developed 360 SAE. The three-speed box was manually operated.

The driver had a sportive bucket seat and if he pressed his foot on the accelerator the car would reach 100 mph (160 km/hour) in just twenty-five seconds. When Chevrolet brought out the Camaro, Delorean responded immediately with the Pontiac Firebird. The Firebird had the same body as the Chevrolet but had a more sporting ride.

The Firebird was improved and made faster through development to make the successful Trans AM. The Grand Am variant though was less successful.

Pontiac sports cars

COUNTRY OF ORIGIN
USA

Pontiac GTO

YEARS IN PRODUCTION
1964–1971

In 1967, Pontiac sold 81,722 of the GTO, of which 9,517 were convertibles.

NUMBER MADE
Unknown

SPECIAL REMARKS
Although the GTO was part of the Tempest range, the car had a different bottom frame and a much more powerful engine. The GTO did not become an apart model until 1966. In 1964, the car was available with either a 6.364 or 6,558 cc engine.

Pontiac Firebird

YEARS IN PRODUCTION
1967–present day

NUMBER MADE
Unknown

Firebird offered six-cylinder 4,093 cc or 5,799 and 6,558 cc V-8 motors in 1968.

SPECIAL REMARKS
The Firebird had the same body as the Chevrolet Camaro but with a different radiator grille and more powerful engine, with an overhead camshaft.

Pontiac Trans Am

YEARS IN PRODUCTION
1970–1985

NUMBER MADE
Unknown

SPECIAL REMARKS
The Firebird got a new body but a smaller engine with a conventional camshaft. Formula 400 and Trans Am racing was new at that time. The Trans Am had a 6,558 cc V-8 engine that developed 350 SAE at 5,000 rpm and had a top speed of 125 mph (200 km/hour).

The Firebird was no longer in convertible form after 1970. This is a 1975 Trans Am with 6,558 cc overhead valve V-8 engine.

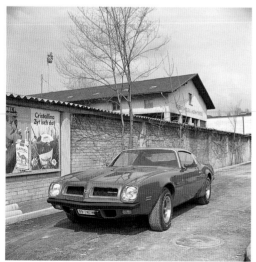

Porsche

The founder of Porsche, Dr. Ferdinand Porsche was not actually responsible for the famous cars that bear his name, When his son Ferry built the first car that was to become the Porsche, his father was imprisoned, having been accused of war crimes. The Porsche firm at that time was operating in Gmünd in Austria, where it had moved in 1943 for reasons of safety. The first Porsche was built with a tubular chassis, had an aluminium open-topped body, and had mechanical parts from the car that was to become the Volkswagen Beetle. The 1,131 cc horizontally-opposed cylinders engine was mounted in front of the rear axle and developed 40 bhp at 4,000 rpm, which produced a top speed of 81 mph (130 km/hour).

The first examples were delivered to a client in Switzerland who had them road tested for a magazine and the resulting publicity led to the car going into production. The factory at that time employed 270 and the production cars had cheaper monocoque bodies. The engine was moved behind the rear axle as Dr. Porsche had drawn it for the forerunner of the VW Beetle. Once fifty-two cars had been built in Austria, Porsche moved back to Germany in the winter of 1949–1950, to Stuttgart.
The new home was the Reutter car body factory, where the bodies of the new Porsche cars were to be made. Production of the 356 got under way smoothly and the car was continuously improved and the engine made more powerful. The engine of the 356 had twin overhead camshafts per cylinder.

Porsche number one is exhibited in a display of Porsche cars at the Schlumpf museum in Mulhouse, France. The body is of aluminium and the engine is mounted in front of the rear axle.

Porsche Speedster, for the American market had spartan equipment: slot in windows for the doors, no insulation, and a simple soft-top hood.

This four-cylinder engine proved to perform well as a sporting and racing power unit.

The 356 was succeeded in 1963 by the 911. The car was intended to be 901 but had to be changed when Peugeot produced evidence that it owned the rights for type numbers with a zero in the middle. The 911 was powered by a horizontally opposed six-cylinder engine. The 912 was a 911 with the newer version of the flat-four cylinder 356 engine.

The 912 was built from 1965 to 1969, when 32,867 were sold.

The model number 911 has been retained even when a totally new car has been produced. In 1997, the 911 had been on sale for 34 years. The first examples had a 1,991 cc engine and its successors had 2,195, 2,341, 2,687, and in 1975, even a 2,994 cc engine. The power output climbed from 140 bhp at 6,000 rpm to 260 bhp at 5,500 rpm in the 3-litre 911 Turbo.

The Stuttgart-Zuffenhausen factory produced an unusual model in 1969 that was not much liked by Porsche enthusiasts. The Porsche 914 or Volks-wagen-Porsche sold extremely well however. The car was aimed as those less well-off. A subsequent "cheap" Porsche 924 was largely the work of Dutch designer Harm Lagaay. Having now returned after a short absence from Porsche, Lagaay is likely to be closely involved in the design of the successor to the 911.

Porsche sports cars

COUNTRY OF ORIGIN
Germany

Porsche 356

YEARS IN PRODUCTION
1948–1965

The 911RS Carrera was intended for both daily use and the track. It was 198 lb (90 kg) lighter than a 911S. It had a 2,687 cc 210 bhp at 6,300 rpm engine.

The first Porsche 356 cars built in Stuttgart had a "kink" in the windscreen. The engines were 1,000, 1,300, or 1,500 cc.

The final 356SC of 1965 was the best of the series. These cars had disc brakes and a 1,582 cc engine that gave 95 bhp at 5,700 rpm.

NUMBER MADE
77,509

SPECIAL REMARKS
The 356 was suitable for a variety of uses, from family car, although the room in the back was restricted, to rally and racing car.
The racing versions had engines with four camshafts.

Porsche 911

YEARS IN PRODUCTION
1964–present day

NUMBER MADE
Unknown

SPECIAL REMARKS
Many Porsche enthusiasts bought one of the final 356C cars because they did not like the look of the 911 and opinions are still divided. It is however an irrefutable fact that the 911 is a commercial success. The model incorporated all the experience that Porsche had acquired through racing.

The 912 was not only cheaper to buy but also to maintain. The Dutch National Police use a Targa version of the 912 for motorway patrols.

The dashboard of the 912 was nothing like either the 356 or 911, which had five dials.

Porsche 912

YEARS IN PRODUCTION
1965–1969

NUMBER MADE
32,867

SPECIAL REMARKS
The 911 was comparatively expensive when compared with the final 356C. When it was clear Porsche drivers were thinking of changing to another make, Porsche introduced the 912. This car was powered by the 356C engine but with a new body.

Porsche 914 (Volkswagen-Porsche)

YEARS IN PRODUCTION
1969–1975

NUMBER MADE
118,978

SPECIAL REMARKS
The died-in-the-wool Porsche fanatic turned his

The commercial success of the 914 was exceeded by the 924 which was introduced in 1975 and disappeared in 1985. The model sold 122,304 cars.

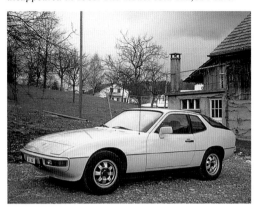

(or her) nose up at the 914 with its Volkswagen 411 engine behind the seats. At Porsche they just laughed at the moaners because Porsche had never sold so many cars in such a short time. A total of 119,000 rolled off the lines of which 3,332 were powered by a "genuine" 2 litre six-cylinder Porsche engine. This version was very popular for motor sport.

Porsche 924

YEARS IN PRODUCTION
1978–1985

NUMBER MADE
122,304

SPECIAL REMARKS
The successor to the 914 did also not enthuse the Porsche fans. The 924 had an Audi 1,984 cc four-cylinder engine that developed 125 bhp at 5,800 rpm. The water-cooled engine was mounted in the front of the car but the five-speed gear box was rear-mounted, by the differential.

Puma

The firm of Sociedade de Automoveis Luminari was set-up in 1964 in Sao Paulo, Brazil, by an Italian, Gennaro Malzoni. The company built polyester-bodied sports cars with front wheel drive using three-cylinder two-stroke DKW engines under licence. When Volkswagen took

This car was sold as the 914 in America and as a Volkswagen-Porsche in Europe, which was to its disadvantage. The 914-6 had a six-cylinder 2-litre that gave a top speed of 131 mph (210 km/hour).

over the DKW factory, Malzoni switched to basing his cars in the VW Karmann-Ghia. The first models were powered by a 1,500 cc engine and later by a 1,600 cc motor. Drive was via the rear wheels. The Puma GTB was launched in 1972, based on a Chevrolet chassis with a 4.1 litre six-cylinder engine under the bonnet. The car was a spacious 2 + 2 that could hardly be regarded as a sports car. The Puma II, as the car with Volkswagen mechanical parts was known, was also sold as a convertible after 1979. Malzoni went bust in 1985 and the business was taken over by Alfa Metais Veiculos Ltda. The Puma continued to be made until 1993 but then had a VW Passat engine.

Puma sports cars

COUNTRY OF ORIGIN
Brazil

DKW-Malzoni GT

YEARS IN PRODUCTION
1964–1968

NUMBER MADE
About 135

SPECIAL REMARKS
The Malzoni GT was assembled from DKW parts. It was a true two-seater and was available

The panoramic rear window of the original Puma was replaced by a flat window when the VW engine started to be used.

with a choice of two 981 cc engines: giving 60 or 68 bhp at 5,200 rpm. From 1966, the Malzoni GT was sold as a Puma.

Puma II

YEARS IN PRODUCTION
1968–1985

NUMBER MADE
Unknown

SPECIAL REMARKS
The body of the Puma had to be altered when the DKW engine was replaced by the four-cylinder VW Beetle engine. This air-cooled engine delivered 55–77 bhp.

The air intake beneath the front bumper was solely for ventilation in the car. The first Puma had a true grille.

Reliant

More three-wheeler cars have been made in Britain than anywhere else in the world. This was due to the preferential road fund licence of these cars. Reliant produced three-wheeler delivery vans from 1935 and these re-appeared after the war. Then in 1952, they brought out a car based on the three-wheeler van. The company did not produce its first "real" car until 1960. This was the Sabre, of which 50 were sold as kits to Israel, 100 as Sabra, and 58 as Reliant Sabres. The Reliant Sabre was available in Britain from 1961.

It was an open two-seater with glass-reinforced polyester body and either the four-cylinder Ford Zephyr engine or six-cylinder Zephyr-Six motor. Reliant introduced the Scimitar at the London Motor Show in 1964. This was a 2 + 2 designed by David Ogle, with a glass-fibre body. Even more interesting was the Reliant Scimitar GTE in 1968 sporting estate body that was the forerunner of cars such as the Volvo p1800ES and Lancia Beta HPE.

Reliant sports cars

COUNTRY OF ORIGIN
Great Britain

Reliant Sabra/Sabre

YEARS IN PRODUCTION
1961–1964

NUMBER MADE
335

With its 2,553 cc six-cylinder Ford engine, the Reliant Sabre could reach 112 mph (180 km/hour.

The Reliant Scimitar GTE had the performance of a sports car with the advantages of an estate car. There was room for four persons and their luggage.

SPECIAL REMARKS
The Sabre was not a success with only 58 of the first series with the four-cylinder Ford engine being sold in Britain. The Sabre Six SE2S with a six-cylinder engine did slightly better with 77 being sold.

Reliant Scimitar GT

YEARS IN PRODUCTION
1964–1970

NUMBER MADE
1,003

SPECIAL REMARKS
The glass-fibre reinforced polyester body of the Scimitar GT was designed by David Ogle. The cars had Ford engines of 2,553, 2,995, and 2,495 cc of which the latter was a V-6.

Reliant Scimitar GTE

PRODUCTIEJAREN
1968-1975

AANTAL
9.416

Technically, the Scimitar GT was identical to the Sabre until 1965, after which it had an improved back axle.

The rear window of the GTE is the third door of today's hatch backs.

SPECIAL REMARKS

The sporting estate car was not invented by Reliant. Chevrolet had already had the Nomad in 1954, which was a Corvette with an estate car rear end but it is immaterial whether Reliant were first: the Scimitar GTE was very successful.

Renault

Louis Renault built his first car in 1898. This car was one of the first cars to be built in the world. Renault then started producing this first prototype and Renault quickly became France's biggest industrial concern.

When France was liberated by the Allies, Louis Renault was accused of collaboration with the Germans and was imprisoned. Soon afterwards he died in mysterious circumstances. His property was taken over by the French state and since that time the business has been Régie Nationale des Usines Renault.

In the post war years, Renault was scarcely known for sporting cars and it is therefore surprising that they have become so closely associated through their engines with Formula One. There have been sporting models in their range of course, such as the four-door Dauphine. This model came fourth in its class in the 1956 Mille Miglia. Besides the standard Dauphine, there was also the Dauphine Floride, designed by Amédée Gordini, which became famous on the track, and the recent Renault 5 Turbo, which is too new for the compass of this book.

A year after the introduction of the Renault 12, the Gordini version appeared, which was very much a sports car, in spite of its saloon body with four doors. The front-wheel drive was powered by the 125 bhp engine from the Renault 16.

Renault Dauphines tuned by Gordini demonstrated how well they performed during the 1950s and now once more on the track at historic events.

Renault sports cars

COUNTRY OF ORIGIN
France

Renault Dauphine Gordini

YEARS IN PRODUCTION
1957–1968

NUMBER MADE
Unknown

SPECIAL REMARKS
The Renault Dauphine had hardly started in production when it won its class in the Monte

Fun for four: the Renault Dauphine Floride.

Carlo rally. Many more victories were to follow. The four-cylinder engine was a mere 845 cc but Gordini managed to get 37 instead of 30 bhp from it.

Renault Dauphine Floride

YEARS IN PRODUCTION
1959–1968

NUMBER MADE
More than 180,000

SPECIAL REMARKS
The Dauphine Floride, which got its name from the 1963 Caravelle, was designed in Piero Frua's studio. The floor-pan came from the Dauphine Gordini. The model was available as both a coupé and convertible.

The Dauphine was a sporty-looking 2 + 2. Its 40 or even 52 bhp engine could take it to speeds of almost 94 mph (150 km/hour).

Saab

The Saab name (Svenska Aeroplan AB) has several associations for different people. Some think of Saab fighter aircraft, while others recall safe, front-wheel drive cars, with two-stroke engines. Others recall the Saab above all as a rally car. The married couple Erik and Pat Carlsson (Pat is the sister of Stirling Moss) contributed to the sporting image of Saab. Despite this sporting image, sports cars have always been an after thought for this Swedish company. The first sports car was more of a hobby activity than business. This car was built on the running gear of a Saab 93 and powered by a three-cylinder two-stroke engine that delivered 58 bhp at 5,000 rpm.

The car did 0–100 km/hour (0–62.5 mph) in twelve seconds and had a top speed of 125 mph (200 km/hour). This car was named the Saab Sonett Super Sport and was launched in 1956 at the New York Motor Show. The firm only made seven prototypes. After that little happened in terms of sports cars until the prototype for the Sonett II, code-named Catherina. This was neither a coupé or convertible but an open car with a Targa-type of roll-over bar for safety. This car too never went into production.

After a Saab 850GT had won the 1962 Monte Carlo Rally, the Saab 96 was called Monte Carlo. The three-cylinder two-stroke engine produced 55 bhp, giving a top speed of 94 mph (150 km/hour).

Despite seven prototypes, the Sonett did not go into production.

The Catherina remained an only child that did not get beyond prototype.

A subsequent Sonett II did make it into production. This two-seater coupé came out in 1966 with a three-cylinder two-stroke engine that produced 60 bhp at 5,200 rpm.

This smelly engine was replaced in 1967 by a four-stroke V-4 from the German Ford Taunus. The final version of the Sonett III was designed by the Italian Sergio Coggiola. It too was powered by the fairly lazy Ford Taunus 12M engine.

Saab sports cars

COUNTRY OF ORIGIN
Sweden

Saab Sonett I

YEARS IN PRODUCTION
1956

NUMBER MADE
7

The Sonett II had a glass-reinforced polyester body made by Malmö Flygindustri.

SPECIAL REMARKS
The Sonett I was designed by Rolf Mellde. It had right-hand drive because Sweden still drove on the left in 1956. Only seven prototypes were made, with the car never going into series production.

Saab Sonett II

YEARS IN PRODUCTION
1966–1970

NUMBER MADE
1,768

SPECIAL REMARKS
The majority (1,510) of the Sonett II sports cars were delivered with the much quieter Ford Taunus 1,498 cc 12M V-4 engine that produced 65 bhp at 6,000 rpm.

Saab Sonett III

YEARS IN PRODUCTION
1970–1974

Despite its bad reviews there, most Sonett III's were sold in America. This is a special edition with a fold-back opening roof.

Sales of the Saab Sonett improved considerably when it got a four-stroke engine.

NUMBER MADE
8,368

SPECIAL REMARKS
The Sonett III was destined for the American market. The press there were very critical with Road & Track writing: "It's a tragedy the styling is so miserable," and "...the styling may bring tears of despair and frustration to the eyes of the serious student of automobile design."

Sabra

The Israeli company Autocars Co. Ltd. of Haifa was yet another to attempt to find a niche in the sports car market.
The company imported Reliant Sabre kits and sold them in Israel and certain other countries as Sabra (see Reliant). About £4,500 was demanded for a Sabra convertible in The Netherlands in 1963 and even more for the hard-top, although the safety belts and a spray can of touch-up paint (creamy-white or fire-engine red) was included.

The wheelbase of the Sabra was 90 in (229 cm) and the overall length 165 in (419 cm). The top speed varied from 94 to 109 mph (150–175 km/hour).

By contrast with their pre-war cars, the post-war Salmsons had headlights incorporated into their front wings.

This car was launched at the Paris Motor Show in 1953 but it could not prevent the company's financial difficulties.
Salmson was taken over by Renault in 1957 and suffered a quiet death.

Sabra sports cars

COUNTRY OF ORIGIN
Israel

Sabra

YEARS IN PRODUCTION
1961–1968

NUMBER MADE
150

SPECIAL REMARKS
Reliant sold one hundred complete cars and fifty Sabre kits to Autocars Co. Ltd. in Haifa, Israel. The four-cylinder engines were from the Ford Consul and produced 74 or 91 SAE.

Salmson

Salmson built a solid reputation before World War II for small motor sport cars and sporting saloon cars. The cars were built at Billancourt. The company restarted production after the war with their 1939 models but there was virtually no demand for these expensive cars, which quickly put the company in difficulties.

The best seller was the S4 which was available with two different four-cylinder engines: 1,730 cc/50 bhp at 4,200 rpm, and 2,320 cc/70 bhp at 3,700 rpm. Both engines had cylinder heads with twin overhead camshafts. The first post-war French design did not appear until 1951.
This, the Randonnée, was a large, luxurious car, that led Salmson to create the 2300 Sport.

Salmson sports cars

COUNTRY OF ORIGIN
France

If there is no heater to keep the windscreen clear, open the roof. This is a 1949 Salmson S4.

The Salmson S4 of 1946 was not an old-fashioned car. It had a twin-cam engine, independent front suspension, but only mechanical brakes until 1952.

Salmson S4

YEARS IN PRODUCTION
1946–1952

NUMBER MADE
2,983

SPECIAL REMARKS
The four-cylinder engines of the Salmson S4 were sportive enough but the body was too heavily built. The convertible weighed about 2,640 lb (1,200 kg) and had a top speed of 81 mph (130 km/hour). This was quite an achievement for a car with only 70 bhp.

Salmson 2300 Sport

YEARS IN PRODUCTION
1953–1957

NUMBER MADE
209

SPECIAL REMARKS
The 2300 Sport was a final attempt at survival by Salmson.

It is a shame the attempt failed, for with a 110 bhp 2.3 four-cylinder tuned engine, the car was fast enough at 112 mph (180 km/hour).

Sbarro

Franco Sbarro moved in 1957 from Italy to Switzerland when he was eighteen years old. Until 1967, he worked as a mechanic, but then set-up in business on his own account. At first he modified Ford GT40 cars for use on the road and built specials that were based on Porsche 908 racing cars. Sbarro then built a Lola T70 for Eric Broadley in 1968 and went on to build thirteen of them. He also exhibited at the Geneva Salon for the first time in 1968 and has remained a permanent feature at the show ever since, with a stand always more extensive than the previous year. Sbarro has shown cars with Ferrari engines but also one with two NSU Ro80 Wankel engines joined together and there has also been a "Bugatti Royale" which was even more impressive than the originals from Mulhouse.

This particular Sbarro car was powered by two V-8 engines mounted one behind the other. All his prototypes are built to order but that does not mean he cannot build cars in small series production. Several hundred of his replica BMW 328 were sold.

Sbarro became internationally known for his BMW 328 replica, which was widely exported.

Sbarro sports cars

COUNTRY OF ORIGIN
Switzerland

Sbarro BMW 328

YEARS IN PRODUCTION
1973–present day

NUMBER MADE
Unknown

Eric Broadley, who built the Lola T70, sold Sbarro sufficient parts to build 13 of them. Customers have to find their own engines.

SPECIAL REMARKS
The Sbarro BMW 328 is of course a replica but so accurate, in spite of its glass-reinforced body shell, that BMW permitted their famous blue and white emblem to be used. The mechanical parts were derived from the BMW 2002 ti.

Sbarro Lola T70

YEARS IN PRODUCTION
1974–present day

NUMBER MADE
Unknown

SPECIAL REMARKS
The Lola T70 can be supplied with a Chevrolet or Ford V-8, or V-12 engine from Ferrari. This Sbarro model has a delivery period of eight to ten months.

Sbarro Ford GT40

YEARS IN PRODUCTION
1965–unknown

The Ford GT40 is available either as a replica shell or a complete car, identical with the original, with chassis number. All the mechanical parts of the complete car are interchangeable with the Ford factory cars.

NUMBER MADE
Unknown

SPECIAL REMARKS
The replica GT40 is built on De Tomaso Pantera underframe. If the client wants a GT40 that is identical with the original, Sbarro has sufficient parts to built entire cars to the original specification. In this case, the car is provided with a certificate of authentication.

Scarab

Scarab was the business of Lance Reventlow, son of American millionairess Barbara Hutton who was married to the former owner of Woolworth Stores. Reventlow started building sports and racing cars in 1958 and even had one attempt with a Grand Prix car. Scarab cars were powered by converted Chevrolet V-8 engines

This is one of the few Scarabs, in a museum at Cunningham in California.

and the final ones of 1962 had the engine mounted in front of the rear axle. Reventlow was killed, aged 37, in an aircraft crash on July 26, 1972.

Scarab sports cars

COUNTRY OF ORIGIN
USA

The Scarab Chevrolet is a rare car, especially in Europe, where this car competed in a race for historic cars at the Nürburgring in 1989.

Scarab Chevrolet

YEARS IN PRODUCTION
1958–1962

NUMBER MADE
Unknown

SPECIAL REMARKS
Scarabs were extremely fast, with their highly-tuned Chevrolet V-8 engines. Chuck Daigh and Lance Reventlow won many races in one in the late 1950s, including the Times GP of Riverside in 1958, where they beat a 4 litre Ferrari driven by Phil Hill.

Siata

The Siata company name was an abbreviation of Societa Italiana Applicazione Transformazione Automobilistiche, which built specials, mainly using Fiat parts, between 1926 and 1970. The small factory was flattened by Allied bombing during World War II but the firm was back in business almost immediately the war was over. They made a convertible based on the Fiat 500 Topolino, known as the Siata Amica. In 1950, came the Daina, based on the running gear of a Fiat 1400. When Fiat introduced their famous and notorious sports car with a V-8 engine, Siata built specials based on the running gear of this very fast car. Siata perished though as so many before them. The company was too small to survive. Fiats were customised to look more

This is how a Siata raced in America, with a strong roll-over bar. Note the exhaust which exits beneath the right-hand door.

A Siata with a Fiat V-8 engine and sports car body by Stabilimenti Farina.

attractive, particularly by adding more chrome and attractive wheel covers but finally there was no money in this and the company was forced to close in 1970.

Siata sports cars

COUNTRY OF ORIGIN
Italy

Siata Amica

YEARS IN PRODUCTION
1948–1952

NUMBER MADE
Unknown

SPECIAL REMARKS
Siata built the Amica two-seater convertible based on the Fiat 500B Topolino. The four-cylinder engine was bored out to 569 cc and given a special cylinder head to deliver 20 bhp.

Siata Daina

YEARS IN PRODUCTION
1950–1958

NUMBER MADE
Unknown

SPECIAL REMARKS
When Fiat introduced the 1400, Siata were able to use it as the foundation for their Daina. The cubic capacity of the cylinders was increased to produce more brake horse power and specialists such as Bertone and Farina ensured the bodies were attractive.

The Daina, seen here as a Farina bodied 2 + 2, had a tuned Fiat 1400 engine with large twin Weber carburettors.

The interior of a Daina was just like that of an ordinary Fiat.

The Daina also looked elegant with its hood up

Siata with V-8 engine.

Siata 208 S

YEARS IN PRODUCTION
1953–1954

NUMBER MADE
56

SPECIAL REMARKS
Siata developed a new tubular chassis for the 208S in which the new Fiat V-8 engine or American V-8 power unit of the customer's choice could be installed, usually a Chrysler. These cars were given fine bodies and both the coupés and convertibles were very sporty.

Siata Spring

YEARS IN PRODUCTION
1967–1970

NUMBER MADE
Unknown

SPECIAL REMARKS
Siata introduced the Spring in a final effort to survive. The nostalgic car was based on the Fiat 850.
When Siata went bust in 1970, Orsa bought the rights to continue making the Spring and did so until 1975.

A classic form and up-to-date technology: the Siata 850 Spring Spyder used parts from the Fiat 850.

Simca sports cars

COUNTRY OF ORIGIN
France

Simca 8 Sport

YEARS IN PRODUCTION
1949–1951

NUMBER MADE
Unknown

SPECIAL REMARKS
The Simca 8 Sport was launched in 1949. The body came from Facel Metallon company which later built their own cars under the Facel name (q.v.). The 1,221 cc four-cylinder engine developed 50 bhp at 4,800 rpm.

Simca

The Société Industrielle de Mécanique et Carosserie Automobile, better known as Simca, was founded in 1935. This French company built Fiats under licence and started in 1946 where they left off before the war, producing the Fiat 500 as the Simca Cinq. Next they built the 1100 with a

four-door body without door posts. The Cinq and 1100 were the final models to look like Fiats with following cars being their own designs, such as the renowned Aronde range, the Vedette, the 1000, and all the other Simcas that were sold in such large volume.

The Simca 8 coupé was a major surprise. The 2 + 2 had very little room in the back.

Simca 1000 Coupé

YEARS IN PRODUCTION
1962–1971

Bertone's styling influence is clearly apparent.

The Simca 1000/1200 with power of 52 or later 80 bhp had a top speed of 100 or 106 mph (160 or 170 km/hour).

Not many specialist car body builders used the 1000 Coupé as a basis for a special. Sibona & Basano are one of the few who did.

NUMBER MADE
24,752

SPECIAL REMARKS
The Simca 1000 appeared as a four-door saloon in 1961 and then as a sports coupé a year later. The body was designed and built by Bertone and shipped by train to France. When 10,011 had been sold, the 1200 was introduced in 1967, with a 1,204 cc engine instead of the 944 cc motor.

When MG developed the MG TC in 1946, Singer brought out an improved version of the Nine, known as the SM (Singer Motors) Roadster. The SM Roadster had a bigger engine, independent front suspension, and hydraulic brakes. This was to be Singer's final sports car.

The company was taken over by Rootes Brothers in 1956, which in turn sold to Chrysler in 1967. The Singer name was not used any more from then on.

Singer

Singer had built up a good reputation as a maker of cycles when they gambled on making their first car in 1905. Singer cars were of good quality, comparable with Rover and Wolseley. In addition to family saloons, the company also made sports cars. The Singer Le Mans was a formidable competitor on the circuits in the 1930s and the company developed the Singer Nine in 1939 to compete with the MG TB.

The same motor was used in the Singer Nine Roadster that was used in the HRG sports car (q.v.). The four-cylinder engine was developed in 1927.

Singer sports cars

COUNTRY OF ORIGIN
Great Britain

Singer Nine Roadster

YEARS IN PRODUCTION
1946–1952

NUMBER MADE
6,890

SPECIAL REMARKS
The Singer Nine had a 1,074 cc engine with overhead camshaft, which was quite special for its time. The power was 36 bhp at 5,000 rpm.

Singer SM Roadster

YEARS IN PRODUCTION
1951–1955

NUMBER MADE
3,440

SPECIAL REMARKS
The SM Roadster had a 1,497 cc four-cylinder engine that initially gave 49 bhp but this was increased in 1952 to 59 bhp at 4,800 rpm.

The SM Roadster was almost identical externally to its predecessor. The most obvious difference was that the wheels which were now closed.

Skoda

Skoda began making cars in Mlada Boleslav in the former Czechoslovakia in 1923 and in 1925 they took Laurin & Klement over, gaining in one go the experience this business had acquired in

building cars since 1906. Skoda made cars in each price range and produced Hispano-Suiza cars under licence for the very rich. Although the factories were destroyed by the Germans at the end of World War II, production re-started in 1946 with the first private cars. The convertibles were soundly built but were hardly sports cars.

The Felicia of 1958 had difficult achieving 81 mph (130 km/hour) in spite of its modern overhead valve 1,221 cc engine that developed 48 bhp at 5,800 rpm.
The Skoda 1000MB saloon with rear engine appeared in 1964 and was followed by a sporting version in 1970. This 110R coupé won many Eastern European rallies.

Skoda sports cars

COUNTRY OF ORIGIN
Former Czechoslovakia/Czech Republic

Skoda Felicia

YEARS IN PRODUCTION
1958–1964

NUMBER MADE
15,864

SPECIAL REMARKS
Skoda's "sports cars", the Felicia, was based on the Octavia. The car was known after 1961 as the Felicia Super. The Super had a 1,221 cc engine instead of the earlier 1,089 cc. A hard-top version was available as an option at additional cost.

The Felicia was indestructible but no racing car with a top speed of 81 mph (130 km/hour).

The water-cooled four-cylinder engine of the 110R coupé was mounted in the rear and had a capacity of 1,107 cc, developing 52 bhp at 4,600. The top speed was 91 mph (145 km/hour).

Skoda 110 R Coupé

YEARS IN PRODUCTION
1970–1980

NUMBER MADE
56,902

SPECIAL REMARKS
Skoda cars were regarded as heavy, well-built, and reliable. This image changed with the 1000MB. The coupé was intended to improve the image but it was only partially successful in doing so.

Spatz

German engineer Harald Friedrich started to build sports cars in 1956 which were intended to cost less than the cheapest Volkswagen Beetle. The new car, which was originally designed by Egon Brütsch as a three-wheeler, was known as a Spatz.

The glass-reinforced polyester body was designed by Prof. Hans Ledwinka. The 200 cc engine was mounted in front of the rear axle. The seat was 57 in (145 cm) wide, giving room for three people and the car had no doors. This presented no difficulties in good weather but when the hood was on, getting in was quite a problem.

Friedrich resigned from the company in 1957 and his partner, the motorcycle manufacturer, Victoria, continued making the Spatz but with two doors.

In fine weather it was easy to climb in the Spatz but very difficult when it rained.

Spatz sports cars

COUNTRY OF ORIGIN
Germany

Spatz

YEARS IN PRODUCTION
1955–1958

NUMBER MADE
859

SPECIAL REMARKS
A further 729 cars were sold with the Victoria name between 1957–1958. This car had a 248 cc instead of 200 cc two-stroke engine and a five-speed gearbox instead of the earlier four-speed box.

A Spatz was a mere 990 lb (450 kg), did 57 mpg (20 km/litre) (2-stroke) with a top speed of 47 mph (75 km/hour).

Standard sports cars

COUNTRY OF ORIGIN
Great Britain

Standard Eight

YEARS IN PRODUCTION
1945–1948

NUMBER MADE
Unknown

SPECIAL REMARKS
The Standard Eight was given a four-speed gear box after the war but the engine remained a side-valve affair. This achieved the minimal power of 28 bhp.

Standard

The last Standard left the factory in 1964 when it had become part of British Leyland. The former owner, Sir John Black, had sold the company to them in 1961. He bought it for little money in 1945.

The Standard factory in Coventry was set-up in 1903 and had built robust cars with outstanding engines. William Lyons used Standard engines in his first sports cars, the SS and Jaguar.

The Standard Eight was a small car at 139 in (353 cm). It was a tight fit for four people.

The Standard Eight dashboard: the winder in the centre opened the front windscreen slightly. The two round knobs operated the windscreen wipers.

Stanga

Sandro Stanga's Officina Meccanica della Stanga in Manerbio, Italy became famous overnight when his small sports cars were so successful in the Mille Miglia. The cars entered in the 1950 and 1951 races were powered by Giannini engines, and these achieved good 750 cc class results in the Mille Miglia and other races. Carrozzeria Motto built a coupé based on a Stanga with a Fiat V-8 engine. At least one car had a Fiat 600 engine installed.s

Stanga sports cars

COUNTRY OF ORIGIN
Italy

Stanga 750

YEARS IN PRODUCTION
1949–1951

NUMBER MADE
Unknown

SPECIAL REMARKS
The Stanga 750 had a twin-cam engine by Giannini.

A Stanga 750 in its element, during the 1997 Mille Miglia Historica.

Stanguellini

Stanguellini became famous for his Formula Junior cars which were unbeatable in the 1950s and still perform well in today's historical

classes. The business in Modena, that is still a Fiat dealer, made sports cars as well as racing cars. Stanguellini used Fiat parts of course. Vittorio Stanguellini began building cars before World War II after he had taken over his father's garage in 1932.

After the war, Stanguellini built sporting coupés and convertibles using Fiat 1100 parts. The bodies of his cars were built by Zagato and Bertone. Stanguellini also built many 750 cc class cars with twin-cam engines.

Stanguellini sports cars

COUNTRY OF ORIGIN
Italy

Stanguellini 750

YEARS IN PRODUCTION
1947–1955

NUMBER MADE
Unknown

SPECIAL REMARKS
Beneath the aluminium bonnet of a Stanguellini 750 was a four-cylinder engine originating from the Fiat 500 Topolino.

The engine was bored out to 745 cc and equipped with a twin-cam cylinder head and twin Weber carburettors.

A Stanguellini 750 on its way to the circuit, The cylinder head and twin camshafts were of aluminium and the compression ratio was 10:1. The power was 60 bhp at 7,500 rpm.

The 1997 Mille Miglia Historica with a Stanguellini 1100 at a control point. The car had a tubular chassis, with its 1,089 cc engine producing 90 bhp at 7,000 rpm.

Stanguellini 1100

YEARS IN PRODUCTION
1939–unknown

NUMBER MADE
Unknown

SPECIAL REMARKS
Stanguellini had already built his first specials using the Fiat 1100 engine before World War II. In 1946 he picked up where he left off, producing superb sports and racing cars, including fine coupés and convertibles. Most of the bodies were built by Bertone.

The dashboard of a Stanguellini 1100.

Studebaker

Brothers Henry and Clem Studebaker began the adventure with cars in 1902. The business had built wagons and other horse-drawn vehicles since 1852. Studebaker was well ahead of the times and in 1930, they were the fourth largest car maker in the United States in turnover, behind Ford, Chevrolet, and Buick. Studebaker were one of the few manufacturers to launch a new model in 1946. This was a car designed by Raymond Loewy, famous for his designs for the Coca-Cola bottle. Studebaker cars had always had a sporting appearance and the Avanti was a true sports car. This was also designed by Loewy and the 2 + 2 was required to save Studebaker from going under but failed to do so. This failure was not caused by any lack of quality on the part of the Avanti, which had a fine glass-fibre reinforced polyester body that was powered by a 4,736 or 4,973 cc V-8 engine with or without turbocharger. The power varied from 240–335 bhp. The turbocharged car had a top speed of 187 mph (300 km/hour). In spite of its exceptional models, Studebaker was unable to hold its own against the "Big Three".
A merger with Packard in 1964 was no more successful in staving off the end and the South Fork, Indiana, factory closed in 1964. The Canadian factory suffered the same fate two years later.

The Avanti had no radiator grille, in common with most cars of the era.

A dashboard like a light aircraft, without unnecessary luxury.

Studebaker sports cars

COUNTRY OF ORIGIN
USA

Studebaker Avanti

YEARS IN PRODUCTION
1963–1964

NUMBER MADE
4,643

SPECIAL REMARKS
The Avanti was available with either the Jet Thrust V-8 engine or Super Jet Thrust with a Paxton turbocharger.
With turbo and quadruple carburettors, the car accelerated from 0–60 mph in about 6 seconds (0–100 km/hour in 6.7 seconds).

Stutz

Harry C. Stutz ran a car parts company when he built a car in 1911 to compete in the first Indianapolis 500 mile race. This car was very successful and became the forerunner of famous models such as the Stutz Bearcat. The company went bust during the Great Depression but the name was not forgotten. On the contrary, many Americans regard Stutz as the only true sports car to be built in the United States. It is not surprising therefore that the name reappeared when the demand for "classic" cars increased. Thus Stutz Motor Corp. launched a Stutz Blackhawk once more in 1970. The body was designed by the famous designer, Virgil Exner (ex-Chrysler) and the chassis was from Pontiac. The car was assembled in Italy. The American public reacted enthusiastically to the car with Elvis Presley and Mohammed Ali being among the first customers. The company changed hands a couple of time but continued making cars until 1989.

The narrow tyres and small rear lights were not unusual in 1963.

Everything that glitters is gold in Curt Jürgens' car.

This car used to belong to German film star Curt Jürgens. Such cars cost almost £60,000 in Europe so not surprisingly they are very rare.

Stutz sports cars

COUNTRY OF ORIGIN
USA

Stutz Blackhawk

YEARS IN PRODUCTION
1970–1989

NUMBER MADE
Unknown

SPECIAL REMARKS
The new Stutz Blackhawk was launched in January 1970 in the foyer of the famous Waldorf Astoria Hotel in New York. The car was 227 in (577 cm) long and 79 in wide (200 cm).

Sunbeam

John Marston was already known in 1887 for his cycles and built his first car in 1899. Several more prototypes followed but production did not get under way until 1905 with the foundation of the Sunbeam Motor Car Co. Ltd. in

Wolverhampton. Sunbeam mainly built family cars but were also known for their sports cars and Grand Prix racers (the latter between 1911–1925). Sunbeam amalgamated with Talbot and Darracq in 1920 and was taken over by Rootes Brothers in 1935. This business was in its turn taken over by Chrysler in 1964, who allowed the marque to disappear in 1974.

The first post-war cars were Sunbeam-Talbot badged touring versions of Rootes Hillmans and Humbers. In 1953, Rootes again produced a Sunbeam.

Sunbeam cars were better than average quality but also more expensive than their competitors. The Sunbeam-Talbot Ten had the Hillman Minx 1,184 cc 40 bhp engine and the Two Litre had the Humber Hawk 1,944 cc 57 bhp engine. Cary Grant and Grace Kelly drove a Sunbeam Alpine in the classic film of the era, To Catch a Thief. The model has its name to thank on victory by

The Sunbeam Tiger with its Ford V-8 engine was aimed at the US market.

The Sunbeam Stiletto was made from 1966–1972. It stood out because of its twin headlights and vinyl roof. The 875 cc engine had an overhead camshaft and produced 60 bhp at 6,000 rpm.

Stirling Moss in the Rally of the Alps in 1952. Subsequent attractive sports cars were also built such as the later Sunbeam Alpine and Tiger.

The Tiger was powered by a 4,260 or 4,727 cc Ford V-8 engine which delivered either 164 or 200 bhp. The same engine was also used in the AC Cobra.

The top speed of the Sunbeam-Talbot Two Litre was only 72 mph (115 km/hour). The car took almost thirty seconds to reach 60 mph (96 km/hour).

Sunbeam sports cars

COUNTRY OF ORIGIN
Great Britain

Sunbeam-Talbot Two Litre

YEARS IN PRODUCTION
1945–1948

The side-valve engine of the Two Litre was simple for the do-it-yourself mechanic. Everything was easy to get at and nothing was complex.

NUMBER MADE
Unknown

SPECIAL REMARKS
The Two Litre was developed before World War II and in 1948 still had a rigid back and front axle. The roadster had the dished doors of a true sports car.

Sunbeam Mark III

YEARS IN PRODUCTION
1954–1957

NUMBER MADE
Unknown

An electrically-operated overdrive was available for the first time in the Mark II for an additional £64. That was relatively expensive for a car that cost £1,198 in 1954.

The Alpine had those things that were missing from the MGA: wind-up windows, comfortable seats, and 13 in wheels instead of 15 in ones. The MGA though could reach 112 mph (180 km/hour) compared with the Alpine's 100 mph (160 km/hour).

SPECIAL REMARKS
The Talbot name disappeared for a time in Britain in 1955, so that the Mark III was just a Sunbeam, whereas the Mark II was a Sunbeam-Talbot. The power-unit was a 2,267 cc overhead valve motor that produced 81 bhp at 4,200 rpm.

Sunbeam Alpine

YEARS IN PRODUCTION
1959–1968

NUMBER MADE
69,251

SPECIAL REMARKS
The new Sunbeam Alpine that became so famous was launched in the summer of 1959. The car was a two-seater with bucket seats and limited baggage space. The 1,494 cc four-cylinder engine produced 78 bhp at 5,300 rpm. The Mk II of 1960, and Mk III of 1963 had 1,592 cc engines.

The Tiger Mk I (1964–1966) had a "small" V-8 engine that produced 164 bhp at 4,400 rpm. The Mk II had a 4.7 litre engine that gave 200 bhp at 4,400 rpm.

Sunbeam Alpine Tiger

YEARS IN PRODUCTION
1964–1968

NUMBER MADE
7,066

SPECIAL REMARKS
The body of the Tiger is the same as the four-cylinder Alpine but the V-8 engine, gear box, and back axle were from Ford of Detroit. The car was less suitable for competition on the track than the AC Cobra but performed well at rallying.

Sunbeam Harrington

YEARS IN PRODUCTION
1961–1963

NUMBER MADE
400

SPECIAL REMARKS
The Harrington was an Alpine with a fixed plastic roof and more highly-tuned engine. Car body builder Harrington was responsible for the body additions and George Hartwell boosted the engine from 90 to 104 bhp at 6,000 rpm.

The Harrington could be recognised by the front end.

The Sunbeam Rapier had a 1,725 cc four-cylinder engine giving 110 bhp at 5,200 rpm. This coupé was sold from 1967–1976.

There was room for two adults in the back of the Sunbeam Harrington. The final 250 of these cars were sold as Harrington Le Mans after the car performed well at this circuit in 1962.

248

The Talbot Lago Record had a wheelbase of 123 in (313 cm). The Lago Grand Sport was 19 in (48 cm) shorter.

Talbot

Clement-Talbot was a British firm, based in France that was founded in 1902. It was taken over by Darracq, also British owned in 1919 and the group bought Sunbeam in 1925. When Rootes purchased the group in 1935, Antonio Lago, a Venetian living in France, bought Darracq and the cars made by Lago were sold as Darracq in Britain and Talbot in France.

The Darracq name disappeared after World War II and the cars were known as Talbot-Lago and also Lago-Talbot. When Lago took over Darracq, he set about making Grand Prix cars but could not compete with the big names but it managed to win three immediate post-war Grand Prix because the cars were reliable.

A Talbot-Lago also won Le Mans in 1951, was second in 1952, and almost won in 1952. The Suresnes factory produced extremely expensive luxury and sports cars but the demand dwindled for such cars. The company was taken over by

The Swiss car body builder Hermann Graber supplied the body for a number of Talbots. This example is from the 1940s.

Simca in 1958 for virtually nothing and the marque disappeared, although it reappeared for a time under Chrysler.

Talbot sports cars

COUNTRY OF ORIGIN
France

Talbot-Lago Record

YEARS IN PRODUCTION
1946–1952

SPECIAL REMARKS
The Lago Record was very similar to pre-war cars but had independent front suspension. The 4,482 cc six-cylinder engine produced 170 bhp at 4,000 rpm. In 1947, the Lago Grand Sport could be ordered with a 190 bhp engine with triple carburettors.

Talbot 2500 Lago Sport

YEARS IN PRODUCTION
1955–1956

NUMBER MADE
54

SPECIAL REMARKS
To keep the price of these expensive cars down, the 2500 Sport was developed with a four-cylinder twin-cam engine of 2,491 cc, giving 120 bhp at 5,000 rpm. The 2 + 2 coupé had a normal four-speed gearbox in contrast to the larger car which had a Wilson pre-selector.

The Talbot-Lago 2500 Sport had a twin-cam four-cylinder engine; these were high-mounted but not overhead camshafts.

The Talbot-Lago 2500 Sport was a two-seater with space behind the bucket seats for luggage.

The Talbot-Lago 2500 became the America after 1957. It was the last real Talbot. The marque re-appeared in 1979 for a time after the Chrysler concern took over in

Talbot Lago America

YEARS IN PRODUCTION
1957–1958

NUMBER MADE
12 and 10

SPECIAL REMARKS
The four-cylinder engine of the 2500 Sport gave lots of problems, so that it was decided to build a better car using the 2,476 cc BMW V-8 engine that gave 125 bhp. Concurrent with this, the car changed its name to Talbot-Lago America. The final ten, which were built after Simca took over, therefore had the 2,351 cc Simca Vedette V-8 engine.

Tatra

The first cars were built by the Nesseldorfer Wagenbaubafrik in 1897. The model was known as President and had a twin-cylinder 5 hp Benz engine. When the borders were redrawn following the Armistice at the World War I, Nesseldorfer was no longer a part of Austria but now formed part of Czechoslovakia. The factory started to co-operate with is former competitors in the same region of Ringhoffer, to form Ringhoffer-Tatra AG. This new company built

Now that the borders are open between the Czech Republic, Slovakia, and the rest of Europe, Tatra T602 cars can be seen participating in races for historic cars.

the final Nesseldorfer models in 1923. From 1926, a new range was introduced under the Tatra name. Hans Ledwinka, who had developed the President in 1897, remained the most important engineer at Tatra. He specialised in streamlined cars with water-cooled rear-engines. Under his leadership, fine cars such as the Tatra 87 and Tatraplan were built. Tatra only built prototypes of sports cars and these cars were only to be seen in rallies after World War II, with the exception of the Tatraplan T602 Sport. Until seventy days before the Czechoslovakian Grand Prix of 1949, this car only existed on paper yet it was ready to race and was driven by Bruno Sojka into ninth place. A number of cars had 1,951 cc four-cylinder air-cooled engines delivering 75–84 bhp. At least one of them was supplied with a V-8 engine used in the Tatra 603.

Tatra sports cars

COUNTRY OF ORIGIN
Former Czechoslovakia/Czech Republic

Tatra Tatraplan T602

YEARS IN PRODUCTION
1949–1950

NUMBER MADE
Unknown

SPECIAL REMARKS
The 112 mph (180 km/hour) Tatra weighed 1,650 lb (750 kg) and had an aluminium body. The engine, with four Solex carburettors, is mounted in front of the back axle.

Thunderbird

There are a number of outstanding moments in the history of the Ford Motor Company, such as the Model-T Ford, which was built in many countries between 1908 and 1925, and which sold 15,000,000 in the United States alone. There was the launch in 1932 of the famous Ford V-8 engine, which cost less then the price of a competitor's six-cylinder engine, and the Mustang that broke all sales records. Thoroughly trouncing Chevrolet following their launch in 1953 of the Corvette would probably rate with Ford as a high-point. At first the Corvette did not sell well (see Chevrolet). Ford's introduction of the 1955 Thunderbird on September 9, 1954 must also rank highly with the company.

During the next five years, these were the sales figures:

	Number sold
1955	16.155
1956	15.631
1957	21.380
1958	37.892
1959	67.456
1960	92.843

For the first year the Thunderbird was in production, it was a two-seater but subsequently it offered ample space for four persons. The second series were nicknamed "Squarebird" because of the angular lines of the new body. The "Cigar Shape" appeared in 1961 and was made until 1963.

The body styling changed about every second year and from 1964 onwards, the cars were no longer sports cars but luxury cars to ride the dead straight highways of America. They were quite unsuitable for motor sport.

Ford announced in March 1997 they were stopping production of the Thunderbird in 1998. Enthusiasts are likely to be interested in the early Thunderbirds for many years to come.

Ford's Thunderbird was a great success unlike Chevrolet's Corvette. This is a 1956 T-bird.

Thunderbird sports cars

COUNTRY OF ORIGIN
USA

Thunderbird Two-Seater

YEARS IN PRODUCTION
1955–1957

NUMBER MADE
53,166

The dashboard of the 1956 T-bird. The radio only receives medium wave.

The new owner of the first T-birds could choose a V-6 or V-8.

The hardtop was available with or without "portholes".

The T-birds, which have become classics, caused the makers of the Corvette some grey hairs. The original T-bird was available from day one with either a V-6 or V-8 engine.

By the final model, the customer could choose between a 4,457, 4,785, or 5,112 cc engine.

Thunderbird Squarebird

YEARS IN PRODUCTION
1958–1960

NUMBER MADE
198,191

SPECIAL REMARKS
Enthusiasts insisted that this Thunderbird was no longer a sports car. Perhaps they were right but the sales figures prove the car's popularity.

Although the convertible was only $283 more than the coupé, Ford sold 57,195 hard-tops against 10,261 soft-tops in 1959.

A 1960 Squarebird. The car was a disappointment for the sports car enthusiast but financially successful for Ford.

Thunderbird Cigar Shape

YEARS IN PRODUCTION
1961–1963

NUMBER MADE
214,375

SPECIAL REMARKS
The third generation of T-birds were only available with a V-8 engine: 6,384 cc with a choice of 304 or 344 bhp. There were four versions to choose from: coupé, convertible, Landau hard-top, and roadster convertible with removable tonneau cover for the rear seats.

Thunderbird 1964-1966

YEARS IN PRODUCTION
1964–1966

NUMBER MADE
226,613

SPECIAL REMARKS
The demand for convertibles dwindled further. Americans would rather drive in a closed car with air conditioning than in an open car. In 1965, 68,126 closed cars were sold compared with 6,846 open T-birds.

The front ends in particular were constantly updated. This is the appearance of the 1964–66 T-bird.

Thunderbird 1967-1971

YEARS IN PRODUCTION
1967–1971

NUMBER MADE
201,037

SPECIAL REMARKS
The body was completely renewed for this model and the headlights now retracted into the

A 1968 Landau model with the headlights retracted into the grill. Note the "pram stays" on the vinyl roof.

radiator grille. No convertibles were built of the 1967–1971 model.

Thunderbird 1972-1976

YEARS IN PRODUCTION
1972–1976

NUMBER MADE
299,146

SPECIAL REMARKS
Although this car was still known as a Thunderbird, it had no relationship with the original two-seater. The wheelbase was now 120 in (306 cm) compared with 102 in (259 cm) in 1955, and the overall length was 219 in (556 cm) instead of 185 in (470 cm).

Thurner

Insurance salesman Rudolf Thurner started making cars in a former fabric mill in Bernbeuren in Germany in 1969. His cars were predominantly sports cars with glass-fibre reinforced polyester bodies and side-lifting "winged" doors, using shortened floor pans from the NSU 1200. The engines were also from NSU and mounted in the rear of the car. There was also a motor sport version with tweaked NSU engine with fuel injection that delivered 135 bhp.

Since the cost of this car was DM30,000, which was twice the price of the standard Thurner, demand was minimal. Thurners with a VW Beetle floor pan and Porsche engine never got beyond prototypes.

Compare the 1973 T-bird with the first two-seaters. This car weighs almost 2 tons (2,235 kg) compared with 3,542 lb (1,610 kg) in 1955. It is 219 in (556 cm) compared with 185 in (470 cm) in 1955.

The performance of the Thurner with its 112 mph (180 km/hour) top speed from its 1,177 cc/65 bhp at 5,500 rpm NSU engine was good. The engine was easy to maintain for those days.

Thurner sports cars

COUNTRY OF ORIGIN
Germany

Thurner RS

YEARS IN PRODUCTION
1969–1974

NUMBER MADE
121

SPECIAL REMARKS
Thurner should have managed to sell more of his cars with their robust tubular chassis, first-class engine, and beautiful body. In 1972, the RS cost a mere DM14,450.

Tojeiro

John Tojeiro was born at Estoril in Portugal, the son of a Portuguese father and English mother. When his father died, his mother took her young children back to Britain and Tojeiro later studied at university in Britain and flew for the RAF.

His career as a builder of special car chassis started in 1951 and he sold his chassis as a kit

The uprated MG TD engine in a Tojeiro with twin SU carburettors for the right mixture.

A 1953 Tojeiro with an MG engine performing well in a race for historic cars.

for customers to build themselves but also sold completed cars. His Tojeiro-Bristol, with a body closely resembling the Ferrari 166 Mille Miglia, was the basis for the subsequent AC Ace (q.v.) from which the famous Cobra was developed. Tojeiro was paid £5 for every Ace and Cobra that Ace built. Tojeiro used Jaguar, Bristol, MG, and Ford Anglia engines.

Tojeiro sports cars

COUNTRY OF ORIGIN
Great Britain

The cockpit instrumentation is typical of the era in this Tojeiro-MG.

Tojeiro-MG

YEARS IN PRODUCTION
1951–1953

NUMBER MADE
Unknown

SPECIAL REMARKS
The best-known of Tojeiro's cars was his Tojeiro-MG. This car also had a body that was clearly copied from Touring of Milan.

Toyota

Toyoda (with a "D") was a company making textile machinery when it turned to making cars in 1933. A number of prototypes were developed before production got under way in 1936 and was soon hindered by World War II. After the war, Toyota (with a "T") started up again but the demand was considerable for trucks at that time and so it was not until 1962 that Toyota showed a sports car.

Like all the Japanese cars of the time, it was a small car with a 700 cc twin-cylinder engine. There were no doors and to enter, the roof had to be slid back. This car went into production with a 790 cc engine in 1965 and since that time Toyota has always had sports cars in its range. In the 1965 Tokyo Motor Show, Toyota revealed a 2000 GT which was an attractive 2 + 2 with twin camshafts, that became famous through the Bond film You only live twice.

Toyota's first sports car in 1962 had a twin-cylinder 700 cc engine. The two-seater got a larger engine before the year was out.

The Toyota 2000 GT was specially developed for the American market. When the headlights were too low for US regulations, the car had two "closed eyes".

The GT Liftback of 1975 with a 1,968 cc twin-cam engine that gave 130 bhp at 6,000 rpm.

The Celica, which has become a permanent feature in car showrooms, was introduced in 1970.

Toyota sports cars

COUNTRY OF ORIGIN
Japan

Toyota Sports 800

YEARS IN PRODUCTION
1965–1969

NUMBER MADE
3,131

SPECIAL REMARKS
The air-cooled twin-cylinder horizontally opposed engine produced 45 bhp at 5,400 rpm that produced a top speed of 94 mph (150 km/hour). Part of the roof could be removed. When Porsche adopted this type of roof in 1967, it became known as a "Targa" roof.

Toyota 2000 GT

YEARS IN PRODUCTION
1966–1970

NUMBER MADE
339

SPECIAL REMARKS
Count Albrecht Goertz, who designed the BMW

The 2000 GT was also available in a motor sport version with a 2-litre engine that delivered 200 instead of 150 bhp.

503 and 507, was also responsible for the body of the 2000 GT. Beneath the bonnet was a 1,988 cc six-cylinder twin-cam engine that produced 150 bhp at 6,600 rpm.

Toyota Celica

YEARS IN PRODUCTION
1970–present day

The Celica was available in three models in 1970: the standard ST, GT with a more powerful engine, and cheaper LT that had fewer accessories and a four-speed gearbox.

Toyota Celica 1600 ST hard-top coupé of 1973, with ST meaning standard model.

NUMBER MADE
Unknown

SPECIAL REMARKS
The Celica was introduced in 1970. Initially, it was a sporting version of the Carina but it soon became a separate model and was sold from the beginning with three different four-cylinder engines: 1,407 cc/86 SAE at 6,000 rpm, 1,588 cc/100 or 115 SAE.

Trident

Trevor Fiore, who used his Italian mother's name instead of Frost, is a British designer who was commissioned by TVR to design them a car with a prototype body by Fissore in Italy. Soon after the car was introduced to much acclaim at Geneva in 1965, TVR ran into financial difficulties. One of the TVR dealers, Bill Last took the project over and the Trident was developed further under him. The car was built from 1967 on an Austin-Healey chassis and then from 1967 on that of a Triumph TR6. The body was of glass-reinforced polyester and the engine was usually an American Ford V-8.
The car was also available with a British Ford V-6, six-cylinder engine from the Triumph TR6 or a Chrysler V-8.
The energy crisis did not help sales and the business was forced to close down in 1975, when about 130 Tridents had been built.

Trident sports cars

The original Tridents were on a TVR Grantura Mk II chassis, which was a sound base for the heavy American V-8 engine.

COUNTRY OF ORIGIN
Great Britain

Trevor Fiore designed the Trident and his friend Fissore built the prototypes in Turin.

Trident Clipper

YEARS IN PRODUCTION
1966–1975

NUMBER MADE
Unknown

SPECIAL REMARKS
Fissore built several prototypes in aluminium. After Bill Last took over, the cars were given glass-reinforced polyester bodies in Britain.

Trident Venturer

YEARS IN PRODUCTION
1969–1974

NUMBER MADE
Unknown

SPECIAL REMARKS
The Venturer was the cheaper version of the Clipper. It had the same body but with a 3 litre V-6 Ford engine of 146 SAE at 4,750 rpm. It still managed a top speed of 119 mph (190 km/hour).

Triumph

Triumph were among the most popular sports cars of the 1950s and 1960s. The company made an important contribution to motor sport in the pre-war years, with cars originating from Coventry such as the Gloria, with which their then technical director, Donald Healey, won his class in the 1934 Monte Carlo Rally.

There were cars such as the 1935 Dolomite which closely resembled the 8C2300 Alfa Romeo and was similarly turbocharged. The Triumph

factory had made its reputation building cycles and motorcycles when it started to build cars in 1923. The company was in financial difficulties in 1944 when Sir John Black bought Triumph from its former owner, Thomas Ward. That same year, Triumph designed its first post-war car, the Triumph 1800, which was launched in 1946 as both a saloon and convertible. The car was an interesting two-seater with a glass cover to the boot that when pulled up formed a screen for a dicky seat for two additional passengers. The engine was a four-cylinder unit from Standard, which Sir John also owned.

A new era of sports cars was begun in 1953 with the Triumph TR2. The car was continuously improved through successive models up to the TR6 which was in production up to 1976. The TR7 and TR8 bore little resemblance to the concept of their predecessors. Their designs were completely different, and the TR8 had a V-8 engine.

The Triumph 1800 Roadster, designed by Frank Callaby, appeared in March 1946. The 1800 was replaced in 1948 by the 2000, which had a 2,088 cc engine in place of the earlier 1,776 cc motor.

The TR5 had a bored out six-cylinder engine from the Triumph 2000, with fuel injection. Triumph was so proud they put PI for petrol injection next to the TR5 logo.

A second line of Triumph sports cars was the Spitfire. These had to withhold the honour of Triumph against the Austin-Healey Sprites and MG Midgets and in this they were very successful. Italian designer Giovanni Michelotti more or less became the in-house designer with his Spitfire and other Triumph designs. The Spitfire was produced from 1962 to 1980 and there was also a coupé version, the GT6, although this was less popular than the open-topped Spitfire. The Triumph Stag 2 + 2 convertible with Targa-style roll-over bar appeared in 1970. The car, with its 2,997 cc V-8 engine that produced 156 bhp at 5,500 rpm, was more suitable for eating up miles on a long journey that a sporting jaunt.

Although it had four doors, the Dolomite Sprint had all the properties of a sports car. It had a sixteen valve engine which was a talking point in 1973 since they had only been seen in Grand Prix cars. Understandably, the Dolomite won many production car races.

The Triumph marque came to an end on June 9, 1984, when the last Triumph left the factory. Will the marque ever return? The MG marque was resurrected by the marketing men and Triumph had at least as many adherents.

Triumph sports cars

COUNTRY OF ORIGIN
Great Britain

Triumph Roadster

YEARS IN PRODUCTION
1946–1949

NUMBER MADE
4,501

SPECIAL REMARKS
The Roadster was a 2 + 2 with the rear seat

The Triumph Roadster was popular with children when the weather was fine.

passengers carried in an external dicky seat. The model was produced in two different series: prior to 1948, 2,501 were made with 1,776 cc 65 bhp engines and after that with a four-cylinder 2,088 cc engine giving 68 bhp at 4,200 rpm.

Triumph TR2 en TR3

YEARS IN PRODUCTION
1953–1955 and 1955–1957

NUMBER MADE
8,628 and 13,377

SPECIAL REMARKS
The deeply recessed radiator grille was characteristic of the TR2 but with the TR3 this was no longer set back.

The TR3 also had handles on the outside of the doors, two small occasional seats in the rear and disc brakes on the front wheels.

The TR2 was an improved version of the TR1 of which only a few prototypes were built. The 1,991 cc four-cylinder engine produced 91 bhp at 4,800 rpm.

Works drivers such as Paddy Hopkirk and Maus Gatsonides won a number of rallies in the TR3. The TR3A had a different grill and was available with an optional overdrive.

Triumph TR3A

YEARS IN PRODUCTION
1957–1962

NUMBER MADE
58,236

SPECIAL REMARKS
The main recognition for the TR3A was the wider grille. The TR3A provided greater comfort and had a more powerful engine that delivered 101 bhp at 5,000 rpm instead of 90 bhp in the TR2 and 96 bhp in the TR3.

Triumph TR4 en TR4A

YEARS IN PRODUCTION
1961–1965 and 1965–1967

NUMBER MADE
40,253 and 28,465

SPECIAL REMARKS
The TR4 no longer had the scalloped doors. Michelotti redesigned the car, which was now both longer and wider. The TR4A had independent rear suspension, a different grill, and sidelights in the wings.

Triumph always produced fine-looking dashboards,
This is from the TR5.

The TR5 engine was 2,498 cc and produced
maximum torque at 3,000 rpm.

Standard-Triumph was bought by Leyland Trucks for £18,000,000 in 1961. The TR4 was given a new body to stimulate sales and the engine was bored out to 2,138 cc to give 105 bhp at 4,750 rpm.

Triumph TR5 en TR250

YEARS IN PRODUCTION
1967–1968

NUMBER MADE
2,947 and 8,484

SPECIAL REMARKS
The TR5 was the first British production car with fuel injection (then called petrol injection). The TR5 and TR250 had the new Triumph 2.5 litre straight-six engine but were in other respects identical to the TR4.
The TR250 for the American market had twin carburettors in place of fuel injection, reducing its power to 104 bhp instead of the TR5's 143 bhp at 5,500 rpm.

Triumph TR6

YEARS IN PRODUCTION
1969–1976

NUMBER MADE
94,619

SPECIAL REMARKS
The TR6 was a TR5 with a face-lift by Karmann of Germany to the front and rear ends. This was the best selling of the original TR series before the concept changed.

A hard-top version designed by Triumph themselves was available at a higher price.

Triumph TR7

YEARS IN PRODUCTION
1975–1981

Standard-Triumph, Austin, Morris, MG, Jaguar, and Rover were all merged into British Leyland in 1967. The Austin-Healey was taken out of production and the TR5 was modernised into the TR6.

The TR7 was designed for the American market to replace both the TR6 and MGB in competition against the Datsun Z.

NUMBER MADE
86,784

SPECIAL REMARKS
The final Triumph TR was the totally different TR7. The completely new design was completely disliked by all the enthusiasts, yet it sold well. A convertible version was introduced in 1979 and a V-8 engine model in 1980, that was designated TR8.

Triumph Spitfire 4 en Mk2

YEARS IN PRODUCTION
1962–1965 and 1966–1967

NUMBER MADE
45,753 and 37,409

SPECIAL REMARKS
The Spitfire was introduced to compete with the small sports cars of BMC and it did so very well. The mechanical parts were from the Triumph

By giving the Triumph Herald engine a new crankshaft, twin carburettors, and increasing the compression ratio to 9:1, the 59 bhp 1,147 cc engine of the first Spitfires was created.

Herald. The engine was 1,147 cc, giving 63 bhp. This was improved to 67 bhp at 6,000 rpm in the Mk 2.

Triumph Spitfire Mk3

YEARS IN PRODUCTION
1967–1970

NUMBER MADE
65,320

SPECIAL REMARKS
The Spitfire, in common with all British sports cars, was primarily intended for the American market. The Spitfire too had to adapt to changing US regulations, resulting in higher front bumpers for the Mk 3. The engine was now 1,296 cc giving 75 bhp at 6,000 rpm.

Triumph Spitfire Mk4 en 1500

YEARS IN PRODUCTION
1970–1980

When the Spitfire body started to look dated, Michelotti gave it a face-lift to create the Mk 4. The large black rubber overriders on the bumpers were quite ugly.

Triumph launched the Mk 3 Spitfire at Geneva in March 1967. The engine was now 1,296 cc with power of 75 bhp at 6,000 rpm and the top speed was 100 mph (160 km/hour).

NUMBER MADE
70,012 and 95,829

SPECIAL REMARKS
To comply with stricter US environmental regulations, the engine of the Mk 4 Spitfire was so detuned that it now only produced 63 bhp at 5,500 rpm. The Spitfire 1500 had a 1,493 cc engine that produced a modest 71 bhp at 5,250 rpm. One crumb of comfort was that first gear of this model finally had synchromesh.

By putting a roof on a Spitfire body, the GT was created and because the car now had six cylinders instead of the four, it became the GT6.

Triumph GT6

YEARS IN PRODUCTION
1966–1973

NUMBER MADE
40,926

SPECIAL REMARKS
The GT was created by putting a roof on a Spitfire body. The car had the 1,998 cc six-cylinder Triumph Vitesse engine. In other respects, the car was technically identical to the Spitfire and benefited from all the improvements to the Spitfire during its life.

Triumph Stag

YEARS IN PRODUCTION
1970–1977

NUMBER MADE
25,939

SPECIAL REMARKS
The Stag was really a mistake. The car was certainly attractive but neither a true convertible or coupé with its "Targa" roll-over bar. The normal reliability of Triumph engines was not upheld with the specially created 3 litre V-8 Stag engine based on two Triumph four-cylinder

The Stag did not sell well, largely because of the poor reputation of its 147 bhp V-8 engine for early wear.

engines instead of using the ideal Rover V-8 power unit.

Triumph Dolomite Sprint

YEARS IN PRODUCTION
1973–1980

NUMBER MADE
22,941

SPECIAL REMARKS
The Triumph Dolomite Sprint was a "wolf in sheep's clothing". From the outside it appeared to be a steady and ordinary family saloon with four doors, real wooden dashboard, and plenty of boot space. Under the bonnet was a 1,998 cc four-cylinder engine with overhead camshaft and four valves per cylinder. This is now commonplace but took the world by storm then. The engine delivered 129 bhp at 5,700 rpm and did 0–60 mph in about 8 seconds (0–100 km/hour in 8.7 seconds).

The Triumph Dolomite Sprint engine had four valves per cylinder but only one camshaft with 8 cams instead of 16 so that one inlet valve and the opposing exhaust valve were operated by the same cam.

The Triumph Dolomite Sprint was a real family racing car. You could drive into town in the same car that was ideal for motor sport.

Turner

Jack Turner, like many other British enthusiasts, built sports cars for his own use. He built his first in 1954 and followed this with a Formula 2 car. Once those who knew him became interested in his cars, he quickly established a works and developed the Turner 950 sports car in 1956. This open two-seater was built using Austin A35 parts and the glass-fibre reinforced polyester bodied car sold well as both a kit and completed car. The second production car was the Turner 950 Sports Mk1 in 1959 which was again built using Austin A35 bits but now with a Coventry Climax or Austin-Healey Sprite engine under the bonnet. The next stage was the Turner 950 Mk 2 which made good use of Ford Anglia parts. The final car, which was built in larger numbers, was the Mk 3 of 1963. This car was sold up to April 1966. Once Jack Turner became ill, he had too little financial reserve to keep

When Turner started to be more successful with his Turner 950, BMC refused to deliver him parts and he was forced to buy them from dealers. The Austin-Healey Sprite was being developed by BMC at that time.

The 1,266 cc Coventry Climax FWE engine produced more than 100 bhp.

his company afloat. This was the unfortunate end for this highly regarded company.

Turner sports cars

COUNTRY OF ORIGIN
Great Britain

Turner 950

YEARS IN PRODUCTION
1956–1959

NUMBER MADE
Approx. 150

SPECIAL REMARKS
In common with all British sports car specials of the 1950s, the Turner had a glass-reinforced polyester body on a light tubular chassis. The Austin A35 engine was converted to produce 40 bhp which took the car to a top speed of 87 mph (140 km/hour).

Turner 950 Mk1

YEARS IN PRODUCTION
1959–1960

NUMBER MADE
Approx. 150

SPECIAL REMARKS
When Turner put an entirely new body on his chassis, the Mk 2 was created. Although a range of different engines could be used, most customers chose a four-cylinder Austin-Healey Sprite or Coventry Climax engine.

Turner 950 Mk2

YEARS IN PRODUCTION
1960–1963

NUMBER MADE
Approx. 300

With its net weight of 1,320 lb (600 kg) the Mk 1 Turner 950 Sports was unbeatable in its class.

The Mk 2 was more suitable for the open road than the track. It was even possible to order a hard-top for it. The interior provided more comfort with a less spartan interior than its predecessor. In other respects, the Mk 2 resembled the Mk 1.

Turner 950 Mk3

YEARS IN PRODUCTION
1963–1966

NUMBER MADE
Approx. 100

SPECIAL REMARKS
After Turner had built nine GT cars, the open sports car had a number of improvements incorporated, leading to the Mk 3. The standard engine was a 1,500 cc Ford Cortina four-cylinder power unit but the Climax engine could be installed on request.

TVR

The TVR company, which was set-up in 1949, has frequently run into financial difficulties causing frequent changes of ownership but has recently seen more settled times and success. The company was founded after Trevor Wilkinson had built his first car in 1947. The company name was derived from Trevor's first name. After TVR Engineering came into being, Wilkinson built sports cars using Austin A40 parts and sold the car as a kit but without an engine. The next stage was to build six open sports cars and the series production of the TVR Grantura Mk 1 coupé started in 1957. The small two-seater had a glass-fibre reinforced polyester body and was available with a wide choice of engines. The standard cars were sold with ordinary Ford Anglia engines or more powerful Coventry Climax four cylinder units. The Grantura Mk 2 was noticeable for the small fins on the rear wings. This car usually had an MGA engine and was very successful in the United States. Wilkinson left the business in 1962 and the first major financial problems arose. The new owners gave the Grantura a new chassis and the MGB engine. TVR built a car for the American

The rear window acted as boot lid or third door with the TVR Taimar

Jack Griffith that was fitted with a V-8 engine in the USA. The model known as "Griffith" won many races.
TVR had a couple of prototypes for the proposed TVR Trident built in Italy (see Trident) but the costs were so high that the company ran into financial problems. The business was restarted by Martin Lilley in 1965 and there was a TVR on show once more at the 1967 Racing Car Show in London. This was the Tuscan, powered by a 271 bhp V-8 engine that was destined for an America customer. The Tuscan was mainly supplied in Europe with a Ford V-6 engine. A further new car in 1967 was the TVR Vixen, which shared the same wheelbase with the Tuscan but was sold with an MG or Cortina engine. In late 1971, the firm introduced the "M" series with the "M" standing for Martin. These cars had both a new chassis and body with a wide choice of engines. The TVR Taimar was surrounded by eager photographers at the 1975 London Motor Show because they found the car so attractive. The rear window, which also served as the hatch or third door to the rear of the car attracted a great deal of attention. In other respects, the car was identical to the "M" series.

TVR sports cars

COUNTRY OF ORIGIN
Great Britain

TVR Grantura

YEARS IN PRODUCTION
1958–1967

NUMBER MADE
Approx. 800

SPECIAL REMARKS
The Grantura was continuously improved so that the model appeared with a whole range of

The Grantura was quite a small car with a length of 138 in (350 cm).

series numbers. The Mk 3 was the first with disc brakes.

TVR Griffith

YEARS IN PRODUCTION
1963–1965

NUMBER MADE
310

SPECIAL REMARKS
Jack Griffith imagined another Cobra: a TVR with a big Ford V-8 engine. He backed the idea by ordering Grantura Mk 3 and then sold the car under his own name in the United States.

TVR Tuscan

YEARS IN PRODUCTION
1969–1971

The Griffith was created and named after the American who decided to put a Ford V-8 in a Grantura Mk 3.

NUMBER MADE
Approx. 175

SPECIAL REMARKS
The TVR Tuscan V-6 was introduced in the spring of 1969. The 2,994 cc Ford V-6 engine developed 146 SAE at 4,750 rpm. For the US market, V-8 engines were installed.

TVR M-series

YEARS IN PRODUCTION
1972–1979

NUMBER MADE
Approx. 1,700

SPECIAL REMARKS
Martin Lilley was 23 years old when his father bought TVR for him. Under his control, a new car went into history as the "M" for Martin series. Martin used 1,599, 2,498, and 2,994 cc V-4 and V-6 engines.
 There was also a 3 litre available with turbo that produced 230 bhp at 5,000 rpm.

TVR Taimar

YEARS IN PRODUCTION
1975–1979

NUMBER MADE
395

SPECIAL REMARKS
The Taimar customer had no choice of engine. He or she had to be satisfied with a Ford 2,994 cc V-6 giving 138 bhp at 5,000 rpm. If more power was wanted, the same engine with a turbo on the exhaust manifold increased power to 230 bhp at 5,500 rpm. Only 30 were sold of this special model.

The successor to the Griffith was the Tuscan. Americans had a V-8 engine fitted while Europeans made do with a Ford V-6.

Vauxhall

Vauxhall started to make cars in 1903. The company made cars suitable for every day use and others which could win races. Think of the superb 30/98 hp sports cars of the 1920s. These cars had 4,224 cc overhead valve four-cylinder engines that produced 120 bhp at 3,300 rpm. They won virtually every race in which they took part.

In 1925, Vauxhall became part of General Motors. GM was primarily interested in making money with cars that could be made in large numbers.

After the war, this policy remained unchanged, although the developers and designers had the courage from time to time to develop sportive concept cars. Occasionally such cars even made it to a prototype or concept car to be shown at exhibitions but nothing became of them to the disappointment of their creators.

But people will find a way. If the factory was unable to build sports cars, then the saloon cars would have to be used for motor sport. The Dealers Team Vauxhall was created that made cars available for drivers in rallies or even entered their own cars. The Vauxhall Firenze was a particularly successful example. It was the coupé version of the Viva and was built at the request of the Team. The normal road version delivered 132 bhp at 5,500 from the 2,279 cc engine, giving a top speed of 120 mph (193 km/hour). Vauxhall conceived a plan to put the car into production and totals of 20,000–50,000 were considered. Eventually, only 204 examples of the "Droop snout", so-called because of its plastic nose, were ever made. The Racing Car Show of 1975 saw a car with twin camshafts with a cylinder head from the Jensen-Healey. This car promised much but this too remained a prototype. The same happened with another "Droop snout" built for Gerry Marshall of the Dealer Team, based on a Vauxhall Ventura. This car had a Repco-Holden V-8 that produced 495 bhp. To keep the weight down this car was partially made of plastic.

The Vauxhall Firenza is a rare car since only 204 of them were built. This one is cornering at Zandvoort.

This Vauxhall Firenza was known as the "Droop snout". The car was very similar to the Opel Manta but had a four-cylinder 2,279 cc engine delivering 132 bhp.

The first three RS type cars had bodies of magnesium alloy, the others had aluminium bodies.

Vauxhall sports cars

COUNTRY OF ORIGIN
Great Britain

Vauxhall Firenza

YEARS IN PRODUCTION
1973–1975

NUMBER MADE
204

SPECIAL REMARKS
The engine in the Firenza had a compression ratio of 9.2:1 and produced 132 bhp at 5,500 rpm. The five-speed gearbox was by ZF of Friedrichshafen, Germany. The car weighed 2,233 lb (1,015 kg) and accelerated from 0–60 in about 7 seconds (0–100 km/hour in 7.6 seconds).

Veritas

Immediately after the war, it was forbidden in Germany to build cars that had engines bigger than 1 litre in the American zone. The former BMW colleagues Ernst Loof, "Schorsch" Meier, and Lorenz Dietrich found a way to get around this ban. When they put their plan to build sports cars into operation, they looked for BMW sports cars to convert to their Veritas cars. In this way, 36 cars were built that were intended solely for the race track. The first production models were named Comet and they were sold as either a coupé or roadster.

When the company moved to the French zone, where the American regulation was not in force, Loof designed his own engine for a Comet S

prototype, which was built by Heinkel. The 2 + 2 coupé was called Saturn and the convertible was named Scorpion. These cars, which were built in very small quantities, had bodies by Spohn of Ravensburg. The Veritas Nürburgring appeared in 1951 as both a coupé and convertible but this time with a six-cylinder engine, again built in the former Heinkel aircraft factory. These 1,998 cc engines had an overhead camshaft and developed 100 bhp at 5,000 rpm. The cars sold, in Veritas terms, quite well.

Between 1951 and 1953, two roadsters, eighteen convertibles, and eighteen coupés were delivered for prices between DM 21,000 and DM24,000 (when a standard VW cost DM 4,400). To increase their turnover, Loof and his partners decided to make a smaller car, the Dyna-Veritas. The car had a twin-cylinder Panhard engine and front-wheel drive.

The production volume certainly climbed but the success was not quick enough to prevent Loof from bankruptcy. Lorenz Dietrich continued making cars under the Dyna name.

Veritas sports cars

COUNTRY OF ORIGIN
Germany

Veritas BMW-RS

YEARS IN PRODUCTION
1948–1949

NUMBER MADE
36

SPECIAL REMARKS
The BMW RS was a true racing car. The car was very fast and won many races (although against low-grade opposition). Veritas built the RS on a

270

This is one of the seven BMW 328-powered Veritas Comets.

tubular chassis with an uprated pre-war BMW 328 engine.

Veritas Comet

YEARS IN PRODUCTION
1949–1950

Veritas built this Comet S in April 1950. It remained a prototype.

NUMBER MADE
9

SPECIAL REMARKS
Only nine Comets were sold: seven as coupé with a BMW 328 engine, one with a BMW 326 engine, and one as a roadster with a six-cylinder Heinkel engine.

The dashboard of the Comet S

The Comet S engine was built by Heinkel and produced 140 bhp.

Veritas Saturn-Scorpion

YEARS IN PRODUCTION
1950

NUMBER MADE
7

SPECIAL REMARKS
The 1,988 cc six-cylinder engine by Heinkel had a compression ratio of 7.2:1 and produced 100 bhp at 5,000 rpm. The 2 + 2 coupé was sold as

A 1953 Veritas RS on the Nürburgring track.

a Saturn, the open 2 + 2 was delivered as a Scorpion.

Veritas Nürburgring

YEARS IN PRODUCTION
1951–1953

NUMBER MADE
38

SPECIAL REMARKS
Veritas moved again in 1951. Production was shifted from Messkirch to a large workshop at the Nürburgring circuit. The final large Veritas cars were built here.

Veritas Dyna

YEARS IN PRODUCTION
1950–1952

NUMBER MADE
169

SPECIAL REMARKS
Until the Dyna, all the bodies had been built by Spohn of Ravensburg. The Dyna-Veritas had a body built by Baur of Stuttgart. The air-cooled twin-cylinder engine of 744 cc produced 28 then, after 1951, 32 bhp at 5,000 rpm.

Vignale

The coachwork business of Alfredo Vignale (1913–1969) was based in the Italian village of Grugliasco, which is a stone's throw from Bertone's home town of Turin. In common with his friend Giovanni Michelotti, Vignale designed and built superb cars. Most of his cars were built on the chassis of Ferrari, Maserati, or Triumph but the Vignale Gamine of 1967 was based on Fiat parts. This small two-seater was built on the floorpan of the Fiat Nuova 500 and had the retro look of a 1930s car.

Vignale was killed in an accident in mysterious circumstances in November 1969 and the company was taken over by De Tomaso but sold on to Ford within a few months.

The Vignale Gamine (loosely a young man with street cred) had an unmodified floor pan from the Fiat Nuova 500. Its 499 cc engine produced 18 bhp at 4,600 rpm.

The Gamine dashboard was simple, like the Fiat 500.

The Gamine was a wonderful car for good weather.

Vignale sports cars

COUNTRY OF ORIGIN
Italy

Vignale Gamine

YEARS IN PRODUCTION
1967–1970

NUMBER MADE
Unknown

SPECIAL REMARKS
The world famous coachwork designer and builder whose name was spoken in the same breath as those of Pininfarina, Zagato, and Bertone, became an unknown car maker with the Gamine.

Volkswagen

Volkswagen came in to being in 1936 to build the "strength-through-joy people's car" (Kraft-durch-Freude Wagen) designed by Dr. Ferdinand Porsche. It is therefore not surprising that the famous sports cars which bear his name should be based on the same concept. The chief characteristic of the people's car was the rear-mounted horizontally opposed air-cooled engine. The classic Volkswagen was used as a foundation of innumerable sporting specials such as dune buggies. Although VW sponsored the Formula VW, the company did not build real sports cars itself although there were sporty cars such as the Karmann-Ghias which were based on the Beetle and subsequent VW 1500 and 1600. The first Karmann-Ghia examples followed William Karmann seeing a prototype on a Ghia stand at an exhibition in Turin.

Is the VW Beetle not a sports car? These autocross Beetles have turbocharged engines.

Beetles are very popular with the public (but not the other competitors) in Super Saloon races.

Karmann was eager to design a sports car for VW but had never been given the opportunity. With Ghia's concept, he was given the go-ahead by the management at Wolfsburg. They allowed him to make the car as designed by Ghia, which was also important recognition for Ghia.

VW introduced the Scirocco as a sports car at the motor show in Geneva in 1974. The "TS" had a 1,471 cc four-cylinder engine producing 85 bhp at 5,800 rpm giving a top speed of 109 mph (85 bhp).

Sportive Volkswagens

COUNTRY OF ORIGIN
Germany

VW Karmann-Ghia

YEARS IN PRODUCTION
1955–1965

NUMBER MADE
445,300

SPECIAL REMARKS
The Karmann-Ghia was built in great numbers. The majority were coupés (364,401). The cars were built on unmodified Beetle running gear that were constantly improved.

The Karmann-Ghia appears to be a smaller version of the Chrysler d'Elegance concept car designed by Virgil Exner in 1953 but the head of Ghia, Luigi Segre, claims the honour.

The Karmann-Ghia's design is similar to the d'Elegance designed by Virgil Exner for Chrysler. The d'Elegance was built in Turin by Ghia.

The Karmann-Ghia convertible was launched two years after the coupé, in 1957.

The type 34 Karmann-Ghia remained in production for eight years ?????. More than 5,000 were sold on average per year.

VW Karmann-Ghia Type 34

YEARS IN PRODUCTION
1963–1969

NUMBER MADE
42,522

SPECIAL REMARKS
The majority of this model were also built as coupés, with only seventeen convertibles being made. The model did not have the same attractive lines as its predecessor and therefore limited numbers were sold. The VW 1500/1600 saloon was also not a runaway success.

Volvo

Volvo was founded in 1927 by Assar Gabrielsson and Gustav Larson in Gothenburg, Sweden.

At first their cars resembled the products from Detroit. It was only in the 1950s that a distinctive Volvo style emerged. Their saloon cars, but particularly the 444 and its successor the 445 made from 1947–1965, were first-class rally cars. They were strong and reliable and could therefore withstand rough treatment. The

first Volvo sports car, the P1900 was a flop. The 2 + 2 car was seen at shows from 1954 but was not on sale until 1956.
The P1800 had the mechanical parts from the 444 with a glass-reinforced polyester body. The body pre-

sented all manner of problems and production was halted after only a few had been made. Volvo attempted once more in 1959 to introduce the P1800 but this car was not available until two years later.
The car was designed by Pelle Petterson, a Swede who had briefly worked for Frua in Italy. The car was robust, like all Volvo cars, and once Simon Templar was seen to drive one in the television series The Saint, everybody wanted one. Most of the first series of P1800 were made in Britain with bodies by Pressed Steel which were equipped and finished by Jensen. This series can be recognised by the curved bumpers.

The P1800 was not so new when it was introduced and after being made for ten years was certainly showing its age. To develop a replacement was considered too expensive and they were therefore delighted to grasp at a solution produced by Jan Wilsgaard who left the design untouched from front bumper to the

The first P1800s were mainly produced in Britain. They can be recognised by the striking front bumper and decorative bright-work on the sides of the car.

The Volvo 122 was not a sports car but people do very sporty things with them in Sweden.

doors but turned the rear of the car into a sort of estate with a large hatched door at the back. The press dubbed the car "Snow White's hearse".

Volvo sports cars

COUNTRY OF ORIGIN
Sweden

Volvo P1900

YEARS IN PRODUCTION
1956–1957

NUMBER MADE
67

SPECIAL REMARKS
The body of the P1900 was far to flexible so that doors flew open when cornering. After the head of Volvo at the time, Gunnar Engellau, took one home for the weekend, the production was halted.

Volvo P 1800

YEARS IN PRODUCTION
1961–1972

NUMBER MADE
39,406

The P1800 E, as this 1970 example, had a top speed of 115 mph (185 km/hour).

The rear window was a hatch-back third door in "Snow White's hearse".

SPECIAL REMARKS
The P1800 was sold with two different four-cylinder engines: 1,780 cc initially 100 bhp then 118 bhp, and 1,986 cc producing 135 bhp. In the P1800 E, the larger engine had fuel injection.

Volvo P 1800ES

YEARS IN PRODUCTION
1971–1973

NUMBER MADE
8,077

SPECIAL REMARKS
The provisional final Volvo sports car until the 480ES of 1985 was more of a sports estate than sports car. There was enormous space in the back that was easily accessible through the rear glazed door. The car was identical mechanically to the fuel injection version of the previous model.

The P1900 was Volvo's first sports car.

WSM

WSM bears the initials of the surnames of its founders Douglas Wilson-Spratt and Jim McManus. These two built their first sporting coupé in 1961 on Austin-Healey Sprite running gear, with an aluminium body but polyester bonnet. The car performed well in rallies and sold well, especially in the United States. The car was followed by a further WSM cars built on the running gear of an Austin-Healey 3000, one using an MG 1100, and at least one based on MGB engineering.

The body of the WSM-MGB was built of aluminium but had a plastic bonnet to save weight.

WSM sports cars

WSM

COUNTRY OF ORIGIN
Great Britain

YEARS IN PRODUCTION
1961–1969

NUMBER MADE
Unknown

A WSM-MGB at Brands Hatch with a Lotus-Buick number six about to retire.

Zeder

Fred M. Zeder Junior raced at Watkins Glen for Allard-Chrysler but was beaten by Briggs Cunningham in a car built by himself. Zeder determined that whatever Briggs could do, he could do better and had drawn designs for a car within a few weeks.

The Zeder took three years to build but was based on a superb chassis with a Dodge V-8 engine that delivered 260 bhp. The aluminium body was made in Italy by Bertone. The car was ready to be shown at the annual motor show in Turin, where it took first prize for "style and design".

Zeder sports cars

COUNTRY OF ORIGIN
USA

Zeder Z-250

YEARS IN PRODUCTION
1953–unknown

NUMBER MADE
Unknown

The Zeder was intended to be a 2 + 2 but Bertone was unable to squeeze in a rear seat.

SPECIAL REMARKS
The Zeder was sold with two different bodies: one for the track and the other for the highway. The bodies were held in place by just four bolts and were easily interchangeable.

ZIL

Owning a private car was a major privilege in the former Soviet Union enjoyed by a very few people so that sports cars were even more unusual.

The ZIL works in Moscow was renowned in Russia for a long time for the huge limousines in which the Party apparatchiks were taken to

The 7.5 litre straight-eight engine in the ZIL 112S produces 300 bhp.

work. These cars still had straight eight-cylinder engines in 1956 and these were used to create the ZIL sports car.

ZIL sports cars

COUNTRY OF ORIGIN
Russia

ZIL Sport

YEARS IN PRODUCTION
Unknown

NUMBER MADE
Unknown

SPECIAL REMARKS
This car has a straight eight cylinder engine of 7,500 cc, producing 300 bhp.

Although the ZIL has no hood, Veldis Branti uses the car daily

Index

Author's and Photographic acknowledgements

The author and publishers wish to thank the following persons who provided photographs for their help in compiling this book. They are acknowledged in alphabetical order.

Albrecht Guggisberg Oldtimer Garage,Toffen/Bern, Switzerland
Dieter Gunther. Hamburg. Germany
Lukas Huni, Zürich, Switzerland
Hans K. Lange, Villach Austria
Rick Lenz. Bloomington, California USA
Reinhard Lintelmann, Espelkamp, Germany
Reinhhard Schmidlin Oldtimer Gallery Toffen/Bern, Switzerland
Ernst Scheidegger, Schwyz, Switzerland
Mat Stone. Glendale. California, USA
Max Stoop. Langnau/Zürich, Switzerland